CAPITALISM, STATE FORMATION AND MARXIST THEORY

ALSO BY PHILIP CORRIGAN

Culture and Control
State Formation and Moral Regulation
Socialist Construction and Marxist Theory:
  Bolshevism and its Critique (with Harvie
  Ramsay, Derek Sayer)
For Mao (with Harvie Ramsay, Derek
  Sayer)
Ideology and Cultural Production (with
  Michèle Barrett, Annette Kuhn, Janet
  Wolff)

Capitalism, State Formation and Marxist Theory
Historical Investigations

Edited by Philip Corrigan

QUARTET BOOKS
LONDON MELBOURNE NEW YORK

In acknowledgement of major debts I dedicate this book to Christopher Hill and E. P. Thompson without whose writings it could not have been assembled in its final form

P.C.

First published by Quartet Books Limited 1980
A member of the Namara Group
27 Goodge Street, London W1P 1FD

ISBN 0 7043 2241 2 (hardcover)
     0 7043 3311 2 (paperback)

Printed in Great Britain at The Anchor Press Ltd
and bound by Wm Brendon & Son Ltd,
both of Tiptree, Essex

Contents

'Capital is a sort of *cabalistic word* like church or state, or any other of those general terms which are invented by those who fleece the rest of mankind to conceal the hand that shears them.'

Thomas Hodgskin, *Labour Defended against the Claims of Capital*, 1825 (quoted by Karl Marx, who thought Hodgskin 'one of the most important modern English economists', *Capital*, Volume 1 of the Penguin edition, pp. 999–1000).

PREFACE

This book surveys the development of the State within England from the sixteenth to the early twentieth centuries, with particular emphasis upon the nineteenth-century dimensions of social experience. The introduction establishes the general approach and comments briefly upon each chapter.

My role as editor has been relatively minor. Authors were informed of the general area I wished them to discuss and editorial comments were provided on any ideas or drafts they submitted. The content of the chapters remains their own responsibility. My task has been one of launching and sustaining the project.

I should like formally to acknowledge both the active support and collaboration of all the authors and the early encouragement and assistance given by William Miller (formerly with the publishers of this volume).

Two technical matters are worth emphasizing for the benefit of readers. All notes (indicated by raised numerals in the text as [1] [2] and so on) arc collected at the end of the book. Similarly we have used a reference system where all the published material is indentified by a name, date (and pages) within the text itself as, Marx, 1867a:719. This indicates that a work by Marx, is to be found in the Bibliography under Marx, 1867 (the Lawrence and Wishart 1967 edition of *Capital*, I) with a quotation or evidence taken from page 719. Unpublished evidence is cited within the notes.

We hope that this book can be taken as a first step in the extensive and increasingly collective work of studying the origins and specific patterns of the social relations that led to where we live and work in the 1980s.

London, March 1979   PHILIP CORRIGAN

NOTES ON THE CONTRIBUTORS

Philip Corrigan worked as a librarian in the 1960s and, after an introduction to sociology at L.S.E. and Durham University (where he was a S.S.R.C. Senior Research Fellow in Sociology), taught at North East London Polytechnic's Department of Sociology and the London College of Printing's Cultural Studies Unit. He is the joint author of *Socialist Construction and Marxist Theory* and *For Mao*; joint editor of and contributor to *Ideology and Cultural Production*; the author of *Culture and Control* and *State Formation and Moral Regulation*, and several articles, chapters and review essays. He is currently employed as Lecturer at the Institute of Education, University of London.

Rachel Harrison took a degree in sociology after four years as a nurse and several more bringing up a family. She is now attached to the Centre for Contemporary Cultural Studies at Birmingham University, where she is working on a thesis on the conditions of existence of romance in three historical periods.

Chris Jones and Tony Novak have worked together for the past nine years on a variety of issues, their major concern being to develop a critique of social policy and thereby the State. This work has been undertaken at the Enfield College of Technology and later at Durham University. With other friends and comrades they help produce the *Bulletin on Social Policy* which is concerned with encouraging the formation of socialist alternatives and critiques of State social welfare. They are currently employed as lecturers: Chris Jones at Preston Polytechnic, and Tony Novak at Bradford University.

Frank Mort is a postgraduate student at the Centre for Contemporary Cultural Studies, Birmingham, where he is currently engaged in research on the regulation of sexuality in the 1950s and 1960s for a Ph.D. thesis. He has contributed to a number of articles and papers on this subject.

Harvie Ramsay is a lecturer on the Industrial Relations Unit of the Department of Economics at the University of Strathclyde. Educated at the Universities of Cambridge and Durham, he is the joint author of *Socialist Construction and Marxist Theory* and *For Mao*. He is currently researching industrial democracy and has published widely on this and related topics.

Paul Richards graduated from Birmingham University with an honours degree in History in 1967 and completed a Ph.D. in 1975 on which forthcoming articles are based. He teaches history at Norfolk College of Further Education and works part-time for the Open University. He is involved in trade-union activities and is a member of the W.E.A. panel of tutors. His main preoccupation is with the education and training of the sixteen to twenty age group.

Derek Sayer is Lecturer in Sociology at the University of Glasgow. Educated at the Universities of Essex and Durham

(where he was a S.S.R.C. Senior Research Fellow in Socio-
logy), he is the joint author of *Socialist Construction and
Marxist Theory* and *For Mao*, and the author of *Marx's
Method*, as well as of several articles and chapters.

Stephen Yeo teaches History at the University of Sussex.
He has published *Religion and Voluntary Organizations in
Crisis* (1976); 'A New Life: the Religion of Socialism in
Britian 1883–96', *History Workshop* (4), 1978; and various
other articles. He is carrying out research on Co-ops.,
friendly societies, building societies and other forms of
working-class association in the nineteenth and twentieth
centuries. He is active in QueenSpark, a community publishing and community action project in Brighton.

INTRODUCTION
Philip Corrigan

The State surrounds anyone who lives in England in the 1980s. And not merely the State whose origins and constructions are studied in this book, but a much more dense and complex *local* State apparatus *and* the instructions and influences of the supranational state of the European Economic Community, the Common Market. Indeed, as I have argued elsewhere (*New Society*, 15 June 1978, p. 615), the State structure these essays discuss and depict has been thrown into crisis and massively transformed from the mid-1960s onwards. This is no longer a heretical position:

> Our Victorian ancestors had a theory of the state, and they based their structure on that theory. One of the reasons why it was so imposing and why it has lasted so long is that structure and theory coincided.
>
> We have no theory; and one of the reasons why the changes we have made in the Victorian structure have so often been damaging and ephemeral is that we therefore have no clear idea of what we are trying to achieve. (*Listener*, 8 March 1979, p. 336)

Professor David Marquand's 'Personal View' is widely shared; long editorials in *The Times* concerning *discipline* (29 November 1975; 27 October 1976 – I drew attention to them in my doctoral thesis, 1977: Ch. 4, section I) point to the same 'problem'.

But that 'problem' is also a resource for understanding our current social situation and the means for its transformation in a direction which will extend the much discussed 'benefits' of the twentieth century more widely among those who live in England. 'England' is quite deliberately stressed here because it is time, once and for all, to recognize that there was an English *empire* long before any stretch of sea 'was crossed'. The subjugation of Wales and Scotland, moreover, was absolutely and not merely contingently related to the 'peculiarities of the English' State formation. Furthermore, that 'problem' has made 'the State' the centre of theoretical reflection for the last ten years or more. But, and some readers will recognize the metaphor, that attention to Theory has become part of our problem and not part of any possible solution. We have a surfeit of theory in this area and in many others. We have a crisis of overproduction (amongst the intellectual élite) and underconsumption (among the general population)! Philip Abrams has drawn attention to this imbalance and to the need to study 'the mechanics of structuring through time' (1972b:10) because

> the identification of structural types, the formal differentiation of past and present, is effected with such élan and internal cogency that it ends up by apparently making unnecessary any further study of the intervening structuring through which the past presumably became the present. Yet, of course, it is only such work that will tell us whether our structural concepts make sense; let alone whether they explain anything. (1972a:32)

It is to begin that work that these essays have been written.

The materials gathered here span the years from the 1530s to the First World War and beyond; but their central focus is upon the origins of the modern democratic Nation State in England (and its imposition elsewhere) which, I am arguing, extended until the mid-1960s. This is not to suggest anything so facile as simple linear continuity; but to point to the enormous enduring *materiality* of symbols, rituals and a general moral ethos which, I am firmly convinced, goes much further to explain what are constantly cited (for instance by commentators as different as de Tocqueville and Marx) as specifically 'English' exceptions. This exceptionalism has been remarked from other directions as well, of course. It formed the basis of two complementary (if differently rooted) critiques of English social activities – those of Perry Anderson and Tom Nairn, on the Left; and those of Sir Keith Joseph and others, on the Right. Both agreed that, in the words of Keith Joseph:

> Unlike some countries in Europe and the New World, e.g. Holland and the U.S., Britain never had a capitalist ruling class or a stable *haute bourgeoisie*. As a result, capitalist or bourgeois values have never shaped thought and institutions as they have in some countries . . .
> Britain never really internalized capitalist values, if the truth be known. For four centuries, since wealthy commercial classes with political standing began to be thrown up following the supercession of feudalism and the selling off of monastic property, the rich man's aim was to get away from the background of trade – later industry – in which he had made his wealth and power. Rich and powerful people founded landed-gentry families; the capitalist's son was educated not in capitalist values but against them, in favour of the older values of army, church, upper civil service, professions and land owning. This avoided the class struggles between middle and upper strata familiar from European history – but at what cost? (1976:60–61)

I find these views quite remarkable, not because of their inaccuracy (on the contrary I think they do contain much that is historically accurate), but because they represent (i) a theoretical voice within English politics which has been noticeably absent – the State is strangely underdiscussed in England; (ii) a general acceptance of much that is marxist (as do *The Times*' editorials previously mentioned); and (iii) a development emerging from the struggles of the radical wing of the bourgeoisie. Richard Johnson has recognized (1975, 1976) the extent to which the arguments of Anderson and Nairn represent the voice of the radical bourgeoisie (against the aristocratic wing of the English party). But Joseph's arguments are salient in the midst of many others: suddenly in the late 1960s and early 1970s, the forms and structures of the English State have come onto the agenda.

This is part and parcel of a wider opening-up of the social vocabulary. Words which for long enjoyed, at best, a shadowy existence (marginalized into purely academic discussions) and, at worst, were censoriously excised from public statements – words like *capitalism* and *class* – have become the commonplace of public statements. 'Like it or not', *The Times* headlined over a statement of the Institute of Economic Affairs (4 December 1974), 'our society is based on the theory of capitalism!'

'To understand how the modern State hangs together' wrote Nicholas Stacey, from the Reform Club, to the *Financial Times* in 1976, 'the production, distribution and exchange functions must be broadly understood by all who, in whatever job, will earn an income.'

Robert Carr could subtly redefine Conservative policy: 'I believe very strongly, with [sic] what I think is genuine Tory principle, that there should be intervention in the economy for social reasons and to deal with a situation where competitive forces are not working properly' (*Listener*, 26 June 1975).

Lord Hailsham's 'Theory of an Elective Dictatorship' (*The Times*, 15 October 1976) places a different emphasis upon the State. Like others, notably Lord Denning, he seeks to strengthen the 'rule of Law' as a means of ensuring that 'the State' does not step beyond its 'proper functions'. Finally, it is important to note a trend of explicitly critical attention to the State; not only from intellectuals and journalists disagreeing with decisions made by their former public school and university colleagues; (and *that* sort of intra-class discussion passes for much 'Great Debate' in England), but also from three important groups: populist newspapers, the Trade Union movement, and socialists who realize that the very rituals and mechanisms of the State have been so constructed that they operate to serve the needs of a small minority. My two favourite quotations are taken from the *Daily Mail*: 'The plain fact is: We're being run by a secret élite that has lost its nerve.' (17 June 1975); 'Our rulers seem to be both blind and deaf. They dwell in a land of their own, living off a diet of Civil Service briefs and party propaganda. *They make pretentious speeches about the British disease. But the truth is that THEY are the British disease. They are the slowcoaches holding back the class.*' (editorial, 18 October 1976, their emphases)

This 'opening up' has been accomplished by a series of quite specific 'revelations' about the internal relationships and work of the contemporary Civil Service (the articles by Peter Hennessy in *The Times* 1976–78 have been particularly useful) and some responses, from within the State, such as Sir Douglas Allen's lecture 'Ministers and their Mandarins' (*The Times*, 14 October 1976).

Taken together, the critical analyses and the 'revelations' are the constituents of a new understanding of the State apparatuses in contemporary England. Whether one speaks of 'Leviathan' (*New Statesman*, 23 March 1979), or 'Pantou-flage' (*New Society*, 22 February 1979), or the extensiveness of *patronage* (now known publicly because of the pioneering work of Maurice Edelman, *New Statesman*, 11 April and 11 July 1975) it is clear there is much more widely recognized similarity between the State today and that of former times;

even if we would not use the term 'Old Corruption'. This is particularly clear in Edward Thompson's admirable tract 'The State versus Its "Enemies" ' (*New Society*, 19 October 1978).

But the arguments advanced in this book suggest that we would not have been *so* surprised by these revelations if we had had a firmer grasp of State genesis and modulation over time – a grasp, especially, of the enormous strength of the 'moral ethos' and major rituals which dominate all affairs of State. The origins of that particular 'spirit' within English State apparatuses has much to do with the continuing control of major positions and responsibilities by those whose affiliations were precisely to those values highlighted by Keith Joseph; above all, the values of a landed aristocracy which continued to be influential in both Cabinet and major State institutions until well into the twentieth century. But *morality* has today become a much weaker term than formerly and many people have written of the history of the State in terms of this weaker version of 'moral concern'. Moral connotes, in my usage, something as general as *social*; it points to the values of a particular class insofar as they understand the requirements of an effective organization of production which sustains their 'way of life'. In that specific sense, of course, as Edward Thompson and others have shown, what we witness in the history this book studies is a displacement of one such morality (that of the 'moral economy') by *two* others. The first is the dominant 'theory', as *The Times* headlined, the logic and 'requirements' of capitalism – *political economy*; the second, originating during the same transformations but totally subordinated and marginalized, represents notions of more collective and conscious (hence egalitarian) forms of life, of socialism – *social economy*.

The 'moral ethos' of political economy has always eventuated in a set of activities of *regulation* in which increasingly secular and national agencies cumulatively act as a State system to ensure that effective and efficient capitalism survives and expands in England. This concern with effectiveness and efficiency has produced real progress for the majority of the population. I stress that, since it is far too easy (for academics and intellectuals) to 'fail to notice' exactly what changes in – above all else – health and housing provision have meant for working-class people in England. Indeed, it is with the ending of England's dominant position as a capitalist power (for which we might take Harold Wilson's July measures of 1966 as a symbolic announcement) that we have seen the relatively accelerating destruction and weakening of a State system which was constructed around a compromise between a social economy of socialism that would have left capitalism behind (since it valorizes all human beings for their qualities and resources) *and* a political economy, which resists the transformation that such a social economy would undertake. This book has been written in order to make the origins of the capitalist State in England more visible, to encourage historians and others to *extend* these provisional insights. Because *as historians* the authors are not merely academics, they are agreed that an understanding of how we arrived 'where we are' is an essential component of understanding how socialist change might be accomplished.

Until recently, a book attempting to trace the history of the State as a feature of the developing relations of capitalist production in England would have been unacceptable to many marxists. This followed from a seriously partial understanding of exactly what Marx's views on the State were – a discussion carried further in the first chapter. As Mary McIntosh has written in her chapter 'The State and the Oppression of Women' (1978:260):

> . . . the state cannot be conceived as external to the dominant mode of production, as is sometimes implied by a mechanical separation of the economic, the political and the ideological in which the state is located in the

political sphere. The idea of contrasting an interventionist with a non-interventionist state – *laissez-faire* versus state control – is a mistaken one, since even *laissez-faire* capitalism depends, for the conditions of its existence, upon the bourgeois state. Capital itself, with its mode of extracting surplus value, is a specific form of property established by a complex set of laws (with an ultimate sanction of coercion) through specific institutions. The 'free exchange' of commodities requires quite different laws from those of, say, feudal production as well as new forms of regulated money and credit. Thus although we may speak of state monopoly capitalism as a relatively late stage in the development of the capitalist mode of production in order to indicate the increasing scale of the state institutions and their direct involvement in capitalist enterprise, we must not suppose that the part played by the state was any less essential in the earlier 'competitive' stage.

Nevertheless such a set of relationships (which we call the State) did not drop from the sky. It was constructed, through complicated and extensive struggles, through time, by human beings grouped together by their differing relationships to the dominant mode of production. Alan Ryan in a review of Quentin Skinner's *The Foundations of Modern Political Thought* (1978), an essential two-volume complementary study to the texts of this book, has pointed to one facet of this moment which forms a theme of the second chapter:

   . . . it was essential that Augustine's *City of God* should lose ground to Aristotle's *Politics*, as from the middle of the thirteenth century it did. To see political science – in the widest sense – as a subject, it was necessary to work towards the idea that the task of governments was to maintain an entity distinct from the particular ruler – the state. By the beginning of the seventeenth century, writers talk about the state much as we do; at the beginning of the sixteenth century they do so intermittently at best, as all commentators on Machiavelli now notice.

But to get the idea of the state as the focus of politics into our conceptual apparatus, more than Aristotle was needed; the sovereignty of the emperor had to be challenged, in order to assert the legitimacy of each political entity in its own right; the church had to be denied any title to secular, coercive authority, and, the other side of the coin, the state had to be seen to exist for secular purposes and not for the salvation of souls. (*New Society*, 8 March 1979, p. 568)

But this 'idea of the state' contains within itself a range of empirical possibilities, different visions of the State as a system. These different visions are discussed in the third chapter, which examines a period when the class structure and capitalist relations of production are more consistently visible. It also addresses the years when – as has been argued elsewhere (Corrigan, 1977; Corrigan and Corrigan, 1978; and references) – the modern democratic Nation State began to achieve its recognizably modern forms: the 1830s. During that decade the specific 'moral ethos' of the English bourgeoisie, with its tendency to atomization as individual entrepreneur competes with individual entrepreneur, is submerged within the *materialization* of a much older patrician form of ideology which argued for the benefits of a longer term perspective than that 'dictated' by capitalist competition.

As is argued in the first chapter any mode of production entails a specific property-form and a particular division of social and technical labour. The modern State within capitalist social formations becomes increasingly concerned with forms of regulation that focus upon the reproduction of all those forms and relations necessary to the expansion of production for profit within that State's territory (*and* that of its colonies and client countries). A property-form and division of labour central to capitalism is that of patriarchy and the family. The State (through, for example, the registration of the population; laws relating to inheritance and the infantalization of the younger generation) has long been concerned with regulating these forms and divisions. This entails an extensive moral classification which operates culturally rather than through coercive means. This complex forms the basis of the fourth chapter.

As Christopher Hill, Edward Thompson and Raymond Williams have consistently argued; there are real limits to the *official* politics and morality engendered by the daily operations of the State. They require, for instance, some leverage upon reality *and* some evidence that, however partially, certain much advertised advantages (progress, access to a better life, respect for the individual, and so on) *are* being furthered by that morality and its rituals. It operates best when it is unremarked; when a particular way of carrying out some social acitivity becomes seen as the only way of so doing; when a particular *schooling* is inflated to become *education* itself. It is easy to suggest that 'the general population' (unlike academics and intellectuals) are fooled all of the time into simplistic reformism and 'mindless' apathy. But there is a tradition (extending over all the centuries of English social experience studied here) of alternative and opposing visions to that of the strategy of the capitalist State, and one strand in that set of visions is discussed in the fifth chapter.

The long established 'gentleman' ideal (service, quietism, a certain amateurism) was modified during the nineteenth century through the increasing (i) employment within the State (at first in a subaltern role) *and* (ii) general involvement with State regulation, *of professionals and experts* (cf. Abrams, 1968). That is to say, a particular way of legitimating the State's activities (and thereby naturalizing a certain range of such actions) increasingly draws upon the evidence and skills of experts from within technical, scientific and medical areas and latterly, from the wider areas of social policy. Such expertise was originally used to justify one course among several others; since the major changes associated with the period of the First World War, *that* set of social skills has been used more and more to set the terms of the debate itself. Recently it has been suggested that government policy 'choices' should be subject to 'participatory democracy', in which a group of experts and advisers (centralized in, for example, the Central Policy Review of the Cabinet Office) establish the policy choices and the people 'choose' *between the alternatives*. The ways in which this completes a procedure begun many centuries ago should be fairly obvious; such a procedure represents the final attempt to reduce politics to administration. The synchronization of that suggestion with the general crisis of the English State seems congruent with the analysis offered here.

These essays are *historical investigations* – attempts to establish the dominant questions (and ways of answering them). They do not constitute answers in themselves, although they suggest that certain explanations are more probable than others. But they also have a wider cumulative purpose within the production and reproduction of knowledge. One of the forms of the division of labour which the State helps to reproduce is that which makes a distinction between mental and manual labour. We have to overcome that if we are not only to understand the State but transform it, along with a more totalizing transformation of ourselves and all those circumstances which currently generate so much needless suffering, pain, anxiety and death in the service of profit and power. But academic life in England establishes a gulf within its own productions (and between itself and 'the general public' whose activity actually sustains academia!) by the personalized career in which individuals *streak* forward with their 'new' knowledge. As the editors of *Ideology and Cultural Production* (M. Barrett *et al.*, 1979:16) argue:

Icons and (significantly) Heroes have been promoted and equally rapidly disgraced with a bewildering ease which, curiously, leaves their earlier acolytes and epigones somehow more assured in their theoretical correctness. This process has been instrumental in the making of a series of individual – predominantly male, white, middle-class – reputations.

By contrast, as well as arguing for specific types of work we would also argue that different styles of work may be (and indeed fruitfully have been) adopted . . . We recognize, for instance, the need for a period of extensive consolidation in which different working groups familiarize themselves with a range of work. Although this consolidating task may involve the risk of repetition, we would argue that it is a necessary stage.

The imbalance in the ratio of women to men in this book should be noted as a serious shortcoming on two levels: that it exists at all, *and* that it exists despite a fairly energetic and extensive attempt to overcome it on the part of the editor.

This book, as noted in the Preface, covers a period until 1914 or so. It is argued that changes, which accompanied 'Reconstruction' during and after the First World War, and particularly during and after the Second Word War, are such that a separate set of essays are required. It is hoped that these will be produced under the title *State Reconstruction and Class Struggle in Twentieth-century England* during the early 1980s, by which time we should have at least a preliminary historical perspective on the major changes of the 1960s and early 1970s which we think will mark as decisive a period in English history as the 1530s, the 1640s or the 1830s (and their associated, complicated changes).

1

The State as a Relation of Production
Philip Corrigan, Harvie Ramsay, Derek Sayer[1]

The major argument advanced here has two facets. Firstly that there are major resources in the writings of Marx which internally relate the State to production. Secondly, recent historiography (both from above, including the form of administrative history, and from below) provides ample evidence to support Marx's analysis, although much of that historical writing does not sufficiently celebrate what it makes visible: the extensiveness but, at the same time, the fragility of the State. Notice, finally, that this chapter begins a work devoted to historical investigations of state *formation*; we stress that we are describing no simple structure, but a changing pattern of relations, primarily between classes, which we can understand as an organization or orchestration of the relations of production.

In this chapter we shall (as we have elsewhere[2]) provide extended quotations, particularly from the writings of Marx and Engels. It is necessary to do this partly to substantiate our own argument and partly to offer the texts which cumulatively show the partial quality of existing ways of understanding the views of Marx on the State. Although there is now a more extensive body of work which takes Marx's work on production as its starting point[3]; (and therefore generates a different understanding of political and cultural history, including State formation and class struggle) it is still necessary to start with some relatively simple premises. These are empirically open-ended, but not abstract, and they are simple. With them, and our quotations, we hope to establish a general historical and material connection between production and State forms.

Production means making things. Things are not made in abstraction, they are fashioned and fabricated in definite, concrete ways and those ways entail particular relations among the people who are engaged in that production or in making it possible for others to engage directly. These relations and, one aspect of them, ideas about the relationships, are produced and reproduced along with the products themselves. For Marx, all human beings 'enter into definite connections and relations with one another and only within these social connections and relations does their action on nature, does production, take place' (1849:80). That is to say, the ideas and relations (among people) are entailed in the production; or, in different terms, the 'production of life . . . appears as a twofold relation: on the one hand as a natural, on the other as a social relation . . .' (Marx and Engels, 1845:43). Speaking of one of the contradictory features of *capitalist* production, Marx argues: 'Forces of production and social relations – two different sides of the development of the social individual – appear to capital as mere means, and are merely means for it to produce on its limited foundation. In fact, however, they are the material conditions to blow this foundation sky-high.' (1858:706).

But the point we stress here is that, for Marx, forms of sociation and cooperation are *productive forces* (1845:43). This has very immediate implications for *how* we understand historical change as is now more generally recognized.[4] In volume 4 (part one) of *Capital* Marx stated quite bluntly: 'In this respect it can in fact be shown that *all* human relations and functions, however and in whatever form they may appear, influence material production and have a more or less decisive influence upon it.' (1863a:288)

That is to say, we are arguing that it is impossible (while remaining true to the historical experience of human societies) to isolate a 'way of making things' which is describable solely in terms of a particular technology, governed by certain economic laws.

A similar error is often found in the desire to establish the essence of a mode of production by abstracting property *ownership*˙ as its defining quality. A change of mode of production, according to this perspective, would be defined by a change of ownership and, possibly, by subsequent changes of use. It is impossible to separate either forces of production (narrowly conceived) or legalistic notions of property control, from the extensive political, cultural and other social relations which make that kind of production possible.[5] Marx and Engels relate these social relations of production by their conception of the division of labour:

> The various stages of development in the division of labour are just so many different forms of property, i.e. the existing stage in the division of labour determines also the relations of individuals to one another with reference to the material, instrument and product of labour. (1845:32)

> Division of labour and private property are, after all, identical expressions: in the one the same thing is affirmed with reference to activity as is affirmed in the other with reference to the product of that activity. (1845:46)

We entirely concur with Engels (in his famous letter of 27 October 1890) that historical materialism 'is easiest to grasp from the point of view of the division of labour'. Indeed, if we forget that perspective – and the practical study of class conflict and struggle (and the differential understanding of production it implies) – we shall only have a very partial understanding of State formation. Marx, as with all his 'abstractions', clearly emphasizes the commitment to investigation implied in his analytical schema. Thus in 1847 he argued against Proudhon:

> In each historical epoch, property has developed differently and under a set of entirely different social relations. Thus to define bourgeois property is nothing else than to give an exposition of all the social relations of bourgeois production.
> To try to give a definition of property as an independent relation, a category apart, an abstract and eternal idea, can be nothing but an illusion of metaphysics or jurisprudence. (1847b:154)

It is a point we shall return to in this chapter.

As far as a different conception of the State is concerned, Marx and Engels have provided ample indications (although as we conclude below, their writings are not free from ambiguity here, a point we have made at some length in relation to Bolshevism elsewhere[6]) of how false it is to abstract a schema or model from their metaphorical use of notions like 'base' or 'basis' and 'superstructure' (and to go further and create 'the economic', 'the political', 'the ideological' and so on, thus not merely 'the instances' of Althusserian theory[7]). For Marx and Engels, specific modes of production *entail* their social forms (including those of the State):

> The conditions under which definite productive forces can be applied are the conditions of the rule of a definite class of society, whose social power, deriving from its property, has its *practical*-idealistic expression in each case in the form of the State; and, therefore, every rev-

olutionary struggle is directed against a class, which till then has been in power. (1845:52)
. . . from the specific form of material production arises in the first place a specific structure of society, in the second place a specific relation of men to nature. Their State and their spiritual outlook is determined by both. (1863a:285)

The specific economic form, in which unpaid surplus-labour is pumped out of direct producers, determines the relationship of rulers and ruled . . . Upon this, however, is founded the entire formation of the economic community which grows up out of the production relations themselves, thereby simultaneously its specific political form. It is always the direct relationship of the owners of the conditions of production to the direct producers – a relation always naturally corresponding to a definite stage in the development of the methods of labour and thereby its social productivity – which reveals the innermost secret, the hidden basis of the entire social structure, and with it the political form of the relation of sovereignty and dependence, in short, the corresponding specific form of the State. (1865:791)

That is to say, to summarize these (and many unquoted) passages, State-forms are related to the social relations and conditions of specific modes of production *in their historical development*. State-forms are not related contingently and accidentally, nor are they externally related – as when the State is considered as a coercive set of relations (e.g. 'bodies of armed men, prisons') but, rather, internally. The forms of State are facets of a given mode of producing things, as essential to reproduction as particular kinds of property or technology – to be thought of, indeed, in the same terms as cultural *eidos* and moral *ethos*.[8] In class societies, State-forms will be both involved in the coercion of the majority *and* appear (phenomenally, i.e. in immediate experience)

as separate from day-to-day production, but we shall generate both partial history and distorted socialism if we take
one set of activities and their immediate appearance as total
explanation.

One final point is in order. Marx concludes the second
quotation given above by stressing the need for 'analysis of
the empirically given circumstances' (1865:792). This stress
upon the need to be historical and empirical is a persistent
theme in his work.[9] In *The German Ideology*, Engels and
he urged against the speculative philosophers of their time:

> Empirical observation must in each separate instance
> bring out empirically and without any mystification and
> speculation, the connection of the social and political
> structure with production. (1845:35)

> Abstractions in themselves, divorced from real history,
> have no value whatsoever. They can only serve to facili-
> tate the arrangement of historical material, to indicate
> the sequence of its separate strata. But they by no means
> afford a recipe or schema, as does philosophy, for neatly
> trimming the epochs of history. On the contrary, the
> difficulties begin only when one sets about the examina-
> tion and arrrangement of the material . . . and its actual
> presentation. (1845:37)

This requires the greatest possible emphasis at a time
when, sadly, many marxists suggest that the act of analysis,
the procedures of abstraction, *alone* explain, in a sudden
flash, the complexities of social experience.[10] Towards the
end of his life, Marx explicitly corrected such a misunder-
standing of his work by stressing that in *Capital* his analysis
was of concrete social forms, not abstractions.[11] One reason
for our starting with simple definitions, and for avoiding the
premature closure (and, we would argue, consequent fetish-
ization) entailed in *a priori* specific of causal primacy to
some allegedly objective/material base (against a supposedly

subjective/spiritual superstructure), is precisely in order to stress the constant need for empircal – above all, historical – investigation. Particular attention has to be given to the ways in which social phenomena are experienced. In turn, to be sure, we have to move beyond experience and its modes, to the structures and relations which make those experiences possible. Although they cannot be our stopping place, they have to constitute our starting point.

State and Capital

Thus far we have discussed the general relations between production and State- (and other social) forms. Let us now turn to that mode of production with which this book is concerned – capitalism.

Marx distinguishes 'capitalist production' by 'two characteristic features':

> *First*. It produces its products as commodities. The fact that it produces commodities does not differentiate it from other modes of production; but rather the fact that being a commodity is the dominant and determining characteristic of its products . . . the relation between capital and wage-labour determines the entire character of the mode of production.
> The *second* distinctive feature . . . is the production of surplus-value as the direct aim and determining motive of production. (1865:879–800)

This statement leads to a question: How does it come about that these specific conditions of production are possible? The answer, briefly, is through conflict a class struggle which turns as much on the construction of new social forms (including new State-forms), as on the desire to utilize existing social institutions. This is discussed in various writings of Marx (notably *Capital*, I: Part VIII and his notebooks for

Capital, the *Grundrisse*; for an excellent terse phrase see the latter, 1858:278) and the same pattern is traced by Max Weber (1920:Part IV). In the case of capitalism, particularly in England, it involves puncturing the 'naturalist' fantasies of the political economists (the notion of 'primitive accumulation'; or, how The Frugal Few 'emerge' from The Spendthrift Many) by tracing 'the forcible creation of a class of outlawed proletarians, the bloody discipline that turned them into wage labourers, the disgraceful action of the State which employed the police to accelerate the accumulation of capital by increasing the degree of exploitation of labour.' (1867a:742)

This anticipates points made in subsequent chapters, for example the stress (drawn there from Christopher Hill's work) on how, in Marx's words, 'the *governments*, e.g. of Henry VII, VIII etc., appear as conditions of the historic dissolution process and as makers of the conditions for the existence of capital.' (1858:507)

It is important to stress that state formation within capitalism is related both to class structure and to the development of nations. To take the first point, the state is 'nothing more than the form of organization which the bourgeois are compelled to adopt, both for internal and external purposes, for the mutual guarantee of their property and interests . . . it follows that all common institutions are set up with the help of the state and are given a political form.' (1845:90; cf. 1847a:319)

In other words *Burgerliche Gesellschaft* – bourgeois civil society – must assert *itself* in 'its external relations as nationality and internally must organize itself as state' (1845:89, our emphasis). But Marx is also clear that this bourgeois class forms 'a class only insofar as they have to carry on a common battle against another class; in other respects they are on hostile terms with each other as competitors.' (1845:77; cf. 1847b:176; 1858:218f.). State formations are *national* States since capitalism (as a global system) involves national organization to secure the *inter*nationalization of its production relations. Marx wrote to Engels (8 October 1858): 'The specific task of bourgeois society is the establishment of a world market, at least in outline, and of production based upon this world market.'

Moreover this internationalization has internal effects. In discussing nothing less than the genesis of the industrial capitalist, we find Marx remarking how the 'different momenta of primitive accumulation' arrived in England at the end of the *seventeenth* century,

> . . .as a systematical combination, embracing the colonies, the national debt, the modern mode of taxation, and the protectionist system. These methods depend in part on brute force, e.g. the colonial system, but they all employ the power of the State, the concentrated and organized force of society, to hasten, hot-house fashion, the process of transformation of the feudal mode of production into the capitalist mode, and to shorten the transition. Force is the midwife of every old society pregnant with a new one. It is itself an economic power. (1867a:751)

Engels notes in a letter of 27 October 1890 that 'Force (that is State power) is also an economic power.'

It is only after this analysis, this comprehension of a whole series of political, economic, and cultural changes, that we can make sense of Marx's and Engels' stress on how State and Market formation are related: 'The bourgeois has at last, since the establishment of Modern Industry and of the world-market, conquered for itself, in the modern representative State, exclusive political sway. The executive of the modern State is but a committee for managing the common affairs of the whole bourgeoisie. (*Communist Manifesto*, 1848:37)

Weber notes that out of these experiences 'arose the national citizen class, the bourgeoisie in the modern sense of the word' (1920:249; cf. 1918:82). For Marx and Engels:

The term 'civil society' emerged in the eighteenth century, when property relations had already extricated themselves from the ancient and medieval community. Civil society as such only develops with the bourgeoisie: the social organization evolving directly out of production and intercourse, which in all ages forms the basis of the state and the rest of the idealistic superstructure, has, however, always been designated by the same name. (1845:89)[12]

But, it is now time to establish firmly that this 'evolving' is not evolution – a naturally developing process linked to some metaphysical notion of the 'logic of development'. It is a constant class struggle *and* a struggle between national bourgeoisie and national bourgeoisie. The State is not a structure, it is an organization; or, better, it is a complex of social forms *organized* so that it inflects all relations and ideas about relations in such a way that capitalist production, and all it entails, becomes thought of and lived as natural.

We shall discuss later how such appearances come to seem natural. First, however, it is important to stress that we have to locate the State's operation (which we wish to consider as *regulation*) within a wider 'field of force' determined, in the sense of sequences and boundaries, by how things are made, distributed and consumed in a given social formation. It is normal to see moral categories as separate from the State, but what the State regulates depends upon such a prior categorization of human beings (sexed, aged, classed, graded, placed, and so on). This cultural realm cannot be ignored, since it amounts to particular forms of the division of labour. State formation and moral regulation are internally related.

Secondly, we have to understand how the social forms of the State are established through (and do not merely result from) continuing intra- and inter-class conflicts and struggles. These struggles themselves, perhaps centring on contradictions inextricably involved with capitalism. Thus actual social forms of education (particularly schooling) or welfare (particularly the 'insurance principle') result from contestations that involve class and other differences. It is literally impossible to discover *what* they are without acknowledging the ways in which the division of labour, class and other structured differences of experience have been compelled to 'live' and 'work' within forms that proclaim their universality and neutrality *vis à vis* empirical difference. This is discussed in different ways in the chapters which follow.

Capitalist production relations in practice (and in many instances this is articulated theoretically as well) entail certain regularly repeated and reliable resources which no single entrepreneur could rely upon. Given the nature of the central capitalist production relations, (division of labour, class, patriarchy,[13] capital's stockpiling of people, and so on) which are not likely to encourage direct organization (at the level of the enterprise) for such requirements, the State increasingly takes over various regulations, producing, and reproducing activities for itself. This does *not* render the State secondary to production or above it – such topographical metaphors have had the most disastrous history in marxism. Increasingly, what should be seen as a *capitalist* cultural revolution is being organized and orchestrated through *State* agencies. But this is, to repeat, always an area of class and other contestations. Marx regarded the pressure of the early trade unionists and others that established the Factory Acts, as a major and progressive *advance* for the working class.

Central to much of this is, of course, the issue of *legitimacy*; as Weber argued (in a far too sexually narrow manner): 'the State is a relation of men dominating men, a relation supported by means of legitimate (i.e. considered to be legitimate) violence.' (1918:78)

For Gramsci: 'The State is the entire complex of practical and theoretical activities with which the ruling class not only justifies and maintains its dominance, but manages to win

the active consent of those over whom it rules . . .'
(1934:244)

'Legitimacy' and '*active* consent' are not static or abstract,
but extremely turbulent descriptions. There is first the problem that neither theorists who speak of 'will' nor those who
speak of 'force' as the basis of the State and/or of law can
deal with the problems of agency and form (Marx
1845:328f.). The problem is that individual will or force has
to be presented as more than individual – and more than
class, of course – but it first has to be established as a basis
for relations among the bourgeoisie. The forms established
here, some of which are discussed in the following chapters,
will be extremely diverse, since the struggle will often
involve different kinds of enemy: aristocracy, church, other
national systems, a unified proletariat, and sections of the
proletariat organized through, e.g. trade unions or music-
halls. This establishes a State *system*, which can be comprehended analytically with coherence and consistency over
time. However, it must be recalled that these analytical
shapes and categories are lived as constant negotiation, fragility and flexibility. The remarks of Edward Thompson on
the limits of hegemony (quoted in the second chapter) are
salient here.

Nevertheless, if the State did not sustain an appearance
of being 'above' sectional interests and 'outside' the economy (just as the law needs its abstract justice-for-all if it is
to operate) it could not operate to further a particular way
of making things *and* the crystallized interests (and not only
those of the ruling classes) of a given national formation.
But these are appearances, *phenomenal forms*: the way reality presents itself through the categories of common sense
and is handled, practised and reproduced in daily life. Furthermore, and Marx has stressed this[14], capitalism generates
and sustains *separateness* and *competition* as its two most
'energetic' categories, along with a consequent series of
classifications and gradings of the 'individuals' and
'instances'. Any analysis which is to go beyond the phenom-

enal forms which surround us (and yet remain true to the experience of those forms, and not attempt false, violent, partial or inadequate *abstraction*[15]) has to make connections with what is experienced as separate and individual, and prise apart that which we live and think of as fundamentally unified.

There are two general views of the State against which we are arguing: the instrumental (the State is there to be used and appropriated by the ruling class or the ruling faction of the dominant class) *and* the superstructural (the State reflects, in the realms of political and ideological relations, the 'facts' of production). The former leads to the notion of the State as a *thing* or *machine*; the latter leads to the idea of the State as ideational, totally false, a mere disguise (velvet gloves) hiding 'reality' (iron fists). There is support for these views in a number of marxists texts, but neither view is congruent with the way Marx and others conduct their detailed analyses, and both lead to the most dangerous political consequences.

Our view begins with the appearance (we might go so far as to suggest 'necessary appearance' providing the term is not misunderstood as a *functional* slip) of State *forms* as separate (i) from production relations, or, more exactly, from 'the economy' (and, often, from 'politics' especially in the case of the law's appeal to abstract and universal principles and rituals); (ii) from each other. The latter is often forgotten, but it is a crucial form of the appearances we are trying to understand, *especially in England*. That is to say, under capitalism the relations of production (the way in which things are made) take the form of separate or loosely connected (e.g. the State *intervenes* or 'the economy' *restrains*) institutional spheres, levels, instances, areas, and so on. That is the way they are experienced. Marx *all his life* (e.g. 1843:167; 1871a, b, c) acknowledged the experiential reality of these separations (what Sartre has called 'pseudo-totalities') *and* argued that (i) analysis had to go beyond them, in order to 'grasp the phenomena' of State, law, cultural relations or production; and (ii) socialism could be defined as (a) that 'going beyond' and (b) the supersession of such separations and false combinations, when 'the public power will lose its political character' in the words of the *Manifesto of the Communist Party* of 1848.

These fundamental forms of separation and false links are cemented into common sense through being *fetishized*.[16] This means, in brief, the denial of the human and historical, i.e. conditional and changeable, quality of social relations in favour of their *naturalization*. In Marx's words, fetishism is a matter of 'metamorphizing the social, economic character imposed on things in the process of social production, into a natural character stemming from the material nature of those things' (1878:229). This is not primarily accomplished by coercion or by cultural 'bombardment'. The production forms which confront us have an enduring naturalness which dwarfs the human population and denies the human history without which they would be dead matter. This dull, repetitive facticity of the obvious ('Well, I mean, that's the way it is, isn't it? – how many conversations end like this, with bafflement *and* dissatisfaction?') accomplishes a great deal, but there *are* idealizations and explanations to accompany and justify those experiences: 'The ruling ideas are nothing more than the ideal expression of the dominant material relations, the dominant material relations grasped as ideas; hence of the relations which make the one class the ruling one, therefore, the ideas of its dominance.' (1845:59)

The two forms of knowledge meet in what we can call a moral topography: unsatisfactory experiences (of feeling less than human, but understanding that's *how it has to be*) are 'explained' theoretically,

> the conditions of existence of the ruling class . . . [are] ideally expressed in law, morality, etc., [conditions] the ideologists of that class more or less consciously give a sort of theoretical independence; they can be conceived

by separate individuals of that class as vocation, etc., and are held up as a standard of life to the individuals of the oppressed class, *partly as embellishment or recognition of domination, partly as a moral means of this domination.* (1845:419–420, our emphasis)

The State within capitalist production, regulates and orchestrates – in short, *organizes* – in such a way that the defining material characteristics of capitalist production relations (individualization, formal equality, and a host of social forms) are made to appear the only way those social activities could be conducted and arranged. *Some* social arrangements become equal to *civilization*. The State regulates relations *which themselves* give rise to the phenomena we have been discussing: an 'economy' which has an 'outtthereness' *vis-à-vis* all other relations and spheres – 'politics', 'culture' and even 'everyday life'. What we are pointing to is that 'the economy', governed by certain laws and understood through certain theoretical propositions, those of 'economics', is one of the phenomenal forms of capitalist production relations; one facet, one 'way-in', to understanding how capitalist production works. Its separateness is not unreal; as an area of social life it is not illusory, a sham, or a delusion. The problem arises from conflating and confusing an 'economy' thus conceived *and* capitalist production relations. The latter are far more comprehensive than the former, not merely making that phenomenon of 'the economy' possible; but also including political (State) and cultural relations as some of the means through which *that* way of making things, in *that* social formation, at *that* time, is made possible.

Equally, as we indicated above, such a perspective has implications (as it clearly does in Marx) for what socialist construction might be thought of as comprising. Communism means, for Marx, when people collectively and consciously (and increasingly in egalitarian ways, we would add) organize production, regulating it for social purposes (it is

in this sense that Marx speaks of 'social control'; 1867b:412).
Under those circumstances, the separations and combinations assumed to be so civilized and yet, conversely, so
natural would *wither away*. It is necessary to argue this with
some force, given the many statements which identify socialism with a larger and larger State apparatus, with more and
more regulation from above, in short with *exactly* the
opposite of what Marx and others intend by socialist construction: 'the rational medium in which . . . class struggle
can run through its different phases . . . It begins the *emancipation of labour*' (1871a:171).

Having said that, it is necessary again to stress the constructed and fragile *nature of official reality*. While Marx
points to the struggles which make 'the relations which make
the one class the ruling one' (1845:59) into 'natural forms
of social life' (1867b:168; another translation has 'natural,
self-understood forms of social life' 1867a:75) he also points
to the always-open-to-discovery *history* of such natural
forms:

> The categories of bourgeois economics consist precisely
> of such forms of this kind. They are forms of thought
> which are socially valid, and therefore objective, for the
> relations of production belonging to this historically
> determined mode of social production i.e. commodity
> production. The whole mystery of commodities, all the
> magic and necromancy that surrounds the products of
> labour on the basis of commodity production, vanishes
> therefore as soon as we come to other forms of produc-
> tion. (1867b:169; cf. 1867a:76)

Marx then moves on (as elsewhere) to criticize all those
Robinsonades – stories of the fundamental first human unit
which, curiously, is always governed by *capitalist* notions –
which push back the relations and conceptions of a historically specific form of production to the origins of human
history. Instead (and this is fundamental to Sayer's *Marx's*

Method where the argument is presented in full) Marx's *critique* establishes analytical categories (or what he calls 'primary equations') *in order to investigate* the historical construction of the relations and forms within which we live. Because, 'from the moment that the bourgeois mode of production and the conditions of production and distribution which correspond to it are *recognized as historical*, the delusion of regarding them as natural laws of production vanishes and the prospect opens up of a new society . . .' (1863c:429; our emphasis. Cf. Sayer, 1978a)

It is that method which, in their different ways, has been employed by the writers here.

We stress (as they do) that the State is constructed and fought over. Central to this is a two-fold set of historical practices: (i) the constant 'rewriting' of history to naturalize what has been, in fact, an extremely changeable set of State relations, to claim that there is, and has always been, one 'optimal institutional structure' which is what 'any' civilization needs; *and* (ii) to marginalize (disrupt, deny, destroy, dilute, 'help') all alternative forms of State, particularly any which announce any form of organization that establishes *difference* at the level of the national social formation (or, crime of all crimes!, that establishes any form of international solidarity along class lines). The State suppression of international solidarity in England against Jacobin ideas in the 1790s and against Bolshevik ideas in the 1910s and 1920s is structurally similar. Although much of this has been effected through coercion-in-general, and particular agencies of regulation (especially State Servants – the organic intellectuals of the ruling class *par excellance* and our real rulers, as Edward Thompson has recently discussed, 1978c,d,e); the real forms of State dominion are the apparently classless and eternal 'rituals of ruling' and the categories of moral absolutism, not least the declarations concerning both 'the national interest' and 'rationality' or 'reasonableness'. What such rituals and categories make possible is a way of discussing political priorities which makes unsayable much of what are lived as political problems. But the same rituals and categories also make much else impossible to discuss *at all*.

The struggle against these State forms therefore involves forms of combination and organization which enable a materialization and discussion of what are otherwise understood as private worries and personal anxieties. Over and over again in English history, such groups have been formed and transformed as the subsequent chapters point out. The problem is further complicated by the historical fact that one rallying cry through which modern State forms were established was that of *Improvement* and (less solidly articulated) *Progress*. Who could be against better sanitation, public parks, libraries or galleries, and the wider provision of education? But these were never offered *in vacuo* as 'social goods'; they were made available in specific social forms of State provision which, moreover, marginalized and suppressed *pre-existing* class and other alternatives. Again, the means used to establish these social forms were acts of categorization and classification – the construction of that social vocabulary or 'public languages', through which social experience is increasingly articulated.

It is as well to interject here a brief cautionary phrase about *intentionality*. Far more than is generally grasped, much of what we have been describing was *intended*; the following chapters (and Corrigan Ph.D. thesis Chs. 3 and 4) show how different strategies and tactics were discussed in class terms, as interventions against alternatives, in relation to production, and so on. But there are also ways in which, as we indicated briefly above, the ruling classes are not fully free to act in *any* way they wish. Firstly, there are (*within* capitalism) necessary laws which can only be ignored at the risk of bankruptcy or minimal effectiveness. Secondly, they face competition within and without – from alternative conceptions of ruling and from other national bourgeoisies. Thirdly, they are far from the unified group that is normally spoken of. Marx argued that the State in this limited and special sense is a far more comprehensive expression of capitalist rule than the enterprise; or rather, to return to our discussion of 'the economy' and 'politics' above, *both* have to be understood as forms of rule *internally related* as front and back of the same complex (to use a figure from Mao Tse-tung).

To sum up before our concluding section: all State forms under capitalism *are* constituted through continuing conflicts, struggles, and contradictions, despite their seeming natural and civilized status *above* society. Although the State regulates capitalist production relations, acting consistently in favour of vanguard production forms and 'national' capitalist interests, its rule is founded upon two prior systems of ritual and category: a wider moral classification which grades the phenomenally separate individuals through certain, often legally defined, forms, and, secondly, the dull and repeated obviousness of the way things can be made in *that* mode of production. That the latter (whose natural obviousness underpins the moral classification) is now the only way to do things, results from a long and bloody struggle to deny the validity of alternatives. That struggle is as much part of the way things are as our language; indeed the two are, of course, inseparable – to call an act 'illegal' (as opposed to unfortunate, scandalous, terrible, or accidental) is to mobilize common sense expectations. But this is not simply the result of 'calling people names', although we often seriously ignore just how material these verbal descriptions are, but because those 'names' do confirm and justify the way we live our lives (so we are told). Socialist understanding of the State – a stage before any transformations are possible – has to come to terms with this very broad canvas of social experience.

Conclusion

We mentioned that there are some 'ambiguities' and 'shifts' in Marx (as in Engels, Lenin, and others)[17] concerning how we should understand the State. One way to illustrate the contrast (but not without its difficulties) is between understanding the State as an *organism* or as an *organization*, i.e. as an evolving natural form of human progress or as a specifically constructed set of social forms particular to a given stage. It could further be suggested, that this difference relates in turn to different conceptions of a wider understanding of society as a whole: those in which, for example, the division of labour is understood philosophically (as establishing different social realms) and those in which it is firmly understood in terms of production relations that permeate the whole social formation. We do not propose to follow this exegesis in detail here.[18]

We wish to draw attention to two bodies of writing which offer contrasting views *and* to the two views of the relation between such State forms and socialism which they make possible. Marx and Engels are often represented as *centralizers*, concerned to make the State responsible for everything. Two texts are often pointed to as evidence for this: the first is the 'programme' at the heart of the *Manifesto* of the Communist Party of 1848, the second is the Address of the Central Authority to the League of March 1850 which ends 'as in France in 1793, so today in Germany it is the task of the really revolutionary party to carry through the strictest centralization' (1850:285). But *within two years* Marx, at the close of the *Eighteenth Brumaire*, is talking of the need to *smash* rather than *perfect* the Capitalist State. Secondly – and it is scandalous that *seventy years* after Lenin drew attention to these 'corrections' we still have to emphasize them – Marx and Engels wrote a new Preface for a German edition of the *Manifesto* in 1872 in which they state explicitly that their programme 'at the end of Section II' of the 1848 text, would, in many respects, by very differently worded today. In view of the gigantic strides of Modern Industry . . . [and] in view of the practical experience gained, first in the February Revolution, and then, still more, in the Paris Commune, where the proletariat for the first time held political power for two whole months, this programme has in some details become antiquated. One thing especially was proved by the Commune, viz., that 'the working class cannot simply lay hold of the ready-made State machinery and wield it for its own purposes.' (1872:31–32)[19]

The last few words are, of course, taken from Marx's tribute to the Paris Commune in his *Civil War in France*. These remain neglected texts for understanding the *capitalist* State – not least because they 'correct' certain formulations of the 1850s, when Marx appears to suggest that any State could *really* rule above Society (the so-called Bonapartist phenomenon). Instead, he stresses that all State formations under capitalism articulate class power. With the drafts and texts about the Commune (1871a,b,c) Marx and Engels announce that there are great costs in any attempt to transform capitalism which makes use of the State innocently. A confusion which Gramsci was to remark many years later: 'The confusion of class-State and regulated society is peculiar to the middle-classes and petty intellectuals, who would be glad of any regularization that would prevent sharp struggles and upheavals. It is a typically reactionary and regressive conception.' (1934:258)

Marx's and Engels's remarks on 'Conservative, or bourgeois, socialism' in the *Manifesto* and Marx's discussion of the 'peculiar character of the Social-Democracy' in the *Eighteenth Brumaire* are extremely relevant to this discussion.

In this context what was remarkable about 'our heroic brothers and sisters' in the Commune, was this. It was essentially a working-class government, the produce of the struggle of the producing against the appropriating class, the political form at last discovered under which to work out the economic emancipation of labour. (1871c:72)

> It was a Revolution against the *State* itself . . . a Revolution to break down the horrid machinery of Class-domination itself . . . Only the Proletarians fired by a new social task to be accomplished by them for all society, to do away with all classes and class rule, were the men to break the instrument of that class rule – the State . . . (1871a:167)

> The Commune does not [do] away with the class struggles . . . but it affords the rational medium in which that class struggle can run through its different phases . . . It begins the *emancipation of labour* . . . (1871a:171)

It is imperative to stress here a partiality shared by so many of the classics of marxism: a tendency to write as if liberation was to be effected by, and for, men alone. We have remarked it elsewhere,[20] but it should *always* be 'marked' and not reproduced. Any system of representation which signifies (by silence or by positive branding) some group as less than fully human has to be transformed on the road – a long and winding road – of socialist construction.

Now this contrast between transformation and reform of the capitalist State should not be read as a new absolutism, a new purity. On the contrary, we have always argued for the greatest possible *tactical seriousness* – working with and within, contesting and combatting, all forms of the State – seeking to 'humanize' and 'open' their working. But we have also stressed that these are a series of tactics, subordinate to a wider political comprehension (i.e. not sufficient in themselves), and not to be confused with a *strategy of contempt*. That is a consequence of realizing that all capitalist relations are permeated with fundamental values of how things are made under capitalism – to reduce all objects (and many relations) to the commodity form *and* to generate surplus value which is privatized or used to perpetuate the system itself.[21] What we have discussed here is also a view of how a socialist strategy is established: through recognizing mistakes. As Lenin said, only those who do nothing never make mistakes. We cited a second text, besides the Manifesto, in which Marx and Engels appeared as *centralizers*. Thirty-five years later, Engels admitted that he and Marx had made aŋ error: 'At that time – thanks to the Bonapartist and liberal falsifiers of history – it was considered as established that the French centralized machine of administration had been introduced by the Great Revolution'; but it was later realized that such State forms were *instruments of reaction* from the beginning. (Engels, 1885:285–286)

Such an analysis and such a perspective are also linked to a wider strategy which is drawn from Marx and others: that socialist construction (i) does not begin from some singular moment called 'The' Revolution, and although it entails a series of such sudden moments of 'overthrow', it also requires a direct challenge and an attempted transformation of all the relations that sustain minority rule for profit; (ii) centres upon the simultaneous transformation of circumstances and selves, a persistent 'irritation of the obvious'; categories and rituals of social life which question the taken-for-granted objectivity of certain facts (in order to discover their historicity) *or*, contrastingly, the seeming subjective (in the sense of personal) quality of feelings, worries and problems. We argued above, that the division of labour is manifest through, and embodied within, all political institutions within capitalism. By the term 'division of labour' we do not merely indicate The Three Great Differences (between town and country, between large-scale industrial and small-scale agrarian production, and between mental and manual labour; in all cases the former hegemonizes the latter and thc third dominates all the others – Marx, 1845; 1871a,b,c) but all the rituals and categories through which human beings are graded and placed. It is in these precise areas that it makes sense to relate (i) the division of labour (normally taken as a matter of 'economics') to political and cultural relations and (ii) the abolition of politics and culture as a separate realm of social life to the abolition of the division of labour. This is what Marx and Engels meant in *The German Ideology* (points recalled in *The Civil War in France* by Marx in 1871): 'It follows from what was said above against Feuerbach that previous revolutions within the framework of division of labour were bound to lead to new political institutions; it likewise follows that the communist revolution, which removes the division of labour, ultimately abolishes political institutions . . .' (1845:380; the 'above' refers to 1845:52–3).

We have tried here (partly in a general sense, and partly in anticipation of the following chapters) to point to the ways in which State forms can be analyzed *relationally*, rather than in terms of their separateness or institutional effectivity. Central to what we have argued is a particular notion of production relations and the centrality, under capitalism, of classes, class struggle and contradictions. We have made our initial definitions simple in order to make possible an opening of doors that have for too long been marked as closed, and to demolish all those far too solid walls which demarcate the 'disciplines' of knowledge that keep us apart from one another. Finally, we have suggested that historical materialism – the resources (made available by Marx and others) understood, however, in the light of historical experience and not as Biblical, Talmudic or Koranic scriptures – provides a more comprehensive body of theory (not least in the work of several generations of historians in England and elsewhere) than any other to enable us to understand our present. For our project is not to move backwards into the past, but to establish the historical qualities of our present and the rich human resources which current 'social arrangements', especially the forms of State regulation, do not allow to flourish. We believe that these resources – the women and men who currently labour unwillingly to sustain production for a profit which is privatized or distributed without their consent or control – are the real resources for socialism and that when they are unleashed we shall see (as history has shown) that *things can be different*. It is to that future that we have dedicated our work.

2

Towards a History of State Formation in Early Modern England[1]
Philip Corrigan

As has been made clear in the introduction, this book does not set out to provide finished interpretations of State formation in any of its parts but *cumulatively* aims to suggest strategies (questions, methods, evidence) for this project. However, this chapter is even more fragile than the others. First, there is the time span: from one 'revolution in government' (the 1530s) to another (the 1830s), even if most of the remarks arise from thinking about the eighteenth century. Secondly, the latter focus shows that we lack a sufficiently firm conceptualization or framework for eighteenth-century English social experience, central to which must be forms and relations of a State/class character. Let us start with this uncertainty and then move backwards to the 1530s and earlier before returning to the crucial fifty years or so before 1776 when Adam Smith's *Wealth of Nations*, Bentham's *Fragment of Government*[2] and certain problems with English rule in North America signify one of those *moments* which this book attempts to illuminate.

In 1964, Edward Thompson outlined a project for tackling the problem of the eighteenth century in his 'Working-Class

Culture and the Transition to Industrialism' when he noted that: 'there is still an unbridged gap between seventeenth-century studies and the industrial revolution. We might see one way of bridging this gap if we followed the problems of labour discipline and of deference. Christopher Hill's *Society and Puritanism in Pre-Revolutionary England* offers the foundations of a bridge from the seventeenth-century side of the gap.' (Thompson, 1964:4).

He was too modest to stress how his own *The Making of the English Working Class* (1963) provides the foundations on the nineteenth-century side. Thompson has followed his own advice[3] and his work, taken together with that of Christpher Hill (as an implicit methodology, as a socialist project, *and* for what it shows which we simply did not know previously), is the basis for anything empirically useful in this chapter. Thompson's work has also resulted in unpublished dissertations and two major texts from the seminars at the Centre for Social History: *Albion's Fatal Tree* and his own *Whigs and Hunters*. There has been much work in areas of culture[4] and crime,[5] both of which provide useful resources for thinking about the eighteenth-century State. But it remains the case, simply and crudely, that we have no stock of *issues for debate* (signifying clashes of paradigm) concerning the specificity of the class structure and State formation of the eighteenth century such as say, the 1640s/1680s or the years after 1780 have generated in modern historiography. Such issues as we do have, furthermore, tend to have their roots in either of those earlier/later periods, with the possible (and very important) exception of work which takes the *overlap* of cultural, property and work *relations* for its prime problem.[6]

A number of recent comparative works[7] (of which Tilly, 1975, is probably the most useful) have drawn attention to the procedures by which modern States are formed, but even the best of these tends to concentrate upon a view from the top and the procedures of administrative history.

There are grave dangers of Whiggery here (the general assertion that everything improves for everyone, technical/ administrative measures 'mopping up' the marginal and localized 'problems'). This ignores the double relations which energize State formation: alternative national groupings or other State systems *and* pressure from within the single social formation. These worlds – without and within – go much further than any abstracted notions of motivation or purely technical solutions. From a very early stage we find crucial Officers of State[8] concerned with discovering what is 'taking place' in those worlds within and without. In the latter case this may be codified (most notably in the case of different Tsars in Russia) into a programme of 'Learning from Abroad'. But care must be taken with developing this line of argument in case we imply that *continuity* appears to permeate English State Institutions; a continuity, moreover, pleasing to Whigs and infuriating to marxist theorists. But it is only an *appearance*; there are quite major discontinuities and fissures allowing old institutions and rituals to be employed in novel ways. Nevertheless such an appearance has some solid material validity; there has never been either a full codification of law or a total rationalization of State offices. A different kind of continuity is also evident: the doctrines that informed oppositions to existing or suggested State practices often drew upon myths of the ancient past, notably that of an egalitarian Saxon constitution *before* 'The Norman Yoke' (Hill, 1954).[9]

One of the best surveys of what its author regards as coherently still a feudal social formation (at least as a polity) is Perry Anderson's limpid chapter 'England' (1974: Ch. 5) which correctly emphasizes (although not in these terms) the manner in which apparently procedural and organizational changes can have the most profound consequences for State forms and strategies. The Norman administrative system, the unitary Parliament as at least a negative check on Royal and baronial absolutism, amongst other changes, established a material groundwork which had enduring consequences. Indeed, traces of that peculiar administrative-legislative 'arrangement' are to be found in England today. The real value of Anderson's survey is his synthesis of the *international* context of the Tudor State. This compensates for his systematic refusal to grasp the complex of forces *within* the English social formation, both those internal to the ruling class alliances and *blocs* and those diffused beyond. Fortunately, we have some excellent, detailed studies of the Tudor State which take these matters for their prime object of study; notably the work of Elton[10] or Loades on the making of the *political nation*[11] – the resources of people and procedures with which coherently modern State forms are constructed in a very complicated and extended movement through until the 1830s or even later. In Hill's direct phrase of twenty years ago: 'The Reformation in England was an act of state' (1956b:41). This is a general theme of this chapter: the closest possible link between productive changes and labour régimes *and* the changing forms of State activity. Hill stresses the economic and social consequences of the Henrician Reformation 'which played their part in preparing for the Revolution of 1640–49' (ibid.)[12] centrally through (i) weakening the Church, (ii) changing the nature of Royal rule, and (iii) creating and sustaining a host of 'new men'. In turn, inasmuch as these 'resulted' from the sale/distribution of Church lands and other Royal patronage, they were also fundamentally implicated in changes in agrarian production and England's 'placing' in the world of trade and manufacture.

Mobility and fluidity represent central problems for the early modern State in England: by the early seventeenth century the phenomenon of 'masterless men' (Hill, 1972: Ch. 1) marks a staging post in the long and bloody history of the relationship between State control and regulation and labour discipline, vagrancy and vagabondage.[13] This relationship between State and labour which has been detailed elsewhere (Corrigan and Corrigan, 1978) stresses *how* Thomas Cromwell's revolution orchestrated and strengthened existing agencies, Erastianized some and created yet others. The range of such agencies available by 1600 qualifies for the name of 'system'. It is important, however, to note the complementary range of controls and regulating agencies/ officials in the areas of recreation, culture and 'mentalities'. The control of printing and the theatre are particularly important areas for study,[14] since the former signifies the circulation of ideas and the latter represents the 'dangerous' area of interpretation-by-performance, which has always been so troublesome to 'the powers that be'. The problem of new forms of labouring/new kinds of property *and* open discussion/commentary are, of course, linked in such pamphlets as Fish's *Supplication of Beggars* (1528).[15]

A central social form crystallizing everything so far mentioned was, of course *the town* (Clark and Slack, 1976; Corfield, 1976) which had particular cultural consequences (not simply those of theatre and the early newspapers, nor yet only the increasing dominance of London,[16] but acute problems of moral regulation: Falkus, 1976; Storch, 1979). Of particular importance within this series of changes is the forming of new solidarities and connections between localized urban élites and the State – which is not at all to suggest any sudden change, nor a rapid displacement of the 'landed interest' which continues to be powerful into the twentieth century. The best sketch of the changing class structure and its relation to State formation in the period under consideration is given in Anderson's chapter (1974: I: Ch. 4) providing we integrate (i) the cultural insights of Hill, (ii) the detail of Aylmer, and (iii) the newly developed area of *economic policy*. This was not even new at this time: works mentioned earlier, (see note 7), taken with Olive Coleman's recent study (1976) of the information available to medieval State officials, show the distant origins of many Tudor, Stuart and Commonwealth *means* to effect policy, although it is also clear how the Tudor era saw the origins of a *system* (including the registration of people) and the Commonwealth-Restoration-Settlement saw the meaning/understanding of that system change. What is now becoming known, however, is the extent of the State's involvement in economic policy, particularly in the distinctive form of *regulation*. What is meant by this is best illustrated from a recent analysis of 'The State and the English Iron Industry in the Sixteenth and Seventeenth Centuries' (Hammersley, 1976) which, although arguing for a pattern of 'modified chaos', has to point to the firm 'basis for restrictive control . . . used sparingly and in response to selective pressures' (1976:180). A pattern of regulation is coherently present in a variety of forms: State employment (e.g. dockyards), the flexible use of administrative rules to benefit certain forms of production or trade, and particular kinds of 'vanguard' labour discipline or payment systems have all been detected.[17] Most recently, Joan Thirsk's 1975 Ford Lectures (published as *Economic Policy and Projects* 1977) discuss 'a deliberate government policy to foster the native manufacture of consumer goods'.

But, as previously mentioned, State concern at the level of cultural relationships is also evidenced in general perspectives upon age or the family (Thomas, 1976; Stone, 1977; Thompson, 1977b; Hill, 1978), upon inheritance (Goody *et al.*, 1976, especially Thompson 1976b), or upon *dress* (Harte, 1976; cf. Buck, 1976). Any theory of the activity and effectiveness of State formation during the early modern period will have to come to terms with the question as to whether or not these different arenas of State action employed a similar 'classification', such that all the policies were inflected not simply toward the preservation or extension of the control of the powerful, but to establish that control in particular ways which also reinforced the 'naturalness' of the power. To mention 'naturalness' is quite deliberately provocative, given the turbulent period under discussion when whole sets of what had been 'natural' (especially collective and customary) rights were being transformed during the two large periods of enclosure. Any new 'natural' order had to be enforced. It was an order, moreover, which could not draw so simply upon divine sanctification or even, after the removal of the King's head, upon the knowledge that there was one 'true' apex to the social pyramid – *a person*. The change signified by Aylmer's two books – *The King's Servants, The State's Servants* – is one of the most important longer term consequences of the English Revolution in terms of conceptualizing the State, completing, in some senses, a set of 'breaks' begun (as mentioned above) with the cutting of the links between the (Roman Catholic) Church and landed property.

Christopher Hill's work, of course, has been centrally concerned to record and understand the English Revolution, especially in the related areas of political theory and class formation. He has stressed (1940a, b; 1956a) that (i) the transfer of property, wealth and power 'from one class to another' (during the Commonwealth) 'enormously accelerated, especially by the intervention of the State' (1940a: 157); and (ii): 'In this new commercial world the King is the most obvious example of the type of big landowner who could not adapt himself: Crown lands had almost all been sold before James II went on his travels. Conformably to the new economic order, the King ceased to be a landlord living of his own, and became a salaried official.' (1940a: 193).

What was also taking place was the enlargement of (and change within) the political nation. At the level of office-holding this has been studied not only in Aylmer's two books but in his recent paper, 'Office-holding, Wealth and Social Structure in England, c. 1580 – c. 1720'.[18] This valuable survey can be complemented by a reassessment of the formation and politics of the New Model Army (Kishlansky, 1978).

Much attention has recently been paid to the Treasury in general (Roseveare, 1973) and to the financial aspects of the Glorious Revolution (Roberts, 1977; cf. Brooks, 1974).[19] Roberts concludes that the financial settlement was a conscious part of the means by which a particular (and new) relationship of King/Queen and Parliament was established: Parliament not only indicated that it paid the Sovereign (in part), it also ensured that there would have to be frequent parliaments. Peter Linebaugh[20] would point to a nexus of new class relationships which cumulatively amount to a forceful set of strategies arching forward over the eighteenth century; central to these is the establishment of State credit and banking institutions, a *labour* policy of maximum flexibility (which could not resolve the central problem of vagabondage following the massive enclosures of the eighteenth century) and normally neglected – the establishment of overseas capitalism in the Americas and in India (utilizing State-sanctioned monopolistic companies). This set of strategies accelerates during the eighteenth century. The agencies of the State are also changed. We now turn to that century – the century whose contours and tensions we still have not fully comprehended – the eighteenth century.

Edward Thompson's 1965 sketch on the 'peculiarities' of English social development (cf. R. Johnson, 1975, 1976) continued in his subsequent work (1967, 1971, 1974, 1975) has recently been complemented by his 'argument' about eighteenth-century English society (1977a). This makes a number of very important points, two of which should be quoted at length. First – to extend remarks made above – the State resonates with the peculiarly capitalist, specifically agrarian-urban, *timbre* and tone of the English bourgeoisie: 'Indeed, that State, weak as it was in its bureaucratic and rationalizing functions, was immensely strong and effective as . . . commercial imperialism, in imposing enclosure upon the countryside, and in facilitating the accumulation and movement of capital, both through its banking and funding functions and, more bluntly, through the parasitic extractions of its own officers.' (1977a: 162; cf. his 1971 study of 'moral economy')

Aylmer has pointed to the specific strengths of that weakness:

The burden of the State on society was undoubtedly greater by the eighteenth century than it had been earlier, but not to an extent which was economically crippling. Nor was office-holding so fatally attractive as to draw too many of the ablest people away from other pursuits. This may well help to explain another puzzle: how it was that an age of aristocratic reaction, of oligarchy, corruption and complacency, seems otherwise a strangely paradoxical prologue to rapid and far-reaching economic change, to the emergence of England as the world's first modern industrial society. (1974:259; cf. Aylmer, 1961: Ch. 7).

The strategic ways in which the State acted for (to 'assist' and to speak for) the agrarian and urban bourgeoisie is one reason for *both* popular resistance, which took traditional forms (one of the major topics of the work of Thompson and the essays collected in *Albion's Fatal Tree*), *and* changes within the 'political nation' including the early forms of electoral politics, such as the growth of Parties.[21] In this way was J. H. Plumb's *Growth of political stability* apparently established.

Secondly, Thompson shows how 'Old Corruption' was done in the king's name *and* in all the 'parasitic' operations of the State, *land was central*: 'It was both the jumping-off point for power and office, and the point to which power and office returned. . . . This was a predatory phase of agrarian and commercial capitalism, and the State itself was the prime object of prey.' (1977a: 139) Money-Land-Politics-Office-Honours-Titles, and much more, formed the class circuits of this State:

> 'Old Corruption' is a more serious term of political analysis than is often supposed; for political power throughout most of the eighteenth century may best be understood, not as a direct organ of any class or interest, but as a secondary political formation, a purchasing-point from which other kinds of economic and social power

were gained or enhanced. . . . Its greatest source of strength lay precisely in the weakness of the State itself: in the desuetude of its paternal, bureaucratic and protectionist powers; in the licence which it afforded to agrarian, mercantile and manufacturing capitalism to get on with their own self-reproduction; in the fertile soil which it afforded to *laissez-faire*. (Thompson, 1977a: 141, cf. ibid., 138–139)

A new kind of public and new forms of policy are made possible through these 'social arrangements' policies which precisely allow the comfort of mutual recognition amongst otherwise very different fractions of the rulers of the English polity.

It is common to contrast the *laissez-faire* of the eighteenth-century State with the *interventionism* of the nineteenth century.[22] This ignores the substantial *presence* of the State, not least in the crucial areas of agrarian change, taxation and law and order, but it also misunderstands the double articulation of capitalist policies through a shared ideology and local systems of rule. Characteristically, Edward Thompson pointed out some fifteen years ago that,

laissez-faire emerged . . . in the great agricultural cornbelt. [Against the new political economy] was the paternalist regulation of the corntrade which whilst in an advanced stage of real decomposition – was nevertheless supported by a substantial body of paternalist economic theory and an enormous force of popular (and urban) feeling. The abrogation of the old moral economy of 'provision' was not the work of an industrial bourgeoisie but of capitalist farmers, improving landlords, and great millers and corn-merchants. (Thompson, 1965: 318–319) cf. his 1971 study).

The century of 'peace and stability' proceeded by a series of savage redefinitions of rights and duties centring upon the monetization and valorization of the whole economy. This was as true outside of England as within it – we shall turn to the events of 1715 and 1745 in a moment. First, let us just register the quantities involved: the total enclosure activity (largely by public statute) between 1760 and the General Inclosure Act of 1845 involved over 6,000,000 acres and over 4,000 acts. This involved two kinds of land: 'open fields' and 'waste'. Before 1760 about 400,000 acres of open fields has been enclosed by some 250 acts; 'between 1761 and 1844, there were more than 2,500 acts dealing with rather more than four million acres of open field. After the General Inclosure Act of 1845 there were another 164 acts which cleared up 2,000,000 more acres of the remaining open field' (Hoskins, 1977: 185; he argues that almost half of the arable land of England was 'converted' from one system to the other *after 1700*). As to 'waste' some 1,800 acts after 1760 covered around two million acres; over a third of what had been 'waste' in 1700 was 'claimed' for cultivation (Hoskins, 1977: 185). It is as well to remind ourselves that 'enclosures' began *before* 1200 and *have not yet ended* (consult Welsh hill farmers and Scots crofters before you claim otherwise).

Before we attempt to sketch the implications of a change of that order for State formation, it is as well to go back fifty years to remind ourselves of other changes. In 1928, introducing Defoe's *Tours* of the 1720s, G. D.H. Cole perceptively noted how the 'English political system was static in appearance, but in reality it was in a process of constant adaptation' – Defoe himself being 'the first great apologist' for the English entrepreneurial middle class (1928:x). Furthermore, 'many households in the eighteenth century subsisted partly by agriculture and partly on proceeds of industrial work' (ibid.: xv). The other great commentary of the same year – another of those masterful surveys of English social experience authored from 'Abroad' – is Paul Mantoux' *The Industrial Revolution in the Eighteenth Century* (1928). This deserves to become as widely known and used as Halévy's history of the subsequent century (the latter's survey of 1815 contains many insights into the 'eighteenth-century world picture', Halévy, 1912). The major stress, in terms of this book, in the work of Mantoux is that of *class formation*, especially that of agrarian and industrial capitalists (chapters of a genesis that can be compared with the briefer sketches of Marx in *Capital*, I (Chs. 29 and 31)). Writers like Marx and Mantoux remind us that *policies mean politics*, that the fields of force associated with the State act for some interests and against others. But, finally, Mantoux' work shows that we have to understand allegedly 'sectoral' or 'technological' changes in terms of a sensitive sociology.

This long 'arch' (to use a figure from Thompson) from the Erastian revolutions of the 1530s onwards was essentially the means whereby capitalist production methods could so extensively and speedily pervade the English social formation. For far too long, marxist historians have searched for some economic base to account for changes which they seek to make secondary or superstructural, whereas as Marx long ago stressed – it is precisely a series of long and complicated class struggles (including, *primum inter pares*, a cultural revolution to make a particular civil society possible) *within which* social forms, technological inventions and applications and the laws of economics are constituted. As Charles Bettelheim pointed out a decade ago: 'capitalist relations of production took shape before machine industry; the latter develops under the domination of capitalist relations of production. . .' (Bettelheim, 1970:87; cf. 1973:91–92).

Perry Anderson now argues that relations of production 'must themselves first be radically changed and reordered *before* new forces of production can be created and combined for a globally new mode of production' (Anderson, 1973: 204). Central to such production relations are the moral classifications and definitions (of property, value, rights, and so on) materialized in State practices. *These are economic forces.* Furthermore, as argued elsewhere (Corrigan, 1977: Ch. 1) and mentioned above, the 1776 writings of both Adam Smith and Jeremy Bentham take a series of State policies and agencies *for granted*. Smith accepts a range of State activities which cumulatively have the effect of making a particular set of market mechanisms operate: it gives them a free hand because alternative forms of sociation or livelihood have been or are being rendered illegal, marginal or 'difficult'. Bentham celebrates the secular power of *Law* (and the reforming capacities of – at least some – human beings): 'Law alone has accomplished what all the natural feelings were not able to do; Law alone has been able to create a fixed and durable possession which deserves the name of Property.' (Bentham quoted Halévy, 1934:503).[23]

Christopher Hill has repeatedly drawn attention to the general significance of legal theory and theorists over the last twenty-five years and more; in 1956 he argued that we should 'take legal history out of the hands of the lawyers. . .' not least because 'Law deals with property relations' (1956a:37). Fortunately this is now being done.

> A ruling class organizes its power in the state. The sanction of the state is force, but it is force that is legitimized, however imperfectly, and therefore the state deals also in ideologies. Loyalties do not grow simply in complex societies: they are twisted, invoked and often consciously created. Eighteenth-century England was not a free market of patronage relations. It was a society with a bloody penal code, an astute ruling class who manipulated it to their advantage, and a people schooled in the lessons of Justice, Terror and Mercy. The benevolence of rich men to poor, and all the ramifications of patronage, were up-held by the sanction of the gallows and the rhetoric of the death sentence. (Hay in Hay *et al.*, 1975:5)

Peter Linebaugh's doctoral thesis[24] and, in contrast, the work of Foucault (especially his *Discipline and Punish*, 1975) reinforce Hay's fundamental argument. The State's direct involvement in the redefinition of property and property rights amounts to nothing less than a reclassification of social structure, a redrawing of the social topography. But it is essential to recall that this enforcement is primarily cultural (rather than coercive) and operates through the class structure. In sum, it is part of the way that the moral ethos specific to the *nineteenth-century* social fabric with its central figure of the landed gentleman and his lady, was constructed. A moral ethos, furthermore, that is an essential constituent of the English State formation through the 1830s and beyond (Corrigan, Ph.D. thesis, Chs. 3 and 4, and Appendices). The State performs as a regulating agency which establishes possible forms of control (cumulatively operating, as it were, in the 'right' direction for the powerful) flowers first in the 'peaceful' years of the early eighteenth century.

From that moral ethos, from those State practices, and with recognition on its part of the 'true rulers', Paul Mantoux has sketched the contours of a manufacturing bourgeoisie in these terms:

In spite of its recent origin, of the dissimilar elements which have gone to its making and of the unequal moral value of its members, the manufacturing class soon became conscious of its own existence. Such class-consciousness, which is based on common interest, can make its appearance only where it is able to find expression. *In this respect conditions in England were more favourable than in any other country*. The freedom of the political system, and above all the traditional habit of petitioning, gave ample scope for advancing collective demands. For many years it had been customary for Englishmen to unite according to their needs or their opinions, to present complaints or suggestions to Parliament. . . Thus it was natural and in conformity with innumerable precedents that the leading manufacturers should unite together for certain practical ends. (Mantoux, 1928: 388–389; my emphasis)

The only qualification of this account is to stress the class specific restrictions of what Mantoux speaks too easily of as 'customary', 'natural' and so on. It was during this period that it was becoming *more* difficult for working-class men and women to group themselves together. In fact the 1770s and 1780s mark a crucial watershed, on the other side of which is 1832 and *both* a modern class structure *and* a dominant form of politics which marginalized certain proletarian forms of activity.[25] It is also essential to 'never forget class struggle' in two senses; first, nothing was (or is) fixed and permanent in ideas or relationships about and between classes; second, the ruling class in England was (and is) an alliance, a set of groups unified at a strategic level despite massive (and sometimes bloody) fissures in terms of tactical politics.

Nevertheless, in this strategic sense, the State increasingly acted (or was used) in one direction. Its directionality stemmed from the changing definitions and practices associated with property and property rights. In this sense (recognized by Marx, 1858:506f. and E. Thompson, 1975, *passim*) the State acts cumulatively to establish, regulate and reproduce the interlocking markets – central to them all is that of the labour market with *its* 'real accumulation' – the stockpiling of workers, as Marx phrases it (*ibid*), which are necessary preconditions for accelerated *capitalist* growth. The 'rights' which are naturalized by the 1780s or so (and sanctified by Law) depend directly upon the destruction and supersession of other rights and the withering away of duties, a necessary decomposition traced by Marx (*Capital*, I, Part VIII; cf. Thompson's work, especially his study on inheritance, 1976b). But these new rights (and the new class structure within which they reside and which they announce) are *not* natural and the State is involved – daily rather than yearly – in regulating their steady, if flexible and modified, reproduction. All this, we might add, before steam engines and the rest of the shuddering and thundering noise of industrial capitalism; but linked to it (Saville, 1969).

If the State, and the class alliances it increasingly speaks and acts for, is thus formed against internal opposition, what of the 'without' of policy? One facet of that 'without' has been mentioned already: the centrality of the imperial connections in English development, especially linked to the 'money interest' (Goodwin, 1979:41f.) which remains, to this day, an identifiable segment determining facets of English social development. Another facet of the 'without' against which State formation can be traced, *was partly within*: the attempted revolutions of 1715 and 1745. These not only solidarized the English bourgeois nation, but through the placing of Crown Agents and other managerialists in charge of forfeit lands, speeded up capitalist development on the periphery and provided an alternative model to the less profit-conscious paternalist moral economy of much of Scotland and elsewhere.

Kiernan (1965) provides an excellent sketch of the links between the rise of nations and State formation in Western Europe. As Barry Supple has more recently argued: 'Frontiers are more than lines on a map: they frequently define quite distinctive systems of thought and action. The state is, of course, pre-eminently such a system; and it is therefore through the history of nations that we must begin any empirical study of the role of the state in the international phenomenon which we call the Industrial Revolution.' (1971:301)

Newman (1975) has shown how nationalism in England became 'empirical, constructive, earnest, moral, comfortably pseudoreligious as well as Evangelical. . . .' (1975:418), at least, we should stress, for the 'middle classes', since it was the Jacobin sympathies of the proletarians which so concerned their *betters* (Thompson, 1963; Goodwin, 1979). There is much truth, in terms of the transformation of eighteenth-century perspectives into the nineteenth century in

England, in Kiernan's argument that nationalism is orchestrated as 'class resentment artificially diverted into xeno-
phobia' (1965:35). A number of writers (e.g. Briggs, 1961;
Finer, 1975) have argued the relationship between warfare
and State formation, especially in regard to social policy
changes. The carnage and brutality of warfare (on land and
at sea) is one side of a social structure; the other side of
which is signified by the common linking of 'Officer' to
'Gentleman' – and with it, the range of duties including
service as well as heroism, 'calmly refusing excitement' as
well as decisiveness – which is found within the local rule of
squire and magistrate and (to look forward again) so many
of the State Servants of the early nineteenth century. Warfare, like Imperialism, is also a great engine of production
as Marx has noted (e.g. 1858:109; *Capital*, I: Ch. 31).

To conclude, whatever the final shape of our understanding
of State formation in the eighteenth century and before (and
of the continuities and breaks as we move forward to the
nineteenth century and beyond) we have to avoid the gross
distortion which any textual rendering of historical experience can so easily provide. Everything thus far indicated is
in a position of fluidity and unclarity; although some of the
actions were motivated (and even those had unintended
consequences), many were not thought through in the way
that we can now suggest. First, there is the complexity of
the State as such, its multicellular opacity, (which all sorts
of reformers were to wish transformed into what some State
Servants agreed to call 'a national system of improvement'
aimed *against* vestralization, jobbery and local powers). As
E. P. Thompson argued in 1965: 'The settlement of 1688
inaugurated a hundred years of comparative social status,
so far as overt class conflict or the maturation of class consciousness was concerned.'
    It is only fair to interject that his more recent work (1971,

1974, 1975)[26] goes a long way to qualify the 'stasis' of the century after 1688.

> The main beneficiaries were those vigorous agrarian capitalists, the gentry. But this does not mean that the government institutions represented, in an unqualified manner, the gentry as a 'ruling-class'. At a local level (the magistracy) they did so in an astonishingly naked manner. At a national level (desuetude of the old restrictions on marketing, the facilitation of enclosures, the expansion of empire) they furthered their interests. But at the same time a prolonged period of social stasis is commonly one in which ruling institutions degenerate, corruptions enter, channels of influence silt up, an élite entrenches itself in positions of power. A distance opened up between the majority of the middle and lesser gentry (and associated groups) and certain great agragian magnates, privileged merchant capitalists, and their hangers-on, who manipulated the organs of State in their own private interest. . . (1965:322)

In sum, 'Old Corruption' could only account for a part of the transformation of an agrarian social formation based upon local forms of patronage and a relatively settled population into a mechanized, urban, industrial social formation, based upon national markets of employment and a relatively mobile population. Hence, on the one hand, the shifting groups within the progressive ruling class (Goodwin, 1979: Ch. 1); hence also, the 'economic reforms' of Fox and Burke (Halévy, 1912: 20f; Gretton, 1913: 85f; Cohen, 1941: Ch. 2f; Roseveare, 1973; Torrance, 1978); the origins of a permanent civil service (Parris 1968); and the institution of budgets, the Consolidated Fund (1787) and the Exchequer Loans Commission (1793; Stern, 1950; Halévy, 1912: 357; Roseveare, 1973). In this process, 'transitional' figures are crucial for example, Sir Henry Taylor (1832) or Sir George Harrison (Torrance, 1968). At a certain point, in other words, 'Old Corruption' became a barrier instead of an aid to great and greater capitalist growth. But the resulting State forms continued to be infused with a moral ethos and a symbolic force which had roots in the early Erastianization of Thomas Cromwell.

Apart from continuing legislation regulating the labour market (such as the Elizabethan Poor Law or the Statutues governing Master and Servant relations, cf. Corrigan and Corrigan, 1978) it is worth stressing that quite novel forms of policy came from the upheavals of enclosures. Mantoux points to the 1757 Relief Act (Mantoux, 1928:171) which empowered the Inclosure Commissioners to levy those who benefited from enclosures, in order to aid those who suffered. In Scotland there were public works schemes which prefigured those of the Public Employment Act of 1817. At work here are signs of the struggle between different ways of working the land which we can categorize as moral economies (depending on a high estimation of 'social capital', that is, the duties considered as part of his role by the local squire) and full-blown political economies governed by full maximization of profits and a constant 'system of improvement'. The recent work of D. C. Moore and A. Brundage has pointed to the continuities in this division in which some local ruling groups are prepared to behave in a way which runs against their interests (of profit maximization), in order to work for what they feel to be the greater values of social stability and public esteem.[27]

There are two further points which it is worth emphasizing in this conclusion. First, there is the important argument advanced by Marx against theorists who postulated either *Force* or *Will* as the basis of *State power*. His first point is that the State itself is created by actual, material relationships concerning property rights, the division of labour, the class structure and the relations of production. But it is his second point which needs to be read back into the history of State formation in England. The individuals who rule have to give their will 'a universal expression as the will of the state, as law. . . Their personal rule must at the same time assume the form of average rule' (1845:329). Debates about what constitutes the 'nation' and 'law' are debates about how the rule of specific groups can be given the form of the rule of all, can be naturalized. Central to this was the open quality *for some groups* – stressed by Mantoux, which is in fact the genesis and articulation of *Public Opinion*. Significantly, the 1780s can be taken as a starting point for the study of Public Opinion (Briggs, 1959: 114), 'the Provinces' (Read, 1964), and 'middle-class consciousness' (Briggs, 1956). Public opinion is a constructed phenomenon subject to classification. That is to say, special agencies were held to articulate 'true' public opinion, since what was otherwise articulated could be dismissed by defining it as 'special pleading', 'public clamour' or '*ill informed shout*', (the last a paraphrase of Chadwick, see Corrigan, Ph.D. thesis, Ch. 3). Public Opinion, for example was defined by W. H. Mackinnon in 1828 as: 'that sentiment on any given subject which is entertained by the best informed, most intelligent and most moral persons in the community, which is gradually spread and adopted by nearly all persons of any education or proper feeling in a civilized state' (quoted by Peel, 1971:70).

In other words, this was an ethos shared within a political nation which, although somewhat enlarged since Tudor times, was still clearly a minority of the total population – a conglomerate of different élite groupings, each apex of the different productive, fiscal, military and simply wealthy communities.

Finally, these groups were far from securely established. Apart from their own uncertainties and the minutiae of social ritual and gradation which covered their social relationships, there was the increasing marginalization of some of the former rulers by changes in the profitability of different 'factors of production'. But there was also steady, well-organized or 'spontaneously exploding', *opposition*. The eighteenth-century State ethos bequeathed to the nineteenth century and beyond was already marked as the ethos of a particular class; the historical experience of the classes who had felt its full weight had baptized it as a non-neutral agency. That contradiction has not yet been overcome. We have to avoid reading back into history the total acceptance on the part of the *apparently* vanquished of the ideals and ends of their victors. The question is worth posing, sharply, in another way – where do the 'Great Leaps Forward' in popular consciousness and action come from? Even to point, as is customary, to the arrival of 'external bearers' of new ideas, simply avoids the question – why did those bearers arrive then? why were their ideas taken up then? These are always historical questions, of course, but I suggest we would do well to avoid thinking of people along a single unitary perspective. People might behave in a particular way because they seriously take note of the *present* powers and controls which 'encourage' that kind of behaviour; but we should never assume a total commitment to the *status quo* from this appearance of acceptance. I suggest that the energies for those sudden upsurges which mark out English social experience come from the reserves carried within seemingly incorporated women and men whom the State thinks it has converted into civilized beings and good citizens.

Christopher Hill's triumphant book *The World Turned Upside Down* and his other writings have shown the sophistication and courage of many ordinary men and women, however much they spoke through the language and ideas of others. These 'organic intellectuals' persist, particularly from the 1780s, and contribute to the making of socialist theory in the 'scientific' writings of Marx and Engels, as both generously acknowledge. I shall close by quoting from E. P. Thompson's recent reflections upon a decade or more of work on the eighteenth century (signposted admirably by his 1971 and 1974 articles). He acknowledges a hegemony by the gentry until the 1790s, but also stresses that for 'a hundred years the poor were not altogether the losers'

(1977a:165). He is also emphasizing not simply the limits of the eighteenth-century State, but the limits of *any* State power:

> it is necessary also to say what this hegemony does *not* entail. It does not entail any acceptance by the poor of the gentry's paternalism upon the gentry's own terms or in their approved self-image. The poor might be willing to award their deference to the gentry, but only for a price. The ·price was substantial. And the deference was often without the least illusion: it could be seen from below as being one part necessary self-preservation, one part the calculated extraction of whatever could be extracted. Seen in this way, the poor imposed upon the rich some of the duties and functions of paternalism just as much as deference was in turn imposed upon them. Both parties to the equation were constrained within a common field of force.
>
> In the second place, we must recall once more the immense distance between polite and plebeian cultures, and the vigour and authentic self-activity of the latter. Whatever this hegemony may have been, it did not envelop the lives of the poor and it did not prevent them from defending their own modes of work and leisure, and forming their own rituals, their own satisfactions and view of life. (1977a:163)

It is in that context that this chapter (and the other chapters of this book) should be read. As Richard Johnson wrote over ten years ago: 'Historians of government may be justly criticized if they fail to distinguish between the growth of the *machinery* of government, and the development of a social philosophy that informs it and really makes it work.'[28]

3

State Formation and Class Struggle, 1832–48
Paul Richards

The condition of the working class is the condition of the vast majority of the English people. The question: what is to become of those destitute millions, who consume today what they earned yesterday; who have created the greatness of England by their inventions and their toil; who become with every passing day more conscious of their might; and demand, with daily increasing urgency, their share of the advantages of society? This, since the Reform Bill, has become the national question. All Parliamentary debates, of any importance, may be reduced to this; and, though this English middle class will not yet admit it, though they try to evade this great question, and to represent their own particular interests as the truly national ones, their action is utterly useless. (Engels, 1845a:51–2)

Since 1945 British historians have been preoccupied with investigating the nineteenth-century origins of the modern Welfare State. It seems agreed that the 1830s and 1840s are

49

the decades demanding research, although this has produced
rival 'Tory' and 'Fabian' interpretations of nineteenth-century State formation. We may call 'Tory' those historians
who insist on the piecemeal and pragmatic character of State
formation and 'Fabian' those who contend that the planning
of Bentham and his disciples has had a major influence on
the shape of the modern State.[1] On the Tory side there has
been much generalization from MacDonagh's pioneering
work on the control of emigrant passenger traffic: 'Without
the slightest spur from doctrinaires or any other *a priori*
influence, experience and the brute facts of the situation
forced those who were concerned with emigration . . .
towards the sort of State we recognise as modern' (Mac-
Donagh, 1958:66)

MacDonagh originated a model to explain how legislative
attempts to blot out 'social evils' identified by religious and
humanitarian opinion failed but sparked 'a revolution in
government', driven by the internal dynamism of State
departments manned by experts demanding increased powers. Against this Tory interpretation, Hart strongly reasserted the case for Benthamism which had been launched
earlier by Brebner and others in debate with Dicey. Chadwick and other State Servants, more or less influenced by
Bentham, are seen as responsible for measures designed to
protect the general interest against the harmful social consequences of an otherwise beneficial economic individualism.
In a brilliant study of Chadwick his biographer S. E. Finer
says of the twenty-five years bounded by the Reform Bill
and the Crimean War: 'It refashioned the machinery of both
central and local administration. It created the modern
police, and brought into being the services of public assistance, public education, and public hygiene. It made a new
start, a modern start, in the public inspection and control of
private economic enterprises.' (Finer, 1952: 1)

The conclusion we are left to draw is that the post-1945
Welfare State has its origins in *either the planning or prag-*

matism of nineteenth-century State servants/experts grappling with 'social evils' thrown up by Industrial Revolution.

The useful work of both 'Tory' and 'Fabian' historians should be recognized, but so should the limitations of the whole controversy. To regard the modern British Welfare State as the consequence of an evolutionary process whereby 'social evils' have been gradually overcome is grossly misleading. In other words, academic orthodoxy has ignored the problematic contained in the term 'Welfare State'. For the German Marxists: 'Increasing interventions by the state for economic and social policy, the concentration of capital and lengthening periods of prosperity, especially before the First World War and after the Second, provide the main basis for that experience, which makes it seem possible for capital to be gradually transformed by means of the State apparatus.' (Müller and Neusüss, 1978:35)

Here the Welfare State is presented as 'an illusion' which masks the form taken by the State at the stage of monopoly capitalism and cultivates working-class reformism. Marxist theory of the capitalist State and its derivation offers a powerful critique of British academic orthodoxy, yet this cannot be successfully challenged without further *historical* research.[2]

'Tory' and 'Fabian' historians fail to come to terms with the capitalist character of the modern State and the qualitative breaks in its formation. To speak of *The Victorian Origins of the British Welfare State* (Roberts, 1960) for a period when the State endorsed the 'sacrifice' of the handloom weavers to an expanding industrial capitalism emphasizes this. At the same time the aggressive capitalist State of the 1830s seems, by the 1840s, to be conciliating working-class opposition to early industrial capitalism. This assertion is supported by Foster's *Class Struggle and the Industrial Revolution* (1974) although this marxist text concentrates essentially on local history. Its conclusions are based on a study of Oldham, a cotton-factory town at the core of early

industrial capitalism, where a revolutionary working-class
consciousness is defused by concessions made by the big
bourgeoisie. Yet Foster admits that a reassessment of economic and social policy begins on the *national* level, in the
late 1830s and early 1840s, *before* Oldham's big bourgeoisie
came out in favour of the Ten Hours Bill and household
suffrage (1974: 186–7). The problem tackled by this essay
is to clarify the interaction between class struggle and State
formation in the 1832–48 period. To do this we need a
national study which will close the space between State and
society postulated by academic orthodoxy.

A useful way to do this is to study parliament. Here we
are inside the State, with the men 'in charge' of its departments, *and* with representatives of 'society' itself. As the
executive power depended for its exercise on a majority in
the House of Commons, a majority often narrow and under
threat at every general election, the political aristocracy had
its crucial terrain here, as well as in the departments
inhabited by State Servants.[3] In nineteenth-century Britain
this representative/parliamentary region of the State was the
national battleground in policy-making. What kind of battleground? For Engels the 1832 Reform Act transformed parliamentary politics into the politics of class struggle.
Certainly the 1832 Act can be seen as a compromise between
the political aristocracy and the bourgeoisie as a whole, to
the great advantage of the latter. To the reactionary political
aristocracy, the Tories, the 1832 Act was tantamount to
revolution. To the liberal political aristocracy, the Whigs,
it saved the country from revolution by closing the ranks of
the properties against the property-less. At the same time
the 1832 settlement began a *working-class* movement for
democracy independent of the leadership of the bourgeoisie:

> The line from 1832 to Chartism is not a haphazard
> pendulum alternation of political and economic agitations
> but a direct progression, in which simultaneous and
> related movements converge towards a single point. This

point was the vote. There is a sense in which the Chartist movement commenced, not in 1838 with the promulgation of the Six Points, but at the moment when the Reform Bill received the Royal Assent. Many of the provincial Political Unions never disbanded, but commenced at once to agitate against the shopocrat franchise. (E. P. Thompson, 1963: 909)

How far can this interpretation of the 1832 Reform Act be sustained? Moore has expanded on earlier work by Professors Gash and Hanham to argue for the importance of its conservative dimension:

The Ministers were not trying to create a political structure in which urban interests would enjoy predominant weight. Nor were they trying to encourage the growth of political individualism. When their handiwork is seen both in its entirety and against the background of the social, political and intellectual movements of the early nineteenth century, it becomes clear that their primary concern was to perpetuate the political pre-eminence of the landed interest and the hierarchical structure of English society in town as well as country. In particular, their efforts in this latter direction are apparent from their attempts to define each constituency socially and geographically – by franchise and boundaries – so that it would provide representation for the interest it principally symbolised. (D. C. Moore, 1967: 46–7)

To some extent the 1832 Act *was* a digging-in on the part of the landed aristocracy against the threat posed to its dominance by the new industrial society and, as such, intensified mutual antagonisms. The Whigs themselves had made the 1832 settlement, as the *leaders* of the popular reform movement, but the county representation was strengthened. A mere forty-two urban and industrial constituencies were created returning sixty-three M.P.s. 1832 did not, therefore, produce a social revolution within the walls of the House. As a certain Mr Murphy informed a public meeting of the London Radical Association in 1835: 'The House of Commons was but the House of Commons of the Aristocracy. He had no hesitation in saying that the House did not represent the feeling or opinion of the people.'[4]

Given this situation, the politics of the turbulent 1831–32 years ('the people' against the aristocracy) were bound to survive and even appear to direct parliamentary business. They were reflected and reinforced by the two major parliamentary parties. After the general election of 1837 Russell counted 338 ministry men or Liberals, 318 opponents or Conservatives and only four doubtfuls.[5] Each party had its own recognized leaders, whips and clubs. In the House Russell assumed the leadership of a progressive urban movement, where Peel defended the Church of England and other traditional institutions. Within the space of a year, Russell's open support of the appropriation of the revenues of the Irish church for lay purposes broke up Grey's government *and* brought to a close Peel's 'Hundred Days' (Prest, 1972: 65–91). The latter had closely collaborated with Wellington, that great enemy of the Reform Bill installed in the reactionary House of Lords. The Lords not only survived the 1831–32 crisis, but soon began to infuriate the Liberals (Turberville, 1958: 320–2).

The hold of formal party politics on Parliament was sometimes tight. But shifting from the politics of town/liberal versus county/conservative, the dichotomy underlying the party system, to the politics of class struggle, to the making of economic and social policy, formal party politics dissolve. The majority of activists in the crucial policy fields were middle-class M.P.s. from urban and industrial constituencies, who were rarely deferential to the aristocratic Conservative and Liberal party chiefs. On the contrary, it was such M.P.s who often made important policy initiatives, men from the constituencies created in 1832, the centres of class struggle and Industrial Revolution.[6] Whigs and Peelites, the men alternately taking charge of the State, *co-operated* against both nominal Liberals and Conservatives. The political aristocracy made initiatives too, often involving large numbers of M.P.s in important divisions. But it was the minority of urban and industrial M.P.s who predominated in policy making, as will be established below.

Can the new capitalist state, as it actually existed in Britain by the 1850s and 1860s, be explained as the product of the class struggle of the 1830s and 1840s? Investigation of M.P.s and policy-making at the two critical conjunctures of class struggle in the 1830s and 1840s (1832–35 and 1838–42) can prepare an answer. Scrutiny of Hansard and committees of inquiry in the key fields of economic and social policy *does reveal* groups of M.P.s or *tendencies*, some of which appear as parties representing classes or class fractions despite their loose organization. At least five such tendencies and/or parties can be identified propagating rival policy programmes within which we can recognize *ideal State forms*. Each tendency and/or party is best explored through a leader or principal activist.[7]

The *Manchester liberals* were those M.P.s with constituencies in Manchester and its industrial regions. Their party leader was C. P. Thomson, a London merchant, elected M.P. for Manchester by its mill-owners and installed by the Whigs as President of the Board of Trade.[8] His supporters included M.P.s from outside the cotton-mill towns of Lancashire, but landed and industrialist politicians centred on Manchester were his closest allies. Among the most prominent were Mark Philips, the other Manchester M.P., and his business partner G. W. Wood who was elected with Viscount Molyneux for South Lancashire. M.P. for North Lancashire was J. W. Patten, spokesman of 'The Master Manufacturers Association' against the Ten Hours Bill, who shared the constituency with Lord Stanley. Through the Manchester liberals, and Thomson in particular, the Lancashire mill-owners and merchants had close links with key state servants such as G. R. Porter at the Board of Trade and N. Senior. (Johnson, 1977: 84). Despite its smallness, the Manchester liberal party seems to have exerted substantial influence and authority in and out of parliament (Bowring, 1877: 302).

The policy of Manchester liberalism is clear from the 1840 report of the commission on the handloom weavers, an answer to the conclusions of the 1835 select committee on the same subject.[9] Thomson had vigorously attacked the 1835 committee report before Senior was given the opportunity by the Whigs to select and organize the commission. One of Senior's 'excellent' assistants, Muggeridge, assured London that he would put before the government and the public 'far more valuable and impartial evidence connected with the condition of the Handloom weavers than the previous inquiry.[10] After four years a report appeared which blamed the Corn Laws and popular ignorance for the chronic condition of the working class, rather than the capitalist economic process itself. Free trade and popular education, as well as curbs on trade-unionism, were recommended by the report as solutions to the national economic and social crisis. There was no mention of an earlier proposal by Torrens that workers who found themselves victims of technology should receive state compensation (Coates 1971: 57–63).

The ideal State form of the Manchester liberals is implicit in all their reports and attacks on popular radicalism. Concern for the general interests of capital, as opposed to the interests of individual capitals, is weak. To emphasize this Thomson, for example, attempted to sabotage the limited 1833 Factory Act which he described as 'an evil' forced upon the Whigs (Hammond, 1923: 42). This attitude was consistent with the conviction that the mill-owner or capitalist was the mainspring of 'national progress' and this excluded State intervention in his activities. Control over the operatives is exercised through the workplace and, in periods of industrial strife, by police and troops. It seems that the dynamic of the economic system itself would 'educate' the rising generation of workers, although a national system of schooling would reinforce the everyday lessons of the free market. A 'Manchester state' would have involved a political revolution:

> You see, to these champions of the British Bourgeoisie, to the men of the Manchester School, every institution of Old England appears in the light of a piece of machinery as costly as it is useless, and which fulfills no other purpose but to prevent the nation from producing the greatest possible quantity at the least possible expense, and to exchange its products in freedom. Necessarily, their last word is the Bourgeois Republic, in which there remains altogether that *minimum* only of government which is indispensable for the administration, internally and externally, of the common class, interest and business of the Bourgeoisie; and where this minimum of government is as soberly, as economically organized as possible. (Marx-Engels, 1962: 359–60)

The Manchester liberals co-operated with the Benthamites, a small group of metropolitan-based intellectuals remote from the new industrial society. No M.P. dominated these self-styled *philosophic radicals* although the lawyer J. A. Roebuck (Bath) stands out.[11] Nearer to C. P. Thomson were C.P. Villiers (Wolverhampton), H. Warburton (Bridport), J. Hume (Middlesex) and J. Bowring (Kilmarnock) whereas G. Grote (London), C. Buller (Liskeard), Sir W. Molsworth (E. Cornwall) and Roebuck kept more apart from other M.P.s. But all the philosophic radicals shared an enthusiam for the works of Bentham rather than Adam Smith as John Stuart Mill conveys in his *Autobiography*: 'But Bentham's subject was legislation . . . and at every page he seemed to open a clearer and broader conception of what human institutions ought to be, how they might be made what they ought to be, and how far removed from it they now are' (Mill, 1964: 6). As legislators, not as political economists, Roebuck and his colleagues acquired a special status in the wider Benthamite circle (Buckley, 1926: 9). This wider circle included that very important State Servant, E. Chadwick, *and*, on its periphery, leading Whig politicians whose patronage was instrumental in opening the way for Benthamite influence (Finer, 1952: 39).

The clearest policy statement by the Benthamites was the education plan detailed by Roebuck almost as soon as the reformed parliament met. An Education Ministry was perhaps the most important of the thirteen in Bentham's Constutional Code or blueprint for a new State. (Bowring, 1838–43: 441–2). And for the Bath M.P. a system of education was the most crucial duty of the State:

> The Government does not often immediately inflict misery on the people by any brutal or bare-faced oppression – but by abstaining from its duty, from doing the good that it ought to do, enormous misery is allowed to continue. By fostering and perpetuating ignorance among the people, it inflicts more injury than by any or all of its direct oppressions – all its immense taxation, considered as a burthen, is a feather in the scale when compared with the ills produced by the ignorance it has engendered.[12]

Roebuck demanded a Prussian-type Ministry of Education controlling the activities of local school committees which would supervise the day-to-day running of what was to be a utilitarian education, clearly designed to fashion a productive and contented working class. The plan was socially conservative, although religion was ignored. But the imprint of the Benthamite tendency is clear enough.

In theory, the philosophic radicals were democrats, but a Benthamite State would have been heavily authoritarian in practice. The 1834 Poor Law régime designed by Chad-

wick would seem to confirm this. Yet the New Poor Law
was intended as only a beginning of a comprehensive policy
to tailor the worker to fit capital's demands *in his own
interest*. This meant State provision for the education and
health of the popular masses, as well as police forces and
workhouses to deter the idle and rebellious. The interpretation of a famous French historian deserves more attention
than it has received:

> The origin of this vast system half elective, half bureau-
> cratic, is easy to recognize: it is the system which Bentham
> had sketched in his 'Constitutional Code'. In 1833, his
> disciple Roebuck had failed in his attempt to set up a
> system of national education embodying his master's prin-
> ciples. Now another disciple. Chadwick, had applied the
> same principles to the reform of the Poor Law. Might it
> not be expected, if the reform proved a success, that
> Bentham's system would very soon be applied univer-
> sally? The task once accomplished which the Poor Law
> commissioners were preparing to undertake and England
> divided into a number of 'unions' sufficiently large and
> sufficiently equal, could not the boards set up in each
> union be used for other purposes, national education, the
> upkeep of the roads and public health? At no distant date
> the entire local government of the country would be trans-
> formed, and a democratic England emerge from the wel-
> ter of aristocratic self-government. (Halévy 1923: 126–7).

England would not, of course, become democratic *until*
the 'ignorance' of the workers had been eliminated. At the
same time, the Benthamite State was to govern in the general interests of capitalism, as opposed to protecting 'the
freedom' of individual capitals which neglected health and
education. The 1833 Factory Act was designed to counter
the disastrous social consequences of intense capitalist competition, although for Chadwick the measure had been
emasculated (Finer, 1952: 68).

Distinct from the Manchester liberals and Benthamites, although connected to them, were the liberal philanthropists whose lack of cohesiveness as a tendency does not detract from their significance. The 'leader' was R. A. Slaney, a Salopian land-owner and lawyer who was M.P. for Shrewsbury.[13] His efforts brought together members of the political aristocracy and M.P.s representing industrial towns and counties. Of the Whigs Lords Duncannon, Morpeth and Normanby, H. Tufnell and W. Cowper should be mentioned, along with members of Peel's inner group including Lords Sandon and Francis Egerton and Sirs E. Knatchbull and H. Inglis. Of the urban politicians E. Baines and J. Marshall of Leeds, J. Parker and J. S. Lister of Bradford, and some Manchester Liberals, including M. Philips should be mentioned. Slaney had numerous contacts within the urban élites of the north and links with important State Servants, such as Dr Southwood Smith and Dr Kay. After 1832, he was dedicated to the creation of a landed-led party committed to social reform in the industrial towns.

The policy of the liberal philanthropists is embodied in the reports of the several select committees chaired by Slaney. The best example is the 1840 Health of Towns report which follows Slaney's initiative of the same year. It was headed in Hansard 'Discontent among the Working Classes' and moved for an inquiry into: 'the causes of discontent amidst great bodies of the working classes in populous districts, with a view to apply such remedies as the wisdom of Parliament can devise, or remove as far as possible any reasonable grounds of complaint, in order thereby to strengthen the attachment of the people to the institutions of the country.'[14]

For 'Health of Towns' we should read a much wider concern for the working class, best explained by commitment to the Industrial Revolution as a progressive force overbalanced by fear of its destruction of social order. The 1840 report declared the emergence of a healthy and contented working class to depend on measures to remake urban environments which had bred pauperism, drunkenness, crime and popular attacks on the new economic and social system. Town boards of health fuelled by *local* effort and finance within a framework of general law and State aid were recommended. Specific proposals for improvements included cemeteries, public bathing, water supply, lodging houses, and parks which were 'essential' to the health and comfort of the urban working class.[15]

The ideal State form of the liberal philanthropists can be grasped through their writings and reports. To Slaney is seemed obvious that, if bridges were to be built between rich and poor in the industrial towns, the chief burden rested on the local capitalists.[16] Local philanthropy was to be promoted and directed by the State *but not stifled by it*. Dominated by the efforts of industrialists fostering independence and self-help, through the provision of model housing, schools and recreation facilities, Manchester and Leeds would become well-ordered, productive and peaceful communities. The emphasis on *personal* class relations (words such as 'benevolence' and 'humanity' illustrate this) strongly suggests that the industrial town was seen in terms of the landed estate.[17] Both kinds of capitalist 'society' demanded that the worker *see* his superiors promoting philanthropy, or class antagonism would be exacerbated. The importance of the State for the liberal philanthropists should not be underplayed, not least in the field of popular education which localities could not always provide.[18] But opposition to the bureaucratic intrusions of a Benthamite State was bound to be strong.

Caught between the Manchester liberals and Benthamites on the one side, and the liberal philanthropists on the other, was the obvious rivalry between urban and rural orders. Very real conflicts existed between the kinds of society represented by the capitalist landowner and industrial capitalist (Johnson, 1975: 25). But it was the Tories or the fraction of the landed ruling class opposed to the 1832 settlement, not the liberal philanthropists, who challenged the dominance of industrial capital. At the same time, the Tories possessed no realistic alternative policy to the liberalism outlined.[19] This seems confirmed by their failure to assert any real weight in the social policy struggles of the 1830s beyond defending the educational role of the Church of England against Benthamite attacks. The success of this counter-attack was important, as will become clear. But we must mention here Lord Ashley whose role as chief parliamentary spokesman of the factory movement sharply separated him from the Peelites. This Dorset aristocrat in no way rejected industrial capitalism, yet this does not deny his service to the children in industrial employments. His successful 1840 motion for a comission into children's employment excited an early biographer to claim that Ashley had attained such power and influence in the House of Commons that it would have been 'unsafe' for any government to resist him (Hodder, 1886: 307). This is an obvious exaggeration despite his real influence. To place policy-making in its real context we must turn to the popular radicals.

The popular radical party was excluded from the expert/departmental region of the state but used the representative/parliamentary one to full advantage. Its members were a motley collection of middle-class M.P.s representing urban and industrial constituencies created by the Reform Act. In most of these, the majority of the small middle-class electorate were shopkeepers, smallholders and publicans depending on working-class custom and open to exclusive dealing. Thus the working class could sometimes exert a major influence on the election of M.P.s. (Vincent, 1966: 138). This was the case with Oldham's election in 1832 of W. Cobbett and J. Fielden, the Todmorden mill-owner, who can be regarded as the leader of the popular radicals.[20] He opened *The Curse of the Factory System* (1836) with a clear statement of his politics: 'I have, all my years of manhood, been a Radical Reformer, because I thought Reform would give the people a power in the House of Commons that would secure to them that better condition of which they are worthy.'

Other principal activists in the party from the Manchester region were J. Brotherton (Salford) and C. Hindley (Aston) whereas J. Maxwell (Lanarkshire) and W. D. Gillon (Falkirk) sat for Scottish constituencies dominated by the cotton textile industry. These northern M.P.s worked closely with T. Wakley and T. Duncombe (Finsbury) as well as D. W. Harvey (Southwark) and T. Attwood (Birmingham).

To the popular radicals, the liberals were responsible for engineering a comprehensive policy through which the exploitation of working people was being intensified. The 1834 Poor Law was regarded as the keystone of this policy, a means to forcibly discipline working people to the basic demands of capital. Fielden insisted that the new Poor Law had driven wages down and the Oldham M.P. believed this 'to have been the object of those who support it'.[21] The popular radicals, and particularly Fielden, were the great *public* enemies to Benthamites and Manchester liberals, who fiercely attacked policy proposals to reform or check industrial capitalism. John Bright linked Fielden with Oastler and Ferrand as 'individuals who . . . had never shown any extraordinary sagacity. . . on public questions' (Ward, 1962: 30). This did not stop Fielden despatching the programme of the Oldham Political Association to Peel in the crisis year of 1841.[22] It included measures for State control of hours, wages, and industrial investment, besides universal suffrage and an income tax (Foster, 1974: 69).

There can be no claim that through Fielden we can discern *the* working-class ideal State form. Due to the uneven development of industrial capitalism, the working class was fragmented and policies hammered out in northern factory towns were not reproduced elsewhere. Yet the Oldham M.P. presented what was probably the most popular and realistic radical alternative to the liberal capitalist state.[23] His *The Curse of the Factory System* was as much an argu-

ment for balanced economic growth as it was the exposure
of industrial exploitation:

> There is no natural cause for our distresses. We have
> fertile land, the finest herds and flocks in the world, and
> the most skilful herdsmen; we have fine rivers and ports,
> and shipping unequalled; and our ingenuity and industry
> have given us manufactures which ought to complete
> these blessings. I am a manufacturer; but I am not one
> of those who think it time we had dispensed with the
> land. I think that these interests are conducive to the
> prosperity of the nation, that all must go together, and
> that the ruin of either will leave the others comparatively
> insecure.

It is clear that Fielden did not look back to a past 'golden
age' nor forward to modern socialism. But he did demand
a balanced and managed capitalist economy, under democratic controls, which would satisfy popular *needs*. This
meant opportunities to choose between the factory or the
handloom, to regain or establish greater control over economic circumstances, as well as regulation of working hours
and wages.

Should the Manchester liberals, Tories, and popular radicals be regarded as political parties representing classes or
class fractions? It is realized that the 'representation' of
classes by parties is problematic. The dislocation of economic and political levels warns against any crude reduction-
ism. And here the problem seems compounded by the
limitations imposed by the political system on 'representation', despite the 'opening up' created by the 1832 Reform
Act. At the same time we can argue for the representation
of classes by parties in the 1830s in the Poulantzian sense
(1968: 247) that they constituted social forces or, at least,
embodied class or class fraction interests. Thus the Manchester liberals represented that fraction of the bourgeoisie
campaigning for the space to conquer international markets

unhampered by any national constraints. The popular radicals represented a working class (however fragmented) opposed to this domination of international industrial capitalism, as did the Tory party or fraction of the landed class; but the former party fought for *alternatives* as well. What is not in doubt is that the Manchester liberals and popular radicals had particularly close personal associations with classes. This was not the case with the philosophic radicals or liberal philanthropists. It should be clear that the Benthamites cannot be labelled as the representatives of the petty bourgeoisie, as Neale concludes (1972: 18–27), but were an intellectual group without a class base. Nor did the liberal philanthropists represent a class or class fraction although the central figures were a few liberal landed politicians. It is more appropriate to see the Benthamites and the liberal philanthropists as *rival tendencies* within liberalism, 'representing' the general interests of capitalism as opposed to the interests of individual capitals.

Where does this leave the political aristocracy 'in charge' of the state? Marx does not appear far wrong when he said that the Whigs were the typical representatives of the bourgeoisie *against* the aristocracy, which allowed the latter to keep charge of the State (Marx-Engels, 1962: 355–6). At the same time, this seems too simplistic an analysis. The Whigs and Peelites are best regarded as the *managers* of all the parliamentary tendencies or parties *in the general interests of the bourgeoisie*, rather than as its representives. Both Whigs and Peelites insisted on the general/national character of representation as opposed to its particular/local roots:

I consider that it is the general interest of the whole country and not the individual interest or wishes of his own constituents, to which every representative is bound in the first instance to look, and the whole theory of a representative Govt. rests upon the assumption that during the period for which he is chosen every member of Parliament should be left free to act according to his own judgment of what is best for the general welfare of the nation.[24]

How should this be interpreted? The task for the political aristocracy was to forge a society torn by class antagonisms into a nation State. In other words, the interests of the bourgeoisie had to be 'nationalized' and to do this the relative autonomy of the State from society was essential. At the same time this meant that the working class too had to be 'represented' within the State if unity was to be attributed to the members of 'society'.[25]

This does not detract from the importance of the expert/departmental region of the nineteenth-century State where its servants, safeguarded from intrusions by the representative/parliamentary region, produced the knowledge/expertise *of the nation*, as opposed to the 'nonsense' propagated by popular radicalism. But the policy clashes between the liberal politicians and State Servants on the one hand, and the popular radicals on the other, reveal two *class* knowledges/expertises – as the next section will attempt to demonstrate. Here we should emphasize the fundamental class character of liberalism as expressed by Dr Kay's reflections on Manchester, that harbinger of a new *industrial* civilization: 'the pauperism of the manufacturing districts does not arise so much from the fluctuations of commercial affairs or from changes in manufacturing establishments incident to the improvement of machinery as from the ignorance and improvidence of the people.'[26]

Faced with this 'national question', the liberals agreed that the stabilization and reproduction of capitalist social relations required the medium of the State as a 'moralizing' or educational agency and not as a repressive one. But what type of liberal State? The rest of this essay will argue that the answer to *this* 'national question' was provided by the outcome of class struggle.

The economic boom of the 1833–36 period and popular organization to resist the capitalist economic process fired the liberals into action to protect and extend 'the freedom' of capital. As the Whigs suppressed Swing and attacked attempts at general unionism, the Benthamite Poor Law Commission set out to discipline the popular masses, while the Board of Trade resisted demands from the handloom weavers and factory workers for controls on production;[27] and Benthamites and Manchester liberals co-operated in the Poor Law Commission's scheme whereby some of the 'surplus' population of the south was encouraged to move north to sap trade union strength (Foster, 1974: 291). The 1833 Factory Act was a concession to popular pressures and, at the same time, a measure compatible with expanded reproduction of capital. It does not represent the 'pure' social seed of a 'Welfare State'. But it is the case of the handloom weavers which best exposes the inadequacy of academic orthodoxy on the character of the nineteenth-century State, and opens the way for the elaboration of an alternative interpretation.

The treatment and struggle of the handloom weavers prove how the 1830s and 1840s mark a *transition* in the economic and political history of modern Britain. The chronic condition of about 840,000 handloom weavers and their families amounted to 'the social cost' of early industrial capitalism.[28] As Marx saw:

> When machinery seizes on an industry by degrees, it produces chronic misery among the workers who compete with it. When the transition is rapid, the effect is acute and is felt by great masses of people. World history offers no spectacle more frightful than the gradual extinction of the English handloom weavers; this tragedy dragged on for decades, finally coming to an end in 1838. Many of the weavers died of starvation, many vegetated with their families for a long period on 2½d a day. (Marx, 1867b: 557–8)

The State intervened to endorse and promote this capitalist economic process rather than to check it. The domestic system and the traditional economy had finally been sacrificed to large-scale industry. Popular experience of this giant economic process, acclaimed by the bourgeoisie, was bound to reshape popular politics. Up to 1832 'the people' included all who worked, including the capitalist, against a minority, the aristocracy, who milked the rest of the population through their control of the political system. This analysis was essentially Cobbettism or the politics of the small property-owner. (E. P. Thompson, 1963: 832–4). But the case of the handloom weavers revealed the industrial capitalist, rather than the aristocracy, as the *popular* enemy. This meant an economic rather than a political analysis of society. John Maxwell, the chief parliamentary spokesman of the handloom weavers, identified his opponents at Westminster for the Scottish workers:

> Mr. P. Thomson and those who supported Mr. Huskisson's principles were opposed to the Bill, so were the Cotton Lords, and the proprietors of the Great Iron Works, who wanted trade to be free. They were likewise afraid that if Mr. Fielden's Bill had passed, that other workmen would likewise apply for the same privileges. He (Mr. M.) believed some of their opponents were far from being inhumane men, but as masters, they looked more to their own interests than to the interests of their workmen, which was more connected with foreign than with English interest. By means of their machinery they calculated that they could furnish all the world with goods at and under price.[29]

State *intervention* in the campaign conducted by the handloom weavers for controls on production (local boards of trade to fix minimum wages and prices) demonstrates the sharp *class* character of the 1830s State. The handloom weavers and their allies did not possess the necessary skill or knowledge, according to the Board of Trade party, to establish the working man's needs and to formulate measures to meet them. In contrast to the conclusions reached by the 1834–35 select committee managed by Maxwell and Fielden, the royal commission of 1837–41 was seen as a model inquiry by the liberals.[30] And the most recent historian of the handloom weavers has reasserted the validity of this 1830s 'expert' opinion:

> And it was precisely because there still existed considerable disagreement what 'the facts' of the weavers' situation really were in the 1830s that the select committee of 1834–5, dominated by committed humanitarians like Fielden and Maxwell, had to be followed by the more sober and impartial royal commission of 1837–41, consisting of Nassau Senior and his fellow economists. The first inquiry was unsatisfactory because it chose facts to fit a case; the second merely sought to establish what had really happened. Whatever his inclinations, the historian must take Senior, not Fielden, as his model. (Bythell, 1969: 127)

Yet it should be argued that the committee was as 'expert' as the commission, that the Bill it recommended could have worked and given the handloom weavers some relief, if only in the short term, and that this whole episode denies the validity of any project to establish the origins of the post-1945 Welfare State in this period.[31] Fielden's Bill was so fiercely opposed by the Manchester liberals, it should further be contended, because it struck at the basic interests of the big bourgeoisie. Labour had to be a 'marketable commodity' with the capitalist buying it at the cheapest rate possible and discharging it when no longer profitable. Otherwise the capital accumulation upon which the expansion of the industrial system depended would have been shackled. What the bourgeoisie feared most was an upsurge of popular demands for controls on the 'freedom' of capital and labour, despite the limited nature of Fielden's Bill itself. At least this was Maxwell's opinion, and he himself was attacked by the liberal press with the warning that 'if he and his class did not have a care Trade Boards might soon be applied to landlords' rents!' (Johnston, 1974: 315).

Despite their experience of industrial capitalism the handloom weavers retained a constitutionalism largely explained by the fact that after 1832 parliament was not dominated by the bourgeoisie, and popular spokesmen could make and follow through initiatives. The capture of the 1834–35 select committee was an important popular 'gain'. Delegates of the handloom weavers from all the major districts and towns gave evidence in London as did several industrialists. Fielden had been optimistic:

> I am busily engaged in Committee on the handloom weavers. I wish we may be able to devise some means of relief for them – the committee is a fair one and will sanction any proposition for redress of the weavers' grievances that can be shown to be practicable and I shall do my utmost to devise practicable measures of relief.[32]

The report of the committee called for the immediate approval by the legislature of Fielden's Bill.[33] This had support from shopkeepers and industrialists worried about falling prices and rising pauperism, as well as the handloom weavers themselves. But the Bill was vigorously opposed by the Board of Trade party, and Maxwell, defeated several times, moved successfully for the royal commission which allowed the liberals to stage a counter-attack.[34] By 1838, popular disillusionment with the reformed Parliament was complete as the Whigs allowed the commission to procrastinate and the New Poor Law to be carried into northern towns struck by depression. A popular constitutionalism, at first strengthened by the 1832 Reform Act, now rapidly transformed itself into a democratic movement threatening rebellion if its demands were not met. (Ward, 1962: 188–89).

The 'sacrifice' of the handloom weavers to industrial capitalism represents a major transformation in British society – a proletarianization of the mass of the population and the rise of large-scale industry at the centre of an expanding world economy – which was rapidly nearing completion by the 1830s.[35] The State promoted this economic process, despite the social upheavals and catastrophes involved; as well as endorsing a Benthamite plan to discipline labour in town and country. In the 1834 Poor Law Commission can be seen the English beginnings of a continental *étatism* geared to engineering an efficient and repressive capitalist society equipped with workhouses, schools, and policemen. Chadwick openly campaigned for new police forces to protect the capitalist from trade-unionism, as well as to enforce the 1834 Poor Law régime (Finer, 1952: 178–80). This interpretation cannot be taken too far. Limitations existed to the policy designs of both Manchester liberals and Benthamites well beyond the antagonism implicit between the two. Aggressive liberalism was obstructed by Tories and popular radicals in and out of Parliament. Thomson's attempt to sabotage the 1833 Factory Act failed and Roebuck's education plan was substituted by a grant system which refuelled the schooling efforts of the Church of England. And the Whigs kept a check on the policy-makers whom they had brought into the State service.[36] Yet the industrial/capitalist character of the nineteenth-century British State was solidified in the 1830s, and moreover, this State was taking on an aggressive and authoritarian form. If 1832–35 was a critical conjuncture in nineteenth-century State formation, however, so was 1838–42.

The significance of the 1838–42 period cannot be realized without emphasizing the interaction of two cardinal facts of economic and political history: the collapse of the 1833–36 boom and the reaching out of the Poor Law Commission into the industrial north. What emerged was a mass democratic movement against the 1832 settlement between the political aristocracy and the bourgeoisie and the disastrous consequences which had *appeared to follow* from it. Here we need to establish the links between this crisis *for* the ruling classes and what appears to be a clear break in national economic and social policy. A series of crucial initiatives was made to stimulate and stabilize the economy (machinery export permitted and the moves culminating in the Bank Charter Act of 1844) *and* also to shift away from the aggressive social policy of the 1830s (the New Poor Law curbed, the 1842 Mines Act and 1844 Factory Act passed, and public health and educational measures taken up).[37]

The case for a policy break in the late 1830s and early 1840s does not rest, however, on any crude correlation between concessions and popular threats of rebellion. It ought to be stressed that the Chartist movement and the 'General Strike' of 1842 *were more severe shocks* to the ruling classes than is usually admitted by historians (Mather, 1974: 115–35) and there was a deep awareness that *a policy* of repression (as from 1815–19) would have been disastrous. The army shadowed the Chartists and new police forces were created, but major confrontations were avoided. The situation dictated some compromise with an organized working class alienated from the economic and political system. But, as Foster says (1974: 187), the real process of change was obviously more complex:

> On the purely economic side there were the govern-
> mental and banking reactions to the increasingly severe
> economic crises of the 1830s and early 1840s (usually
> blamed on domestic industrial speculation), a recognition
> of the gains to be won by making London *the* interna-
> tional banking centre, and the emergence of the necessary
> technological conditions for large-scale capital export.
> Socially, there was the very real perception of the dangers
> presented by the existing economic course. And as far as
> the industrial bourgeoisie was concerned – not so much

a change of analysis as a loss of will to oppose changes
which still cut across their basic interests. It was the interlocking of all these factors that brought the national
change.

Foster seems to lay too much stress on qualitative changes
of economic policy (the curbing of the 'factory sector' and
shift towards capital export) whereas there seems little
doubt that the Whigs and Peelites agreed that the basic
solution to national crisis was a revival and expansion of
industrial capitalism (Gash, 1972: 359–62). At the same
time, there was a conviction that renewed industrial *and*,
therefore, urban expansion had to be subject to greater
'physical *and* moral' regulation of the working population.
A policy break at national level almost certainly began
after the general election of the late summer of 1837 when
the Benthamites suffered defeats and the Whigs were
alarmed by the anti-Poor Law politics evident in many urban
constituencies (Prest, 1972: 118–19). Then the failure of
Fielden's February 1838 motion to repeal the 1834 Poor
Law Act seems to launch Chartism into a broad-based popular movement which pushes key M.P.s and State Servants,
such as Ashley, Slaney, Chadwick, Dr Kay and Horner,
into a close co-operation. But a response to the threat of
popular rebellion cannot be easily disentangled from a
response to 'the physical and moral' degeneration of the
urban and industrial working class, as revealed by private
and state inquiries (Cullen, 1975: 139). These inquiries, by
urban statistical societies and State Servants, aided and
abetted by M.P.s were both a consequence of social crisis
and a stepping-up of existing activity. Slaney was particularly busy absorbing the findings of the inquiries and organizing their presentation to parliament, as was Lord Ashley
and a few other M.P.s, some of whom belonged to the
statistical societies.[38]
To illustrate that we are dealing with a policy break, a
reorientation away from the aggressive liberalism of the

1830s, the policy makers in the crucial public health/education field should be studied. Chartism was seen as an explosion of popular ignorance which could only be tackled if the younger members of the working population were protected from exploitation and slum environments. Horner, the factory inspector, wrote:

> Now unless every possible chance be given to the child of growing up healthy and strong, unless his natural intelligence be cultivated and drawn out, unless moral and religious principles be early implanted in him, so to become part of his nature, what chance have we of his growing up to be a healthy, strong, intelligent, ingenious, honest, and right-principled man, a useful and orderly citizen?[39]

Slaney endorsed Horner and informed Brougham that the health of towns was:

> . . . closely connected with the moral as much as the physical state of large masses of the working classes in our populous districts. The Report and Evidence show how little probability there is of any effectual prospect of Education amid these multitudes unless some strenuous efforts are made to improve the state of their dwellings in decency and comfort.[40]

Through Horner and Slaney, we can see what was now a typical response by the ruling classes to social crisis.[41] This *was* an awakening to 'social evils' but an awakening best *explained* by Gramsci's concept of hegemony. This refers to the function of the capitalist state to win and keep 'the consent' of the dominated classes to their own domination. This has to be achieved and regularly maintained through the promotion and extention of 'moral' education, although coercion is always present.[42]

In the 1830s the British ruling classes experienced *a crisis* of hegemony. The working class was not simply ignorant but possessed its *own* knowledge:

> The prevailing want of the present day seems to be a want of correct information as to the true interests of society. The progress of popular education has already infused a mind into the masses heretofore but passive instruments in the hands of those who were the exclusive possessors of knowledge. The people now read: the people reason; the people think for themselves. What do they read? What are their thoughts? From what principles do they reason? These are questions of deep import. For the answers to them must determine the ultimate result of the revolution, hitherto a tranquil and bloodless, but yet a complete revolution, which has long since commenced, and is in active progress throughout Europe. By education the people are everywhere acquiring knowledge; and knowledge is power.[43]

The foundation of the Education Department in 1839 was an important moment in the formation of what Gramsci calls 'the cultural state' as the ruling classes closed ranks against the threat to their domination (Gramsci, 1934: 258). Although 1839 was not the strong dose of State intervention demanded by some liberals, it did cement the alliance of rural and urban orders against Chartism.[44] The reality of the alliance was both the cause and effect of the 1841 election victory of Peel and the Conservatives, marking the rightwards shift that liberalism had taken since 1832. A *modus vivendi* was agreed between the Whigs/Liberals and Tories/Anglicans bringing into official play what has been described as the co-existence of conservative and liberal ideological repertoires 'pressed into the service' of capital as a whole:

> So throughout the century genuine attempts at a real popular emancipation always faced a double armoury: the economic power of manufacturer *and* farmer/land-

lord; the ideologies of 'deference' as well as those of bourgeois 'independence', self-help and thrift; High Tory Anglicanism *and* Methodism (in its unnaturalized forms), militant Dissent and popular anti-catholicism; Chadwick's and Peel's newly professionalized police *and* the gentry justice; popular political economy *and* 'moral and religious education'; utilitarian political philosophy *and* an anti-democratic conservatism; bourgeois special constabulary *and* an aristocratically-led plebeian army. Elements in this dual repertoire came to the fore according to circumstance and need. (Johnson, 1975: 26)

The argument is that the late 1830s and early 1840s do witness a redirection of national policy to solve an economic and social crisis of major proportions. Concessions to the working class and measures to stimulate industrial capitalism should be seen as part of *a wider strategy* to contain class struggle and give cohesion to the economic and social system. This interpretation can explain the form of capitalist State as it existed in the 1850s and 1860s after the battles of the 1830s and 1840s. Any attempts to fully implement a Manchester or Benthamite policy programme would have forced the working class into a revolutionary strategy and split the ruling classes. Instead the compromise between the rural and urban orders – only temporarily upset in 1846 – kept political power and authority localized while a central political scene dominated by the landed gentry masked rule in the interests of industrial capital.[45]

To summarize, the early nineteenth-century State endorsed and promoted the capitalist economic process despite its chronic social consequences. The sacrifice of the handloom weavers to that process cleared the ground for large-scale industry and competitive capitalism. In other words, the 1830s and 1840s condensed the capitalist character of the modern British State. At the same time this intensified the class struggle generated by early industrial capitalism and threatened the cohesion of society itself. This threat can explain the policy break of the late 1830s and early 1840s involving the abandonment of aggressive liberalism and measures designed to recharge the system. The railway boom of 1843–46 guaranteed the success of this ruling-class *strategy* and encouraged the disintegration of a Chartist movement fuelled by ideas seeking *alternatives* to industrial capitalism. The final collapse of Chartism as a mass movement in 1848 confirmed the permanence or acceptance of the new economy and society. Thus working-class movements in the 1850s and 1860s were characterized by reformism. The only alternative to capitalism was now modern socialism.[46]

The common ideology of 'Tory' and 'Fabian' historians has prevented them from recognizing the capitalist core of the mid-nineteenth-century State and its formation within the context of class struggle at a *particular stage* of capitalist development. This charge can be substantiated by reference to the failure of academic orthodoxy to question the concept of expertise as used by the nineteenth-century State. Official 'knowledge' asserted its superiority over working-class 'knowledge' as being 'scientific' as opposed to the 'nonsense' expounded by popular representatives. Yet the ideological content of State expertise and its use to legitimize the interests of the bourgeoisie is clear from the case of the handloom weavers. It is also true that the application of official expertise could realize an improvement in working-class conditions, emphasizing its relative autonomy from individual capitals. The Factory Acts are the obvious example, albeit as attempts to contain class struggle *and* to promote a healthy and productive working class as against the effects of capitalist competition. The genuine humanitarianism of some policy matters should not be denied. But nineteenth-century State Servants cannot be regarded as neutral social scientists better equipped than anyone else to administer to *social need*, however well-intentioned and intelligent some of them may have been.

This critique of academic orthodoxy should beware of being the stick too far in the other direction. The nineteenth-century British State was not a crude apparatus at the service of capital against labour, nor was it the central site of a ruling-class conspiracy to defuse revolution. The British capitalist State, as it actually existed in the 1850s and 1860s, derived from the class struggles and compromises of the 1830s and 1840s. *These struggles and compromises took place within the State as well as outside it.* The suggestion is that the modern State condenses class relations and allows the men 'in charge' to work for the overall cohesion of capitalist society. By the 1850s and 1860s a British nation State deflected class struggle at home and challenged other nation States abroad. This national/capitalist State was embodied in a landed-dominated legislature, supreme within a State whose promotion of bourgeois hegemony was largely obscured. The *relative* autonomy of the State from the interests of industrial capital appeared as a clear *separation* between the two, encouraging a popular anti-aristocratic liberalism and/or popular nationalism. But this *resulted* from the real contribution of landed, *and especially popular, power* to the defeat of the aggressive capitalist State which had begun to emerge earlier.

4
Patriarchal Aspects of Nineteenth-Century State Formation: Property Relations, Marriage and Divorce, and Sexuality
Rachel Harrison and Frank Mort

This chapter examines particular aspects of patriarchal State legislation in the nineteenth century, governing the regulation of familial property relations, marriage and divorce, and sexuality (particularly sexial 'deviance'). In the recent theoretical focus on the State there has as yet been little attempt to conduct an analysis of sexual and moral practices as they act as determinants on the structures of legislative intervention in specific historical moments. One is at worst reading through total absences, or at best left merely with indications of possible developments, signalling the position of women or sexual relations, which are not elaborated (e.g. Jessop, 1978, Poulantzas, 1978).[1] These absences may be generally defined as a failure to recognize that the State not only stands in a particular economic, political, legal and ideological relation to the contradiction between capital and labour, but also that its legislative action secures continuation and definition of specific forms of patriarchal relations involving the subordination of women and the construction and regulation of particular sexualities.[2] The insistence on the patriarchal organization of the State has come from feminists working in the field, (e.g. Political Economy of Women Group, 1975, Holcombe, 1977, Wilson, 1977), who have attempted to explore the marked economic, legal and ideological intervention of the State in constructing and regulating women's position in the spheres of property relations, marriage and the family and sexuality. These key areas have emerged as a central focus for feminists in understanding the nature of the connection between the continuing patriarchal organization of those practices, within the state apparatuses, and the history of the development of capitalist relations.

The beginnings of an attempt to understand historically the articulation between patriarchal relations and capitalist development has formed one of the major focuses of our work on the nineteenth-century State. Functionalist analyses tend to pose the relation between the two structures in a mono-causal way. Changes in the history of the capitalist mode of production are seen to 'require' or necessitate periodic revisions in those spheres (including the family and sexuality) which contribute to the continuing expansion and reproduction of capital (generally referred to as the areas of social reproduction). The interventionist State is seen to function as the 'ideal total capitalist' (Mandel, 1975: 479), serving the interests of capitalist production and social reproduction as a whole, as against the competing interests of individual capitals. Such arguments insist that it is the 'logic of capital' which determines the nature and effectivity of State intervention in the areas of social reproduction (e.g. the family, education, 'welfare' provision), and which wholly secures the continuing subordination of women.[3]

However, what has informed our analysis here is a consideration of some of the problems posed by a functionalist reading of the State in relation to patriarchal relations. Gramsci's generalization that the operation of the capitalist State serves as 'the instrument for conforming civil society to the economic structure' (Gramsci, 1934) is useful as a point of departure for understanding the effectivity of cultural, moral and sexual determinations on State formation. But it has been an awareness of the history of partriarchal relations and the structures of sexuality as they pre-date capitalist development, that has led us to question any notion of a simple functional fit between patriarchal State intervention and capitalism. The State can be seen to draw on, transform and modify particular sets of patriarchal relations, through legislation governing the transmission of property, marriage and sexuality, but it cannot be seen to *create* those relations. Furthermore, specific ideologies and legal practices which are the inherited structures of previous social formations, still act as determinants on the formation of particular apparatuses governing sexuality and the family throughout the nineteenth century. (For example, ecclesiastical apparatuses and religious ideologies still structure the civil regulation of marriage and divorce in the period.) Our particular analysis attempts to comprehend *both* the internal and relatively autonomous history of specific structures and practices governing sexuality and the family prior to the development of industrial capitalism, as that history influences nineteenth-century legislation in this area, *and* the ways in which forms of State intervention are determined by the more immediate changes in the sphere of capitalist relations. It is clear, for example, that legislation addressing particular forms of patriarchal legal relations in the nineteenth century, governing property and inheritance, is as much determined by the structures of its own history prior to the shift into industrial capitalism, as it is by the specific historical developments in the period. Moreover, not all practices relating to marriage, sexuality and the transmission of property, stand in an equally direct relation to capitalist development in the nineteenth century. Legislation governing marriage and divorce and the sexual division of property stands in a more immediate relation to the wider economic, politico-legal and ideological developments of the period than legislation regulating forms of sexual 'deviancy' such as homosexuality and prostitution.

Finally, it should be stressed that functionalist accounts of the history of State formation often fail to consider elements of contestation and struggle as fundamental determinants on the construction and implementation of legislation. Specifically, the history of State intervention is itself not only the history of forms of class struggle, but also of struggles conducted against patriarchal relations institutionalized through the State. For example, State intervention in the nineteenth century in the sphere of property relations, and in the regulation of prostitution[4] is directly influenced by demands and pressures made on the State by early feminists. In the attempt to be more specific about the political analysis of struggles around the State, we should note that the State should be seen not as a monolithic and unified 'subject', but as a differentiated set of practices and institutions which at specific historical moments may stand in contradiction or opposition (see Jessop, 1978). The point is particularly important in analysing the relation of women to the State: the construction and definition of women's subordinate position will vary across particular apparatuses and institutional sites, it will not remain constant or unchanging in the form of its appearance. We concentrate here on the way in which the *legislative processes* of the State construct and articulate particular sets of patriarchal relations, rather than on the effectivity of that legislation as it is implemented and 'lived' within specific practices and institutions.

The legislation we consider takes as its primary focus the *explicit* regulation of familial property relations, marriage and divorce, and sexuality. We do not specifically deal with what can be seen as a second legislative tradition, which focuses on areas other than marriage relations and sexuality, but which contains within it regulative structures governing the position of women, and the control of sexual practices. *The Poor Law Report* (1834), for example, contains specific statements on bastardy and illegitimacy, and on the position of women in the family (cf. Thane, 1977; Corrigan and

Corrigan, 1978; and Ch. 6 below). Also, *The Factory Acts* (1844 onwards), *The Education Act* (1870), and *The Sanitary Report* (1844), articulate specific moral assumptions on the nature of female sexuality and working-class sexual practices, and construct particular definitions of women in the family and in the sphere of social production.

Legislation on the Sexual Division of Property

In bourgeois law a distinction is frequently made between public law which deals with economic relations of production (e.g. the expansion of capital, or the regulation of labour) and private law which deals with areas 'outside' production (e.g. the family[5]). The purpose of the first part of this chapter is to show that an understanding of women's subordinate legal status, especially in relation to property ownership, depends on a historical examination of the interconnection between these two areas.

The ownership of the means of production (productive property) by the aristocracy and the bourgeoisie in the nineteenth century was patriarchal in character, but differed according to the nature of the property which was owned. The growing importance of productive capital as property meant that certain principles of common law which had been developed primarily to deal with rights to lend, were becoming increasingly anachronistic; they addressed *freemen*, meaning owners of freehold land, rather than shareholders. The changing nature of property and the rigidity of the old principles of common law ownership rights encouraged the development of a new more flexible body of law which was based on the principles of 'equity' and practised in separate courts; the courts of chancery. From the 1830s there was a movement to establish the rule of equity, that is, the justice of the individual case, more generally, adapting to a world in which 'real property' took the form of stocks and shares (Harding, 1966:375).

The common law was not made redundant, however, for the ownership of land (freehold real property) to which it applied remained important economically, politically and ideologically, particularly during the first half of the nineteenth century: 'The cohesion of the traditional English landowning class rendered their power extensive. They were in ultimate control of all institutions . . . in rural areas they held, either individually or as a class, a virtual monopoly over employment opportunities' (Davidoff, *et al.*, 1976:24).

Common law laid down rigid rules of succession based on primogeniture and entail for the inheritance of landed property. This involved the transmission of ownership through the oldest legitimate son in order to preserve the integrity of estates: that is, to pass them on intact in the male line. If a daughter inherited land in the absence of male heir, it passed under common law into the control of her husband on marriage. In this way, the differential division of property between man and wife on marriage justified the differential transmission of property to sons and daughters: for unless the husband was a close cousin, the estate of an heiress would inevitably become alienated from the male line on her marriage. The exclusion of daughters from the land was therefore 'an indispensable means for keeping the patrimony in the lineage' (Goody, 1976a:18). This was important politically, because any system of property distribution that allowed women to own land would disturb traditional hierarchical attitudes to the 'legitimacy' of aristocratic ownership based on inherited titles or names: 'Where women receive land, the basic means of production, its ownership is drastically reorganized . . . it changes hands at every marriage' (Goody, 1976a:20).

Therefore as Bourdieu comments, it was only in exceptional circumstances that landed property was transmitted through the female line: 'Only the absence of any male descendant . . . can bring about the desperate solution . . . of entrusting to a woman the task of transmitting the lineage' (Bourdieu, 1976:119). Provision was made under common law for younger sons and daughters; the 'portion' allotted to younger sons and the dowry allotted to daughters on marriage were devices for compensating them for disinheritance from the means of production, but allowing them a means of subsistence.

Primogeniture was not a universal practice among landowners.[6] It was favoured by the owners of large estates because it enabled a continuation of their political power. New landowners, however, with small estates were inclined towards partible inheritance (F. Thompson, 1963:119). In some instances, notions of 'fairness' (a particular form of the ideology of equality) worked against the interests of these smaller landowners; in their anxiety to provide for all their children, some yeomen withdrew capital from the land and prepared the means of their own destruction (E. P. Thompson, 1976b:349).

With respect to capital, the shift into machinofacture in the first half of the nineteenth century saw a massive increase in the rate of capital accumulation. Marx estimated that between 1838 and 1850 the wealth of manufacturers, based on the increasing exploitation of labour power, increased by an average of 32% (Marx 1867b:540–41). He noted two opposite tendencies associated with this expansion: one was the tendency for 'an expropriation of capitalist by capitalist, the transformation of many small into a few large capitals', the other tendency was towards 'a division of property within capitalist families', so that 'portions of original capitals disengage themselves and function as new independent capitals . . . with the accumulation of capital, therefore, the number of capitalists grows to a greater or lesser extent' (Marx, 1867b:623).

These shifts in the history of capital accumulation, as well as the shift from the primacy of landed property to that of industrial capital, underlay legal changes in patterns of inheritance. The common law had operated with fixed rules of succession and little freedom of testation, but during the eighteenth and nineteenth centuries an increasing freedom of testation allowed fathers to leave their productive property to a successor or successors of their choice.[7] 'Parents could determine the distribution of capital among the children of remoter issue as they thought fit, even to the total exclusion of sons' (Crane, 1957:236).

While the passing of property to daughters was no longer explicitly prohibited by law, as it had been under the system of primogeniture, it remained customary for daughters to inherit only in the absence of male heirs. The division of property which Marx noted within capitalist families was accomplished by a system of partible inheritance. This system was a more egalitarian division than primogeniture as far as sons were concerned.

Marriage law (prior to 1882) still dictated that a daughter's property must pass to her husband on marriage, alienating it from the male line. The perpetuation of the common law practice which allowed a husband to appropriate his wife's property enabled fathers to continue to justify their practice of transmitting their property to sons; it appeared both 'natural' and logical, given the marriage laws, to exclude daughters in the interest of preserving continuity of succession in the male line. Only rarely in the absence of male heirs, did a daughter inherit the means of production and the accompanying rights of appropriation of labour power.[8] Only as a single person, as an unmarried heiress, could a woman become a member of the bourgeoisie in her own right. On marriage the heiress became the legally dependent bourgeois wife, whose husband owned the means of production.

During the nineteenth century it was not so much the differential distribution of property to sons and daughters (laws of succession), but the division of property between husband and wife (marriage law) which became a principal focus of early feminist struggle. Under common law a husband assumed legal possession and control of all his wife's real and personal property on marriage, and any that she might inherit during her marriage. Common law distinguished between real property, which was freehold land, and personal property which included leasehold land and chattels (Holcombe, 1977:4). Under common law it was possible for a daughter's dowry to be dissipated by a spendthrift husband, so a system of marriage settlement developed during the eighteenth century which allowed a wife to hold a 'separate estate' in real or personal property free from her husband's common law rights of possession and control (Holcombe, 1977:7). One of the characteristics of this equity protection, as it was called, was a legal distinction between possession and control. This meant that while the wife *formally* possessed the separate estate, it was lawyers who drew up each individual pre-marital agreement and held the power of investment and control.[9]

In the attempt to preserve the interests of the wife's family of origin, marriage settlements curtailed the common-law rights of husbands, who, unless they persuaded a daughter to elope, had to consent to her 'separate estate' at bethrothal. Settlements gave aristocratic daughters some protection from patriarchal structures of matrimonial property law, in that they allowed a wife some income for her own use; but they should not secure her economic independence by means of her formal possession of an inheritance.[10] Though marriage settlements gave to lawyers extensive powers and remuneration, the principal beneficiary of the 'separate estate' was the wife's father: 'The essence of the arrangement which equity upheld was the preservation of wealth within the (paternal) kinship group which provided it . . . It also protected the capital against incursions of the husband, his family and the recipient herself' (Finer, 1971:97).

The expense of the proceedings in the chancery courts meant that settlements were only available to one woman in ten (Holcombe, 1977:7–8). During the 1850s efforts were made to extend the system of equity to all women who had real or personal property, or earnings; for earnings too were subject to the common-law provision whereby all money that a wife earned automatically passed to her husband. The movement to extend equity beyond the minority of aristocratic women grew out of frustrations experienced by bourgeois and middle-class married women. A Law Amendment Society was formed which drew up a bill recommending that all married women should have the right to keep their own inherited property or their earnings. A reduced form of these recommendations was hurriedly added to the *Matrimonial Causes Act* of 1857 in an attempt to forestall any wholesale reform of property law in favour of wives. The additional clauses allowed property rights to divorced women or women who were legally separated: they gave legal protection to 'injured' women only, leaving a married woman's husband free to squander her property or appropriate her earnings as before.

Because of the limited scope of the 1857 Act, struggles for wider reforms continued. Women were active members of the reform group, but it was men who put the case to the Select Committee in 1867–8. They stressed that their proposals were not only designed to benefit bourgeois and middle-class women, but working-class women too. Moreover their arguments in favour of property and earnings reforms were couched in such a way as to counter the fears expressed by the Select Committee that a more equal distribution of rights between husbands and wives would have adverse repercussions on marital relations. In the case of working-class women the Committee was anxious that if a wife did control her earnings she might excite increased brutality from a drunken husband; in the case of women with property the Committee focused persistently on the question of whether the authority of husbands would be diminished by the fact that they did not possess *absolutely* both their own property and the property of their wives. Barristers representing the Law Amendment Society argued that England was the only civilized country in which marriage operated as a transfer of the property of the wife to the husband.[11] They attempted to reassure the Committee that giving the wife a settlement under the system of equity would not reduce the husband's authority because 'authority comes from property' and the husband inevitably had 'greater business opportunities' (*Report of the Select Committee on Married Women's Property 1867–68*: 24, 83). Even in the minds of lawyers the principle of equity had little to do with equality between the sexes.

Though it was much amended in the House of Lords, the *Married Women's Property Act* of 1870 did extend to all women who owned property the principles of equity in the form of the marriage settlement: 'Married women were to have their "separate property" . . . the earnings and property they acquired by their own work . . . money invested in several specified ways . . . and with qualifications, property coming to them from the estate of persons deceased' (Holcombe, 1977:20). But the qualifications were important because although there were no restrictions on the transmission of property to unmarried daughters, its transmission to married daughters was strictly limited. A married woman could only independently hold property which came to her as next of kin of an intestate (a person who died without making a will); she could hold no legacy larger than £200 left her by will (Holcombe, 1977:21). Thus a father could not leave productive property to a married daughter by will: if he did so, it passed to her husband as before under common law.

After much effort by the Married Women's Property Committee and its supporters, the *Married Women's Property Act* of 1882 was passed. For the first time it allowed a married woman to own all the property that she possessed at the time of marriage from whatever source it originated, and any she subsequently acquired. The relaxation of the legal restrictions on the division of property within marriage went hand in hand with the relaxation of restrictions on the transmission of property from father to daughter. But even though a daughter could hold her property as a separate estate and a father could transmit his productive property to a married daughter by will, it remained the custom for fathers to pass their property to their sons as before, in order to retain the means of production in the family name. In practice, therefore, a daughter was only likely to become an heiress in the absence of sons.

The Married Women's Property Act of 1882 was progressive in the sense that it lessened the economic dependence on their husbands of those women who possessed property. For the majority of women who did not own property, even personal property, the Act marked an advance in that their earnings could no longer be legally appropriated by their husbands. To find out how much this meant in practice would involve an investigation of the implementation and effectiveness of the legislation. (It is likely that only bourgeois wives, married to owners of the means of production, and middle-class wives, married to men in professional occupations, would have had the resources to take a case to court.)

The changes effected by the legislation on property reform can be seen as the result of early middle-class feminist struggle conducted against a particular set of patriarchal relations institutionalized by the State. In that respect they form an example of the way in which particular social groups, other than those involved in economic and political *class* struggle, come to perceive their oppression as maintained and reproduced through the operation of the State. Yet Holcombe (1977) alerts us to a different, seemingly contradictory, tendency of the legislation: namely its *compatibility* with the changing economic, political and ideological conditions of the mid-nineteenth century: 'in demanding reform of the married women's property law feminists were fortunately not swimming against the currents of the time' (Holcombe, 1977:26). More generally, it could be argued that the structures of a fully industrial capitalism had come to 'require' some revision of the moral, cultural and sexual practices and institutions, which were largely the inherited products of previous social formations.

That is to say, the shift from the dominance of agrarian capital and aristocratic politics to the ascendancy of industrial capital and the emergence of secular 'democratic' ideologies implied the possibility of a more progressive legal and economic position for bourgeois and middle-class women.

Yet, in fact, the Married Women's Property Acts, together with the innovatory 1857 legislation on divorce law reforms, are illustrative of the deeply contradictory tendencies of much State legislation as it affected the position of women in the nineteenth century. They reveal the ways in which new ideologies, emerging with industrial capitalism, had progressive implications for certain classes of women, while still being articulated through patriarchal structures. The legislation governing property reform, and the struggles surrounding it, were clearly influenced by variants of the ideology of economic individualism (that world characterized by Marx as encompassing the rule of freedom, equality, property and Bentham), in as much as it marked the first stages of the extension of the concept of *homo economicus* to bourgeois and middle-class women. Furthermore, it is clear tham many of the early feminist struggles (including the struggle over political representation) were conducted on a predominantly middle-class terrain, in that feminists were attempting to achieve the same status as middle-class males, often by exposing the contradictions in an individualist ideology which still remained patriarchally structured.[12]

Moreover, the articulation of patriarchal ideologies coupled with ideologies of individualism is illustrative of the transformation effected in the nature of patriarchal relations as they are incorporated into State legislation, as the State works over and modifies pre-existing patriarchal structures. The Married Women's Property Acts – or rather the ideological ground on which they are constructed – marks the emergence of a type of patriarchal ideology which comes to form the organizing principle of much twentieth-century legislation addressing women: notions of difference combined with ideologies of equality and complementarity.[13] As Sachs points out in discussing the ideological implications of the property reforms: 'the two sexes were neither the same with regard to rights, nor even separate but equal, but rather different and complementary. In other words, women were to complement men, not to compete with them' (Sachs, 1978:27).

We have attempted to indicate that, within the general history of capital accumulation in the nineteenth century, there occurred a generational transmission of particular capitals, which was effected through patriarchal structures of family relations, as they were constructed both in law and in customary procedures of succession. Capitalists, we would argue, were not only capitalists, they were at the same time sons and fathers; their insertion into nineteenth-century relations of production as agents of capital, was closely bound up with their insertion into relations of procreation (or family relations) as agents of transmission of capital. We have seen that the nature of the property owned directly influenced these patterns of transmission: on the one hand there was the association of land with primogeniture, and on the other that of capital with partible inheritance. Both of those patterns of inheritance were patriarchal, though their forms were distinct.

At the most abstract level it could be argued that capital is as indifferent to the sex of the capitalist as it is to the sex of the labourer. Historically, however, capital worked on and benefited from the cheaper cost of female labour power and its different cultural and ideological value; these factors were a consequence of the patriarchal family and work relations that preceded industrial production.[14] We would suggest that, historically, capital also benefited from the subordinate status of the bourgeois woman with respect to property ownership. Firstly, under certain circumstances, the *appropriation* of a wife's property on marriage aided capital accumulation in that it augmented the husband's capital resources. Secondly, the *transmission* of property to male heirs facilitated the economic stabilization and political legitimization of the ownership of the means of production by individual named families. Historically, the passing of property to legitimate sons was a method of preserving the private, family nature of the competitive self-interest that was the ideological structure of nineteenth-century capital; the necessary form taken by the inherent tendency of capital to self-expansion.

Legislation Governing Marriage and Divorce

The mid-century legislation on marriage and divorce carries with it the continuity of concern over bourgeois property transmission and inheritance. In attempting to emphasize the line between legislative changes governing this area of sexual/moral practice and wider historical developments, we would generally insist that it is misguided to pose any direct or functional relation between divorce law reform and the 'needs' or 'demands' of capitalist relations. Rather, it is through an examination of the shift in the apparatuses of regulatiom from Church to State, together with an awareness of the political and ideological significance of that movement, that we have sought to locate legislation on marriage and divorce in the context of wider historical determinations.

Before the changes enacted by the 1857 *Matrimonial Causes Act*, the power to pronounce divorce '*a mensa et toro*' ('from bed and board' – amounting to the modern legal separation) lay in the hands of the ecclesiastical courts. Only Parliament could dissolve marriages absolutely, allowing re-marriage, through a complex and highly expensive procedure involving a private parliamentary bill.[15] The Cambell Commission established in 1853, on whose recommendations the 1857 legislation was largely carried through, itself noted two significant factors affecting the use of that parliamentary procedure. It stressed that under exceptional circumstances the spiritual jurisdiction of the Established Church was overridden by specially created parliamentary machinery, and that those exceptions characteristically concerned the transmission and inheritance of property. As Finer and McGregor point out, individual parliamentary divorce acts had their origins in the need for the continuance of peerages, together with the attendant real property, in the male line (1971:92). The Commission noted that the first divorce act passed in 1666 was granted to the husband under circumstances in which: 'there was no probable expectation of posterity to support the family in the male line.' (p. 7)

More specifically, though, the use of divorce procedure usually expressed the husband's concern that the wife's adultery allowed for the possibility of implanting illegitimate offspring in a legitimate aristocratic family. Often the explicit needs of legitimate property transmission were stated in the proposed parliamentary bills, with reference to the threats of patrilineal inheritance posed by the wife's adultery. The Commission argued that adultery should be seen as sufficient grounds for absolute divorce because it 'introduces a confusion of offspring' and cuts off all 'hope of succession' through diverting 'the affections and feelings into strange channels, which reason and religion forbid them to flow in' (ibid.: 15). A similar concern was expressed in the parliamentary debates surrounding the 1857 bill, particularly over the question of allowing to the wife the right to petition for divorce. The proposal was eventually withdrawn on the grounds that accessibility to divorce procedure was seen to be far more necessary for the husband than for the wife; because of the need for the legitimate transmission of property through the male line. As the Commission noted: 'the difference between the adultery of the husband and the wife (socially speaking) is boundless' (p. 16). The Lord Chancellor's argument in the House of Lords over the passing of the Act is characteristic in its expression of this dual morality:

A wife might without any loss of caste, and possibly with reference to the interests of her children, or even of her husband, condone an act of adultery on the part of the husband; but a husband could not condone a similar act on the part of a wife. No one would venture to suggest that a husband could possibly do so, and for this, among other reasons . . . that the adultery of the wife might be the means of palming spurious offspring upon the husband, while the adultery of the husband could have no such effect with regard to the wife. (*Hansard*, 1857, vol. 145, quoted in McGregor, 1957:20)

Effectively, what the 1857 Act did was to extend the possibility of obtaining absolute divorce settlements to the bourgeoisie and professional middle classes – legal relations which had previously only been accessible to the aristocracy. This was primarily achieved by cheapening and simplifying the procedure: removing the expense of a parliamentary bill, and instituting the newly-created civil divorce courts capable of pronouncing absolute divorce and legal separation. There is little evidence to suggest that there was any direct campaign in the 1840s and 1850s for divorce law reform on behalf of a bourgeois and middle-class clientele; most of the directly expressed dissatisfaction with the existing procedures came from the legal profession itself. However, the connection between the increased accessibility of divorce for those classes and the economic and political shifts of the early nineteenth century involving partial bourgeois ascendancy should be noted as significant.

Yet the influence of the new legislation on the structure of working-class marital relations was minimal. Though Lord Resedale had argued in a minority statement to the 1853 Commission that the proposed legislation would create a demand from the working class for 'cheap laws' for divorce (ibid.: 28–29), even after 1857 the expense of the proceedings made divorce an exclusively aristocratic and middle-class privilege. However, with the renewed panic and concern over working-class poverty in the 1870s and 1880s, attention was focused on the increase in violent crimes in working-class districts, and particularly in relation to cases of physical assault by men against their wives. The 1878 *Matrimonial Causes Act* (a result of the findings of the 1875 Law Commission on brutal assaults, and of the pressure and influence of Frances Power Cobbe's campaign, and her exposé in *Wife Torture*) gave magistrates' courts the power to grant legal separation with maintenance, together with limited rights over custody of children, to a wife whose husband had been convicted of aggravated assault on her. Further Acts followed in 1884, 1886 and 1895 which consolidated and extended the powers of magistrates to grant separation orders. By the end of the century there were, in effect, two separate and class specific legal apparatuses established for the regulation of marital relations: the divorce courts proper, used by the aristocracy and middle class, and the magistrates' courts, which were the working-class remedy for matrimonial difficulties (though of course legal separations did not allow for remarriage). As McGregor points out, the latter facilities were widely used: between 1897 and 1906 'magistrates' courts granted over 87,000 separations and maintenance orders' (McGregor 1957:24). It was not until the appointment of the Gorell Commission on Divorce and Matrimonial Causes in 1909 that the problem of the dual class morality began, even summarily, to be addressed.[16]

Yet it was not so much a newly enshrined middle-class morality that was enacted by the 1857 legislation, but rather the increased availability of a set of legal practices governing sexuality and the family which had their origins prior to the nineteenth century. The legal and ideological definitions surrounding marriage and divorce remained relatively unchanged by the new legislation; certainly no new criteria for divorce were introduced. Nevertheless, there was perhaps the beginnings of a more clearly secular, less spiritual, emphasis placed on the significance of marriage; the 1853

Commission stressed the fact that marriage and its dissolution were the direct concern of 'the moral order of *civil society*' (p. 13), involving 'the morals and happiness of the whole *community*' (p. 24, our emphases). Previous parliamentary acts of 1753 (*Lord Hardwicke's Marriage Act*) and of 1836 (the *Marriage Act* and the Births, Marriages and Deaths Act) introduced legislation recognizing marriage as a specifically civil contract, and removed the right to determine what constituted legal marriage from Church to State.[17] If the prevailing ideologies and moralities in the field were slightly differently inflected after 1857, it was primarily due to the shift in the apparatuses of control from an ecclesiastical form of regulation to a predominantly secular legal code.

Yet, while it is important to be alert to any ideological repercussions involved in this shift, we should also be aware that religious and moral ideologies remain primary determinants in the ideological construction and regulation of marital relations and sexual practices. There is little evidence here, in State legislation in the nineteenth century, of the influence of secular ideologies of individualism, which we noted for the transformation of property relations; no belief that the breakdown of marriage is a matter of purely personal concern between the individual contracting parties. There is no corresponding ideological shift here, at least within official discourse, from a religious and public morality to the private individualized ideologies of purely civil contract. Individualist ideologies do surface heavily in the structures of romance (particularly in romantic fiction) during the period,[18] but that type of privatized, 'person-focused' inflection does not begin to influence legislation governing marital and sexual relations until a century later.[19] The 1857 Act combined a new 'moral economy' of secular regulation, while largely maintaining the earlier moral and ideological configurations which had been developed under an ecclesiastical tradition.

As to the wider determinations and repercussions on the

shift from an ecclesiastical to a civil form of regulation, we can, at this stage, only begin to suggest points of departure. At a specific level it would be difficult to argue any *direct* connection between the innovatory legislation on marriage and divorce and the changes effected, largely by progressive middle-class intellectuals, in related spheres such as Education and Poor Law reform during the period. There appears to be no Chadwickian or Benthamite equivalent in the field of sexuality and marriage relations; no similar advocate of utilitarian forms of state intervention who is opposed to the older ecclesiastical tradition of regulation. Yet at the level of broader generalities, similar patterns can be distinguished. It is the changing position of religious forms of regulation in a number of practices during the nineteenth century, (Poor Law reform, Education, and marriage and divorce) and their ultimate transformation by apparatuses of the State, which has led us to consider the wider political and ideological implications of that shift. It turns up necessarily to examine the position occupied by the Established Church both in the political arena and in the ideological field during the first half of the nineteenth century.

As we have noted, the parliamentary acts of 1836 established a national system of registration for births, marriages and deaths, (with a General Register Office and a network of local offices throughout the country) which replaced the old system of parochial registration. The immediate reason for that change appeared to concern the difficulties that ecclesiastical registration caused for religious dissenters, as prior to 1836 legally valid marriage could only take place in an Anglican Church (Finer and McGregor 1971:89). However, we should also be alert to the beginnings of the massive general growth in State bureaucracy and personnel, which had its repercussions here in the creation of a centralized and secular system of registration replacing the fragmented and less coherent form of ecclesiastical administration. William Farr, the first statistician at the Register Office, commented that the 'obvious importance' of the new system lay in the fact that: 'the records of the events [births, marriages and deaths] should be brought together into a safe place of deposit, where they may be easily accessible to any one wishing to consult them' (quoted in Finer and McGregor, 1971:89–90; cf. Ch. 3 above and Corrigan 1977).

More generally, though, the shift in apparatuses of regulation instituted by the Acts of 1836 and 1857 should be seen in the political context of the aftermath of the debates over the 1832 Reform Bill, during which the Established Church was identified by radicals as a part of the system of 'Old Corruption'. As Richard Johnson notes, established religion, based on the hegemony of gentry paternalism and the rule of agrarian capital, was an integral part of the whole conservative Anglican repertoire of the class-cultural relations of the eighteenth century (Johnson, 1976:24). In the period after 1832 many Tories joined forces with the Benthamites, fearing that the Church might be wholly disestablished, and eager to prove 'how the efficiency of a religious institution mischieved by pluralism, non-residence and nepotism might be increased by utiliarian organization' (Finer and McGregor:90). Yet certain of the secular, administrative powers of the church were annexed by the newly-created State apparatuses after 1836 and 1857. It is significant in the light of the identification of Anglicanism with corruption and incompetence, that the 1853 Commission rejected the possibility of utilizing the old ecclesiastical courts as the site for the new secular divorce courts.

More generally, the analysis of legislation on marriage and divorce leads to an awareness that the formation and expansion of particular State apparatuses and practices in the nineteenth century (and the emergence of ideologies of statism) is often achieved through the displacement and transformation of an earlier ecclesiastical administrative system. The precise political and ideological significance of that transformation, and its effects on the formation of the nineteenth century State, remains to be investigated. Examination of the more detailed histories of the secular influence of the Anglican Church, and its position in the construction of mid-Victorian hegemony, could well begin to provide points of clarification.

The Regulation of Sexual 'Deviancy'

It would perhaps appear that legislation governing homosexuality forms a less significant element in the structures of patriarchal State intervention during the nineteenth century. Legislation in this area does not crystallize debates over the ethics of State intervention in sexual and moral practices, as is the case with the *Contagious Diseases Acts* on prostitution.[20] Nor are there any major commissions or reports to act as points of departure. Further, the regulation of homosexual practices presents particular theoretical problems for an analysis which attempts to trace a link between the structures of sexuality and the development of capitalist relations, in that with regard to sexual 'deviancy' there exists no direct and immediate relation between the two spheres.

At a general level it should be clear that, as a form of non-procreative sexual practice, homosexuality is constructed and classified in a subordinate legal and ideological relation to the primacy of heterosexual relations, organized around procreation. But we should be aware that the regultion of 'deviant' sexualities, including homosexuality, pre-dates the development of capitalist relations. Nineteenth-century State legislation addressing homosexuality is as much determined by pre-existing legal structures governing forms of sexual 'deviancy' as it is by particular social and cultural developments during the period. We have come to define the significance of the legislation in this area by locating the beginnings of a shift in the *modality* of State control of particular sexualities, which is more generally related to the way in which sexual meanings are constructed within specific practices and institutions.

What we possess at the outset is a series of discrete and seemingly unrelated processes of legislation, spanning much of the century. As Jeffrey Weeks has noted, homosexuality (or rather the legally undifferentiated act of sodomy, which was defined as involving unnatural intercourse between man and woman, man and beast, or man and man) had long since been brought under the jurisdiction of the State for the purposes of regulation. The shift from ecclesiastical to secular forms of control had occurred much earlier in this area of 'deviant' sexual practice. It was the 1533 Act, reaffirming the death penalty for sodomy, which effectively transferred jurisdiction to Statute Law (Weeks, 1977:12). What took place in the nineteenth century was a series of modifications to the early statute, which still provided the basis for all convictions up to 1885. Slight amendments were effected in 1826[21]; and the death penalty for sodomy was abolished in 1861, when it was replaced by imprisonment for between ten years and life. The most radical legislative innovation was the *Labouchère Amendment Act* of 1885, which extended the scope of legal regulation to cover *all* homosexual acts between males that could not be classified as buggery:

> Any male person who, in public or private, commits, or is a party to the commission of, or procures or attempts to procure the commission by any male person of any act of gross indecency with another male person, shall be guilty of a misdemeanour, and being convicted thereof shall be liable at the discretion of the court to be imprisoned for any term not exceeding two years, with or without hard labour.
> (*Criminal Law Amendment Act*, Section 11, quoted in Weeks, 1977:14)

Finally, the *Vagrancy Act* of 1898 attempted to control homosexual soliciting.

That brief summary provides the necessary chronology

and covers certain of the areas in which the nineteenth-century State intervened to regulate particular forms of non-reproductive sexuality. But given the fragmented nature of the evidence, what can such elements reveal about the structures and modalities of control exercised by the State in the field of sexual and moral practices? Further, given our warnings against functionalist analyses, in what ways do these legislative moments relate, if at all, to wider historical developments in the period? Can we, in fact, move the listing beyond the merely aggregative and descriptive?

Clearly, at one level, all the legislation dealt with in our analysis was affected by specific determinations relating to the administrative apparatuses of the State. Political changes in the parliamentary arena, the emergence of key individual figures, press debates etc., all had significant influence on the passage of a bill through the legislative machinery. The 1885 Amendment, for example, was an addition to the Act raising the age of consent for heterosexual sex acts, and was designed to clamp down on the incidence of child prostitution. It was sponsored largely through the individual efforts of the radical M.P., Henry Labouchère, in the wake of renewed campaigns over moral purity, and of a number of prominent homosexual scandal trials.[22] Yet, as Stuart Hall has pointed out in a related context: 'Concentration on the moment of political appropriation must not be allowed to distract our attention . . . from wider historical contexts' (Hall, 1978a:4). In attempting to locate the immediate historical terrain on which parliamentary acts and reports are grounded, we should also note that attention to significant elements of empirical detail does not wholly *explain* the reason for the appearance of a particular body of legislation. That is to say, any account of the historical location of legislation must also utilize, beyond a certain point, a more structural and comprehensive history of the State regulation of sexual and moral practices; a conceptual history, pitched at a different level of abstraction, and involving a theoretical understanding of the position occupied by 'official discourses' around sexuality, morality, the family and procreation in particular social formations.

As we have noted, 'deviant' sexualities are constructed in a particular legal and ideological relation to the key issues of marriage, the family and procreation. The latter part of the ninteenth century saw the growth of ideologies of childhood (see Ariès, 1973), domesticity, (see Davidoff, Esperance, and Newby, 1976), motherhood (see Davin, 1978), and campaigns around moral purity, and it is clear that legislation governing homosexuality should be seen in relation to these developments in familial and moral ideologies. Furthermore, the late nineteenth century marked the emergence of ideological configurations around the themes of Nationalism and Imperialism, which had particular implications for the structure of sexual ideologies. As Anna Davin has convincingly argued, the emergent subject 'mother' was linked to the expansion of racist and imperialist ideologies, which centred on notions of national efficiency and planned reproductive strength, together with panics over class specific underpopulation. Paralleling those constructions, homosexuality also began to be articulated and constructed through ideologies of national decline and of 'race suicide'. The comments of the Fabian socialist Beatrice Webb illustrate the type of connection made between sexual 'degeneracy' and imperial decline: 'It is the rottenness of physical and moral character that makes one despair of China – their constitution seems devastated by drugs and abnormal sexual indulgence. They are essentially an unclean race.' (Beatrice Webb's *Diaries*, vol. 30, 6 November 1911, quoted in Weeks, 1977.)

Clearly, changes in familial and sexual ideologies did act as determinants on the implementation of State legislation governing sexual 'deviancy' in the late nineteenth century. But we should be aware that the *regulation* of 'perverse' sexualities does not necessarily imply any simple notion of sexual *repression*. To argue that 'deviant' practices were merely repressed, or wholly denied recognition by the State, is to oversimplify the developments. Much of the recent work on nineteenth century sexuality operates with an understanding that links the repression of non-procreative sexualities to the demands of bourgeois sexual respectability (see Marcus, 1966; Pearsall, 1969; and Cominos, 1973). Broadly speaking, the argument runs that with the development of bourgeois society non-reproductive forms of sexuality were driven underground, and refused access and public visibility. The private sphere of the conjugal family became the only recognized place for sexuality within the dominant culture, where sexual practices were rigidly channelled into their reproductive function. The analysis is often extended to suggest that the reason for such severe sexual repression relates to the threat posed by sexuality to the reproduction of bourgeois social relations. Non-procreative sexuality is seen as incompatible with capital's demands for an ordered and disciplined labour force.

But a simple notion of sexual repression often also implies an 'essential' sexuality which, though it is denied access and visibility, is basically taken as pre-given. What such a position fails to consider is the fact that particular sexualities (e.g. notions of sexual difference and sexual 'deviance') are *constructed* within specific practices such as the law, literature or medicine. For example, the 'homosexual subject' is constructed by a variety of discourses and institutions, some of which may differ in their inflection, and all of which will be historically specific. As Foucault (1976) and Weeks point out, what occurred in the nineteenth century was the differentiation and minute classification of 'deviant' forms of sexuality. The homosexual of the nineteenth century became a person with a history, a childhood and a way of life: 'with an indiscreet anatomy and perhaps a mysterious physiology' (Foucault, 1976:59). For example, the Austrian pyschiatrist and sexologist Krafft-Ebing, in his *Psychopathia Sexualis*, constructed a detailed catalogue of deviant identities, with speculation on the aetiology and pathology of sexual perversion.[23]

Similarly, an examination of nineteenth-century legislation on sexuality reveals not so much the absence through
repression of non-procreative sexualities as the beginnings
of a proliferation of categories or subjectivities of sexual
deviance within official discourse. As we have noted, the
Act of 1533 governing unnatural sexual practices did not
differentiate between *forms* of sodomy, nor did it attempt
to construct a particular 'deviant' subject. The 1885
Labouchère Amendment Act marked the beginnings of the
concern with specificity and particularization: henceforward
legal distinction was made between homosexual intercourse
between males, and other forms of homosexual behaviour.
The homosexual began to acquire a particular identity
within legal practice; a form which comes to structure legislation in this area into the twentieth century, and finds its
most developed statement in the *Wolfenden Report*. In the
same way, the main section of the 1885 Act raising the age
of consent, implicitly constructed the sexuality of 'the child'
as a differentiated category; while parliamentary reports and
commissions in the 1860s and 1870s, surrounding the repeal
of the *Contagious Diseases Acts*, gave a new visibility to
prostitution and to the prostitute.[24] Generally, it was the
greater differentiation of forms of deviant sexuality within
legislation, rather than their monolithic repression, which
emerged as a characteristic feature of State intervention in
this area in the latter part of the nineteenth century.

Moreover, we would argue that the classification and
nomination of differentiated sexualities marked the beginnings of a partial shift in the moral economy of punishment
(and the exercise of State power) in the overall regulation
of sexuality. Though deviant sexualities were not absent
from State legislation in the period, it is also clear that they
were still strictly regulated. Traditional structures of disciplinary punishment and power continued to form the principal strategies for the control of sexual practices (e.g.
capital punishment, imprisonment and hard labour). Furthermore, it would be misguided to suggest that the period

saw any real movement away from a 'criminalizing strategy' in the field of sexuality and morality; the regulation of 'perverse' sexualities still draws massively on the coercive and repressive apparatuses of the State. However, Foucault, in his attempt to locate the changing patterns of the regulation of sexuality in the nineteenth century in *La Volonté du Savoir* (1976), argues that we should attend not merely to the level of tolerance or quantity of repression exercised over 'deviant' sexualities, but to the *form of power* that is implicit in their minute classification and differentiation. Increased specificity and individualization, Foucault insists, is the necessary corollary to a more finely developed system of power relations and punishments: 'What was beginning to emerge was a modulation that referred to the defendant himself, to his nature, to his way and his attitude of mind, to his past, to the "quality" and not to the intention of his will . . . In short, power does not simply "check" illegalities; it differentiates them, it provides them with a general economy' (Foucault, 1975:99, 272).

Foucault's analysis of the innovatory strategies of regulation is most clearly exemplified in the newly emergent, extra-legal, disciplines; the 'small-scale legal systems' that are to be found in medical practice, psychology, social-work, etc., where 'individualization' forms a characteristic feature of the exercise of disciplinary power. (The 'deviant' subject is not absent from the discourse, but she /he is only permitted to speak from a subordinate position; as 'patient', 'pervert', etc.) Yet, we should also be alert to the fact that similar principles of regulation began to emerge within the legislative apparatuses of the State. Traditional forms of punishment remained as the principle strategies here, but much of the legislation does exhibit the tendency towards the differentiation of sexual identities and acts of transgression (e.g. sodomy, other homosexual practices, and homosexual soliciting). It is that tendency which, at a much later moment, comes to form one of the principal techniques for the legal regulation of sexual 'deviance'.[25]

Conclusion

However, certain difficulties raised by Foucault's analysis of
sexuality return us, by way of conclusion, to the wider set
of historical questions encountered in our investigation.
Foucault notes the increase in the number and type of sexualities within particular discourses at specific historical
moments during the ninteenth century. Further, he indicates
that the differentiation of those sexualities facilitates the
operation of a more finely developed set of power relations,
through which sexual 'deviance' comes to be regulated. Foucault's attention to the specificity of regulative structures
does provide, at one level, a more sophisticated model for
understanding the form of power relations within particular
practices and institutions. Certainly his model marks an
advance over simplistic notions of 'social control.' However,
particular questions which appear to be integral to Foucault's analysis remain unaddressed. Specifically, it does
seem crucial to investigate the set of wider historical determinations which are effective in structuring the new organization of sexualities that Foucault locates; together with a
more particular understanding of the form and derivation of
the 'power' that is exercised over them. Foucault's analysis
consistently refuses the marxist-feminist approaches to those
questions which have framed our own work. He is insistent
that the determinants on the organization of sexuality and
its regulation in the nineteenth century are not reducible to
the demands of capitalist production and its reproduction,
articulated through the power of the bourgeois State. Yet
in making that insistence, he fails to investigate the historical
relation of discourses constructed around the family, morality and sexuality to other economic, legal and ideological
practices. Foucault's analysis of the changing patterns of
organization of sexuality is largely conducted as an examination of the *internal specificities* of particular discourses
addressing sexuality, rather than as an attempt to locate the

wider sets of relations which also structure sexual and moral practices in the nineteenth century.[26]

Our own investigation has attempted to hold to a two-fold formulation in analysing particular items of legislation governing sexuality and the sexual division of property: both to the internal history of legal structures, as that history is not synchronic with the development of capitalist economic relations, and to an awareness of the particular economic, political and ideological shifts in the history of capitalist organization in the nineteenth century. Both elements should be seen to act as determinants on the structuring of legislation. The capitalist mode of production, at a particular historical stage of development, may be seen to 'require' that certain conditions are met by political, legal and cultural forms – conditions which include the structures of sexuality, morality, the family and procreation. But those conditions are abstract and general, in as much as a determinate set of productive relations do not specify directly the form and content of particular cultural or sexual practices.[27] The structure of specific apparatuses or institutions outside the sphere of economic relations cannot be 'read off' from any general concept of the mode of production and its abstract conditions of existence. As we have seen, the regulation of sexual practices through legislative intervention may be determined as much by the prior internal history of legal discourse, as it pre-dates capitalist relations, as by specific shifts in the history of capital accumulation. Moreover, certain areas of sexuality addressed by ninteenth-century legislation (e.g. homosexuality and prostitution) stand in a differentiated, much less direct, relation to capitalist development than State intervention governing the sexual division of property, where there is a more immediate concern with the transmission of productive capital. General theories, positing abstract conditions of existence of the capitalist mode of production, fail to grasp the differentiated internal histories of particular sexual and cultural practices. Our study here forms the beginnings of an attempt to construct one such history.

5

State and Anti-State: Reflections on Social Forms and Struggles from 1850
Stephen Yeo

'Won't people say then
It could never have worked?
The heaviest laden
Will wish they had shirked.

What will remind them
Of all the killed?
Wounds still unhealed
Those will remind them.
– Brecht, from 'In Times of Extreme Persecution'

Needs and Forms

Producing, distributing and using basic goods such as food, soap or clothes; learning in general about a universe as well as in particular for a life; entertaining and being entertained; getting and embellishing shelter and places of assembly; finding ways of dealing with old age, infancy, sickness and periods of less or no productive work . . . are all material human needs. In any existing human society the manners of meeting, or exploiting, such needs are deeply connected with each other and resistance to arrangement in neat hierarchies with fixed 'economic' bases. But such needs have been met in some forms of association distinguishable from 'society' at most times and in most places in human history.

Near to our own time and place, as soon as a brief list is made: workshops, factories, farms, allotments, schools, families, chain stores, co-ops., corner shops, pubs, clubs, music-halls, cinemas, television, friendly societies, private insurance companies, welfare states, council estates, trading estates, garden suburbs, mutual building societies, permanent building societies, promoter building societies . . . the *varieties* of product and social relations involved in meeting or exploiting such needs cry out. What kind? For whom? How much? How patterned? By whom? In what relations with each other? How can they be 'read'?[1] (Davis, 1975: xvi–xvii).

For example, 'co-operative factories of the labourers themselves', the Co-operative Wholesale Society (1863) and local retailing Co-ops., have been ways of producing, distributing and using basic goods such as food, soap or clothes, as have Unilevers and Marks and Spencer. However, they are obviously not the *same* ways. The various methods have not remained static throughout their history, nor has the relative presence of any or either of them been constant. A society in which one was dominant and the other recessive would not be the same as one in which the roles were reversed. The same could be said of mutual insurance (for fraternity, through friendly societies), private insurance (for profit, through companies), or National Insurance (for 'social security', through the State), each of them ways of dealing with old age, infancy, sickness and other contingencies. Similar distinctions could be made within each of the needs and forms listed.

Struggle and History

Ways of life (whose?), in societies like our own, clash, co-exist, compete, are killed, survive, change . . . as different ways of associating and producing for meeting and exploiting such needs are developed.

From a conservative point of view, one uninterested in change or in history except as a ratification and celebration of the present, attempts are always being made to collapse 'ways of life' into a single 'society' or 'system'. And then the way is open to say that the ways we meet, define, multiply or divide needs, constitute a single 'culture' – 'our' way of life, *the* system.

The function of so doing is to remove from view ownership, power, struggle, interests. It is to conceal alternative, latent potentials and achievements, in the interests of existing, manifest facts and ideologies. Above all, it is to devalue memory and its collectivization in history. Competition and struggle involve loss and defeat as well as growth: presents involve running over unrealized but partly-surviving pasts and temporarily blocked futures. As is often the case, a poet puts it most succinctly – William Carlos Williams, in the first part of his poem called 'The Descent':

> The descent beckons
>   as the ascent beckoned.
>   Memory is a kind
> of accomplishment,
>   a sort of renewal
>   even
> an initiation, since the spaces it opens are new places
>   inhabited by hordes
>   heretofore unrealized,
> of new kinds –
>   since their movements
>   are toward new objectives
> (even though formerly they were abandoned).

No defeat is made up entirely of defeat – since
the world it opens is always a place
   formerly
      unsuspected. A
world lost,
   a world unsuspected,
      beckons to new places
and no whiteness (lost) is so white as the memory
of whiteness.

Needs involve *things* or usable products and entail (as we
are human) *social* relations. But neither 'society' nor forms
of association constituting 'it', neither any particular whole
set of social relations nor sub-sets, can be read off from
needs such as the ones listed in the first paragraph of this
chapter, or from usable products ('satisfying the needs of
the stomach or the imagination') involved with those needs.

If they could, it would be possible to abnegate struggle
and say, 'if you are going to have basic goods x y or z (say,
cheap soap or mass insurance), you must have form a b or
c (say, Unilever or the Prudential).' It would be possible to
say that things *are*, in their very nature, commodities, rather
than that they become so with the development of particular
dominant social relations and forms. In this way a terrifying
closure between possibility and what *is* would have been
effected, and it is precisely this closure which a careful study
of history can prevent.[2]

Still less should history be read as if it were the story of
even higher Stages in Progress towards meeting Need and
supplying usable products. If it is so read it becomes possible
to hold social relations constant and to say, 'if we are to
have adequate food supplies or other 'wealth', then we must
have the existing retailing industry or 'economy', with all
the costs and prices entailed.' Such attempts, by capital, for
capital, to underwrite existing social relations are always
being made. They involve, quite explicitly now, making the

whole social relation into a contract: something *given* to 'society' by the individual/family (like restraint, economic or political, or like work) in return for something else (like privacy, or leisure, or life). Such public social relations are not, it is widely admitted, the best that are humanly or materially possible. But, say the suppliers of basic goods x y and z, they are all we can have if the world is to be made safer for forms a b and c. A whole history is involved here: a history which sees earlier relations and forms only in so far as they feed into later ones, as forerunners rather than as hopeful, rational, and available resources for a better future. In the end, history itself can be dispensed with. After all, as a pioneer of a particular form, that of mass production, designed to 'take out' as many earlier forms as possible in order to exploit in a specific way the human need to travel, suggested, 'All history is bunk'.

Class and Change

To change social relations from labour's point of view requires a somewhat finer perspective. To change social relations, for labour rather than for capital, means to realize them in one of the other forms they make materially possible at any one time, as opposed to 'understanding' them or 'explaining' them from the point of view of what they predominantly are. This means operating through the facts and with a particular conception of class. 'Nothing', as a British pioneer of mass production remarked, 'could be more dangerous.'[3]

Contrary, perhaps, to expectations, a class perspective is neither mechanical nor structural. It is not the view which says 'show me the basic needs /products – i.e. the "economic" – change these, and all the rest will follow.' Only in the crudest capitalist, and hence mechanical marxist, view of humanity could some forms of production which are seen as the only truly necessary or material ones, be held to explain all others or to provide the forms to which all others can be reduced. Nor is it the view which says 'uncover for me the laws and structures of which events are mere illustrations, and through that disclosure we, the conscious ones, will direct the only possible change'. Only in the most élite capitalist – and hence structural marxist – view of the division of labour between thinking and doing could such a search for the single, scientific fulcrum hold such priority among so many thinkers wishing to be on labour's side.

No such magics will ever or have ever worked, even for capital. Those were not the spectacles worn by capitalists creating *their* world, nor will they be the spectacles worn by socialists if ever we are to create ours. Social relations are what they say: social *relations*, not one-way traffics from basics to secondaries, and *social* relations, productive, specific and thus determined, but not puppets unable to pull their own strings. We have to look to particular humans and classes of humans, to their/our choices, past and present, to their/our ways of producing usable things (including ideas), to their/our acquired positions and powers in relation to other humans across very wide and increasingly inclusive areas of social activity. If we are to help to change needs and forms through struggle in a place and over time, we have to find ways of seeing them such as class ways, which make them vulnerable to our associated, co-operative interventions and creativity.

This, in the end, is the only justification, for labour, of the historical category, class. Incidentically, it is how and why the category first came into active use, for capital in the 'middle-class' politics of the first half of the nineteenth century (Briggs, 1956). But I am aware that I am using 'class', when I write 'for labour' or 'for capital' in what increasingly seems to be an idiosyncratic way. I shall now define my terms.

Class may be the best tool we have for pin-pointing the limits and possibilities of associated, collectively-conscious activity and production in and beyond capitalist modes. As a historical category it has been and can be used to point to the necessity, opportunity and difficulty of association first, then, for capital, now for labour. Its test of usefulness in action is whether it points to the real constraints and potentials, for capital and for labour, through time and place, better than other categories and whether it shows, more helpfully than other categories, what can, as well as what cannot, be done. It is, however, not talismanic. It can neither explain, without the detail of the story, what has happened; nor can it predict, leaving aside the heat and chance of the struggle, what will happen. But it can, if it can do anything, *enable* the history and the struggle, for labour. As a means of understanding social relations which constitute it, 'class' can be used to change those relations.

With the development of capitalism there is also the unavoidable-by-capital (unless it resorts to slavery, fascism, or some other increasingly technically possible closed mutant)[4] development of the material possibility, for labour, of making things in ways which can transcend capital's dominant mode. Capitalism has built-in and of-its-essence limitations to the forms it can adopt, to the distribution or sociology of the articulation of needs within it, and to who can share its highest promises and possibilities. 'The capitalist mode of production, by its very nature, excludes all rational improvement beyond a certain point.' Its development is bounded by its own dynamics: private, or at least minority controlled/owned accumulation; private or at least privately disposed surplus; competition; the subordination of labour through forms of wage payment and the maintenance of labour power as a commodity and the labour process as an 'economic' activity within the constraints of 'the self-valorization of capital . . . by means of the "free" purchase and consumption of labour power.' Capitalism's very essence and dynamic is that some people (indeed a whole class) cannot be what others are and all cannot be what some have become. Times of desire, imitations, aspiration towards 'producing fully developed human beings' are dangerous to it: more so than its own economic crises. Inequality is its core and it is this which it must protect against Christianity or any other form of humanism. It must, in the end, destroy or provide permanent ideological channels for the insistent, nagging comparisons humans make between each others' situations. The facts and human conceptions of class will make it hard, but not necessarily impossible, for this protection to be permanently achieved.[5]

Labour's potential and limitations are necessarily harder to spell out. But they explain my interest in class struggle and associational form in Britain, particularly from the mid-nineteenth century onwards. It should be possible to imagine and even to describe the material possibilities for labour, not in idealist or historicist ways, but as visibly possible, partially achieved, partially destroyed, outlines. And not just in a negative, reactive way to capital either; not just as the opposite of everything that capital stands for. Ways of producing, which change through time and through struggle and in specific locations, are ways which are in some sense linked, even if only in contradiction, or through the unity of opposites. They are also ways which are amenable to our agency, our wills, associations and forms, to the ways we act in relation to the facts and concepts of class, using past struggles as capital for ourselves. This is not to deny constraints and determinations. But such constraints are not transcendent, they are contextual, particular to social formations, places and times and vulnerable to (because they are made up from) associated creativity.

So, Where Are We Now?

We (most readers of this book) are now in a period of capitalism which, over the last hundred years or so, has been momentous domestic (social) and international (geographic) extensions of the capitalist mode of production and portentous extensions of human attempts to grasp its history, its beginning and its ending. These human efforts have included large associations of working people trying to *change* or move beyond social relations as they found them (including such consequences as unventilated workshops, adulterated food, pauper funerals or rented slums), as well as heroically grand theory and attempts at 'general over-turn'. All these kinds of extension have been located in Britain – wider social and geographical penetration by capitalism, *and* Marx-Engels writing with significant reference to Britain from 1842 through to the early 1890s, *and* what an Austrian observer during the late 1880s called 'the theatre of a gigantic development of associated life which gives to her [England's] labour, her education, her social intercourse, nay to the entire development of her culture, a pronounced direction, a decisive stamp' (Baernreither, 1893: II).

For Marx, the material outlines of a social economy (in the line moral, political, social; Corrigan 1977) were visible in Britain while he was writing. More strongly than that, we can now see that such outlines were part of the determinations of his work; components of the tensions which gave it life and growth without which it could not have been the same. Marx did not make the mistake (however he *presented* a finished book like *Capital* I) of believing that what he was thinking/writing had primacy over what he was thinking/writing about: nor were Manchester working people, agitators for factory reform, Chartists, Co-operators, First Internationalists, Communards . . . mere examples of what he or Engels already knew.[6] By 1854 and in capitalism 'the working millions of Great Britain' had 'first laid down the real basis of a new society'. Capitalism had 'called into life the material means of ennobling labour itself' (Marx, 1854: 278).[7] Capitalism, like any other mode of production which has not effected total closure, included and includes more-than-capitalist *humans* as well as factors of production (like labour or capital) and classes: it also changed and changes through alterable forms (e.g. factories, credit, stock companies) over time. If it is important for cognition (under-standing the world), not to collapse capitalist relations into human relationships, it is also important, for revolution (changing the world), not to collapse human relationships into capitalist relations. By 1867 The Scientific Socialist in his great work of Science called on 'us' (the readers of *Capital,* I) to '*imagine*, [my italics] for a change, an associ-ation of free men, working with the means of production held in common, and expending their many different forms of labour power in full self-awareness, as one single social labour force' (Marx, 1867b: 171).

Marx could see space between predominant modes of production and society: spaces for other forms and relations to have 'influence' – their own limited, determined 'specific gravity' (Marx, 1858: 107). 'When the development of the material forces of production and of the corresponding forms of social production has reached a certain stage', new modes, 'as forms of transition from the capitalist mode of production to the associated one' may 'naturally grow'. According to *Capital,* III, this was actually happening in Britain, negatively in capital's own forms, positively in working-class social products such as the co-operative move-ments. It had always been, in Marx's view, the 'labouring classes' singular opportunity to emancipate themselves and hence 'man'. Once the 'productive powers of modern indus-try' had, 'thanks to the sweat of their brows and brains' reached the 'inexhaustible' stage even of the early 1850s, they no longer lacked the strength and 'real basis' for such a task. What they 'wanted' then were adequate forms for 'the organization of their common strength', and on a national rather than merely local or episodic scale. So Marx was on the look-out for initiatives with potential in this direction, like the anti-Parliament of 1854 (Marx, 1854).[8] Hence his excitement when looking back, from 1864 to 1848, at the 'great facts' of working-class achievement in Britain during those years and the possibilities for transition they constituted (R. Harrison, 1964). The greatest of these facts was 'the co-operative movement, especially the co-operative factories raised by the unassisted efforts of a few bold "hands".' 'The value of these great social experiments cannot be overrated.' They had shown 'by deed instead of by argument' that existing social forms and relations were *not* essential to 'production on a large scale and in accord with the behests of modern science' and that 'associated labour plying its toil with a willing hand, a ready mind and a joyous heart' could make 'hired labour' as archaic as slave or serf labour (Marx, 1864: 79–80). Such were the real goals of emancipation, for which political organization was vital, but to which it must be subordinate.[9]

Marx knew the difference between first victories and whole campaigns – what student of the rise of capitalism could not? In the very act of announcing his great facts in 1864 – in the very next paragraph – he began the analysis of their active containment and their false friends. He was never slow to denounce deformations, of Co-operation or of anything else (Marx, 1864: 80; Marx, 1867b: 413, n. 58). But the first victories in broad daylight of the political economy of labour ('social production controlled by social foresight') over and against that of capital, had, in his view, been won in 1847 with the Ten Hours Act. They were 'the product of a protracted and more or less concealed civil war between the capitalist class and the working class'. 'What a great change from that time!' (Marx, 1867: 412–13). In such partial, preliminary victories – 'modest Magna Carta's' – which quickly turned into defeats and each one of which aspired to seem total and permanent; it was not only *what* was fought for, but *when* and *where*. Who held the initiative? This is a different question from who is in formal, or even real, control. Whether a reform was 'bourgeois', 'reformist', or not, depended not only on the substance but on the form. Each initiative had to be 'read' and related to politically. In what context? England or France? Successfully counter-attacked or not? This was the case with suffrage reform which could be revolutionary, as much as with factory legislation.[10]

By the late 1880s it had become transparent in rotten-ripe Britain how much of the initiative even in narrowly-defined 'economic' production and even in self-imprisoning rationalization and modernization of industry – leaving aside 'social production' – was owed to labour. It was irritatingly clear to Engels particularly, how otiose British capital*ists* had begun to look by the end of his life (Engels, 1889). 'If we could but see a day of it . . .' To understand our own century (let alone the moods of late nineteenth-century socialists in Britain such as Engels or Morris), we have to see, against all the narrowing of vision, privatization, mass killings, world wars, social sciences, State National Socialisms, minutest divisions within and between intellectual and manual labour which have characterized it, that such a day was indeed no dream but had a real basis. It could have been Somewhere, not far from Here. Indeed, the narrowing of vision, mass killing, world wars, social sciences, etc., are inexplicable without this real possibility.

This, presumably, is what contradiction is about. Even in the very act of 'really' subordinating labour, with all the technical development of the forces of production that implied, the possibilities of a division of labour which was a division of work not of humans – a state of complex rather than merely simple co-operation – were being created. Even as head was separated most visibly from hand and from humanity itself, the possibility of 'educated' labour and a withering away of older reasons for the division of labour were coming into being.[11] Even as a determined, structured, monstrous 'system' was growing up – evidenced in Empire as well as in entertainment, linked through capitalist uses of communication – and even as the eye was being battered by more and more appearances in commodity form; human efforts to comprehend and resist were (are) being made and it was becoming materially possible to supersede such a system in a way never before possible in human history.

Hence the image of the sorcerer in the *Communist Manifesto*: 'modern bourgeois society . . . no longer able to control the powers of the nether world whom he has called up by his spells'.

This reading or emphasis within a reading of Marx which cannot be singular, does not suggest a voluntarist, or any other naughty-ist, perspective, leading one to say: 'It's all easy. Just look at things differently and go out and make socialism.' It is a reading which calls for the politics of detail: building, federating, linking, articulating on the basis of what is there (here) for labour. This is just as hard a task as *theoretical* practice, although practitioners in that mode make it look uncomparably difficult, as priests do salvation. But at least it is scientific, unlike the utopian alchemy which tries to turn epistemological breaks into social ones, immaculately.[12] And there are resources, outside ourselves and outside books like this. 'Already' as Brecht told his Danish working-class actors in his Speech on the Art of Observation:

> Many of you are studying the laws of men's life together,
>> already
> Your class is determined to master its problems and thereby
> The problems of
> All mankind. And that is where you
> The workers' actors, as you learn and teach
> Can play your part creatively in all the struggles
> Of men of your time, thereby
> Helping, with the seriousness of study and the cheerfulness
>> of knowledge
> To turn the struggle into common experience and
>> Justice into a passion.

The reading of Marx in the context suggested here might

even explain why all this has been and is so difficult. Of course labour is really, rather than just formally, subordinate; of course the working class an *under*-class. But because it is an under-*class*, it also has a possible future. That this has not yet become the present, has been attributed by modern Marxists in Britain, moralistically, to the inadequacies of workers. Their 'level' of consciousness has not been high enough; they have been 'reformist', 'apathetic', 'corporate', etc. So they need more of the 'level' of consciousness of modern Marxists in Britain, . . . instead of those Marxists (us) needing to develop more creative ways of seeing forms of struggle, with and for labour, and *as* the labourers (albeit mental) that we are. As Marx and Engels wrote four years before Marx's death:

> For almost forty years, we have stressed the class struggle as the most immediate driving power in history, and, in particular, the class struggle between the bourgeoisie and the proletariat as the great lever of the modern social upheaval; therefore it is impossible for us to ally ourselves with people who want to eliminate this class struggle from the movement. When the International was formed, we expressly formulated the battlecry: the emancipation of the working class must be the work of the working class itself. We cannot ally ourselves, therefore, with people who openly declare that the workers are too uneducated to free themselves and must first be liberated from above by philanthropic big bourgeois and petty bourgeois. (Marx-Engels, 1879: 374–75).

Of course it can help to expound the logic of a system of commodity production at the level of Marx's most elevated abstractions. Such a way of seeing capitalism as a whole is essential for getting behind its myriad and all-present results, into the labour processes and class struggles which compose and decompose it. Indeed, that is what Marxism pre-eminently *is*, a way of getting behind results in capitalism into process and struggle. Of course there is a nightmare clinging to the known and old, a 'world historical necromancy', pulling us back at critical moments 'just when they [we] appear to be engaged in the revolutionary transformation of themselves [ourselves] and their [our] material surroundings, in the creation of something which does not yet exist' (Marx, 1852: 146–7). But there is also a more positive inheritance, known or unknown we cannot escape it. 'It must be kept in mind that the new forces of production and relations of production do not develop out of nothing, nor drop from the sky, nor from the womb of the self-positing Idea but from within and in antithesis to the existing development of production and the inherited traditional relations of property' (Marx, 1858: 278). There were (are), spaces away from the State, but not entirely behind its back, perhaps pre-eminently in Britain, for thought and activity with and for working-class associations directed towards a new state of affairs, rather than the old State modernized and rationalized and captured – as it will need to be in Britain to do this – by State Socialist rulers. The reversals of our own times, carrying middle-class liberalism with it as much as working-class socialism and threatening to carry marxism too, and the resources we may have for dealing with it, cannot be grasped without some exploration of labour's (and hence humanity's) stored capital, for itself. We need to know among other things, how far labour was travelling down a possible road for itself through the second half of nineteenth-century Britain – the most bourgeois society, we are told, the world has ever known – in order to get some helpful bearings on where we are now.[13]

'English Associations of Working Men'

At this point detail would help. 'Reading' associational forms, as they constitute class struggle, requires episodic analysis and narrative concentration – i.e. history – of a kind which cannot be attempted in this space. Trade unions, co-operative societies, friendly societies, building societies, educational associations, etc. – by no means all male – each have their own complicated, particular histories gathering permanent institutional momentum rapidly from the mid nineteenth century on. In what follows I am going to use, argue with and trespass beyond existing research on some of these particular histories, in order to see their subjects as a whole. The hope is that their history can then be seen more creatively, for labour, by me and others elsewhere.

One justification for this procedure is that my assertions will not be one-sided. They will be not-only-but-also points, seeking for a dialectical rather than functional, way of seeing associational form and change. Functional ways of seeing the second half of the nineteenth century have themselves functioned to excise, for capital, whole areas of class struggle from twentieth-century British history.

If associational life c. 1850–90 simply functioned (in cahoots with imperialism) to 'incorporate' 'labour aristocrats' and to divide them willingly and comfortably from other workers; if such life never constituted any threat or potentially displacing growth within 'the system'; if it was subject anyway to universal, brass 'laws' of bureaucratization . . . then what is my problem, where was the struggle?[14] Associations such as the Co-ops., in this perspective, gave way through relative affluence and human attributes like 'apathy' to business modes and consumerism – surrounded by the 'law of value' their chances of success were slight from the very beginning. Then, lo and behold, there came the technology of the modern 'mass entertainment' industry, available at exactly the right time – the mid-1890s, (Briggs, 1960) to serve 'demand', alongside a freshly benevolent 'welfare state'. *Tit-Bits*, Empire Music-Halls, chain cinemas, and National Insurance Benefits were 'what people really wanted'. The whole project of a person like J. T. W. Mitchell (who's he?) – or John Stuart Mill for that matter – was a huge, if noble, mistake based upon false ideas of 'what people are really like'.[15] Human Nature has hitherto been hidden, owing to lack of Progress: however it has now been revealed in Modern Societies, for the whole world to see.

Against such a parody, not-only-but-alsos fight to do justice to great facts. Not only were there forms of working-class association which constituted evidence of different, possible futures for labour, but also, admittedly, such evidence was heavily overlain even *within* the forms themselves. That is one of the good reasons, alongside the many bad ones, why these forms have not been recognized by historians. There was material evidence of different futures in the sense that, for example, the giant Affiliated Orders of Friendly Societies tried, in practice and with some success, to unite the contradictory imperatives for working-class association of economies and equities of scale with local autonomy and accessibility to control from below.[16] Indeed the *affiliated* form, characteristic of many working-class associations from Trades Councils, to the T.U.C., to the pre-1918 Labour Party, to the Miners' Federation, has been, at its best, at attempt through federation to displace the from below/from above dichotomy. There would be Congresses not to pass down leadership from above, and not to advertise to 'the general public', but to associate opinion.[17] Co-ops. also tried in practice to unite production and consumption, to make the working class their own employers, and to educate for a Co-operative Common-wealth and against Competition. One can choose whether to affect surprise at their 'failure', or build on the fact that the attempt was (still is) made at all. All forms of working-class association characteristic of the second half of the nineteenth century in Britain, including Working Men's Clubs, explicitly fought for unities and mutualities, against divisions and 'structural differentiation'.

In addition such evidence *was* overlain within the forms themselves. That is to say, there was struggle, with class implications, *within* such forms as trade unions, clubs, building societies, as well as between them and unambiguously

capitalist forms.[18] For example, the incipient giants of the
Permanent Building Society movement clearly had a vested
interest in suppressing more mutual and accessible Promoter
forms, as they also did in discouraging, in the early days,
Municipal mortgage schemes.[19] Not only did the State nur-
ture such internal tensions within the forms themselves
through a process of artificial selection and legislative
encouragment of some forms (and *therefore* discouragement
of others), but it also made it possible for a whole branch
of social production (e.g. building societies or the Labour
Party) as it were, to go over to capital's side. A whole
branch could start to act explicitly and mainly for capital,
which is not to say that there would be no room in it for
further struggle for labour. A whole branch could start to
act itself as a chartered, licenced, 'registered', 'official',
'legitimate' monopolist, preventing and policing for capital
the possibility of more challenging forms of association
developing in that branch. Thus the Labour Party has occupied a lot of the space available for politics-for-labour during
this century (Wainwright, 1977); Clubs a lot of the space for
sociability-for-labour, Co-ops, co-operation, and so on.
Such huge 'legitimate' presences have recently been crack-
ing, although the forms of struggle for labour, against them
or within them, have not yet clearly emerged.

Associations of collective self-help – indeed continuous,
formal movements/associations of all kinds – were, to vary-
ing degrees, confined to an upper stratum of working
people. Given the constraints on time, money, and spare
cultural resources of any kind in most nineteenth- and early
twentieth-century working lives, there was no way except
through charity, 'vice-presidential' or public subsidy, that
participation in such associations could have been available
on a majority scale.[20] Given the deformation and scarcity of
direct charity, and the constraints which followed vice-presidential domination (which was what the 1880s revolt in the
London Working Mens' Clubs was about), *some* form of
public (State) financial aid was a real temptation, even a

necessity, for associations with universalizing ambitions. Creative ingenuity over forms of membership, forms of payment, the goods that were offered and organizational modes, was necessary in order to achieve any kind of economic autonomy combined with wide availability (members unlimited) among working-class associations. Some branches of social production were more open to such ingenuity than others. It was easier to think of going through groceries into the Co-operative Commonwealth ('eating their way into the future' as a Royal Arsenal Co-operator put it), or through the bar takings into the wider goals of Clubland, than it was to find an equivalent vehicle for the goals of, for example, relatively autonomous education. Even Co-operation needed a State-defined tax position (won in 1880) and clubs a State-defined licensing position (continually attacked from the 1890s through to 1908); education, however, was recalcitrant to privacy on any scale for capital, let alone for labour. Sheer scale was one way out in some branches; checking off almost unnoticed sums from very large numbers has been a way into mass 'free' trade-unionism, for example, or mass Labour electoral politics.[21]

In this inherently limited, difficult situation for labour, with quite specific determinations operating, the degree of 'success' or 'failure' imputed depends on how one looks at it contextually as opposed to moralistically. It also all depends upon politics. It depends upon whether you wish to take a creative part in the construction of associated enterprise for labour, or to be a party to its emasculation. There is a continual and in the end political choice to be made, from within such enterprises today, whether to emphasize what is being achieved (however small) and could be achieved (however visionary), or to stress what has not been, is not being or cannot be achieved.

Given the above constraints, I find the amount of involvement in associations of working people during the second half of the nineteenth century in Britain more remarkable than the degree of confinement. In the same way, given the economic, systematic determinants in capitalism of the stratification and uneven development of the working class, I find the extent to which class associations kicked against these obstacles more interesting than the extent to which they 'functioned' to reinforce them or 'reflect' them.[22] I also find that, to a significant extent, the degree of confinement was not willingly accepted. There was a search for devices to overcome it, a search which had to risk sacrificing class content, for labour, to universalizing ambitions and expansion in a necessarily recalcitrant (since mainly for-capital) context.[23] This search may even be interpreted as the search, on behalf of an embryonic mode of production, to overthrow an existing 'ready-made foundation' and 'create for itself a new basis appropriate to its own mode of production.'[24] There is a *history* to complaints about 'apathy'. In the Reading Co-op., for example, in the years before 1914 at least, such complaints were a register of active aspiration towards something else, in a situation (to us) of extraordinary participation and vision, rather than the moralizing ratification of permanent rule by the few which such complaints have since become.

It is also important not to measure actually-existing class formations against Platonic working-classness. There are good class struggle reasons why the working class cannot become an 'it' perfect and entire, until the moment(s) of abolition of class as such, sometimes called The Revolution.[25] Until then, ruling-class struggle necessarily prevents more than partial class formation. The facts that English Associations of Working Men were not pan-class, that they degenerated early on, that the society their visionaries believed in did not come about, have been attributed, in a moralistic manner, to their intentions. They have become a reformist 'gap' in labour movement development between 1848 and the 1890s. They have then been seen as 'giving way' to higher forms, rather than as having been destroyed in a grinding series of twentieth-century counter attacks. In this way, the struggles within them and against them have been removed from view.

Thus, at a strategic moment of possible state-supported generalization of some of the mutual achievements of Friendly Societies in 1911, the private industrial insurance industry twisted the State its way in an explicit struggle between rival class forms.[26] Thus, a period of impressive Co-operative consolidation, in Britain between the wars organized private retailing capital tried, through the Royal Commission on Income Tax (1920) and the Raeburn Committee (1932), to get Co-ops, registered under Industrial and Provident Society legislation, assimilated to private capitalist forms, registered under the Companies Acts. If one asks, 'so how did the Co-ops. become the businesses they now are, with their mimetic responses to capitalist competition?' one of the answers, admittedly, is internal: their own self-appointed Dr Beechings, oligarchic degeneration, and the inadequacy of attempts from inside to organize for any rival vision. But another answer, the history of which remains to be written, is *through the law*. Thus, again *c.*1890 and 1908 a period of multiplicity of Club forms and some remaining energy of vision and desire (at least compared with that of today), there was an active struggle through the State and over forms of Licensing, between Working Men's Clubs and private licensed victuallers allied with temperance enthusiasts, (Hall, 1912: Ch. XI). Such struggles have been no less determining in relation to labour's potential during the twentieth century than the better-known offensive on trade-unionism at the same time (Saville, 1960). Across the whole range of associational forms, there has been an active process of artificial selection and incorporation, in its legal sense. This process long preceded the intense period of counter-attack by capital from the late nineteenth century on. I am not suggesting a period of autonomy followed by one of regulation. Very early on, almost simultaneously with their autochthonous creation, associations for the working class were licensed by the State in some forms rather than others, and lionized – in such a way as to try to breed lambs – by social reformers of many varieties. Even to expound the Acts of Parliament involved would exceed the space available for this chapter. Again, *timing* was important, with legislation sometimes running along behind, trying to baptize already born bastards. But in many branches of cultural/social production an attempt to discriminate between 'chartered', 'legitimate', 'official', 'licensed', 'registered' forms, *and* 'illegitimate', 'sham', 'bogus', 'unofficial' forms can be traced. Often, the association itself in its 'legitimate' form (e.g. C.I.U. affiliated clubs) would be incorporated as the main policeman against less desirable forms in the same branch. Often, too, the overt reasons for such legislative selection would be entirely rational, e.g. fire hazard in the case of the smaller music-halls in London in the 1880s, and cinemas in the Cinematograph Act of 1910. But the consequence was the same. As in the sphere of material production, more conventionally understood, there has been a decrease of space and resources available for less lionized forms. Big trees help to determine the undergrowth in any forest.

Characteristic means of growth for nineteenth-century working-class associations – schism, secession, federation, horizontal alliance, local innovation – became more difficult. They gave way to twentieth-century means such as take-over and ecumenical merger. The rising technical or organic composition of capital in material production has its direct – and of course linked – counter-part in social production. This is not to say that space for partial or total challenge to dominant forms ever gets blocked completely: indeed through the contradictions of any particular branch at one time, or across the whole 'system', they may suddenly open up in ways for which it is vital to be prepared. Nor is this rising public or bureaucratic or State composition of social (or associational) capital a 'natural' growth, or even an 'iron' law: it is constituted by, unintelligible without, and unchangeable except, through class struggle, whether 'privately' competitive ('economic') or publicly coercive ('political'). Indeed this is what class struggle *means*.

Not only has there been this process of attempted subordination, there has also been autonomous life. Resistance to registration was often noticed (Supple, 1974: 227). Indeed the legislation and direct competition, boycotts etc., faced by working-class associations cannot be explained as an ongoing story except by reference to vigorous independence. Class struggle is not only labour against capital, with capital in its fixed, achieved, 'capital*ism*', positions. It is also constituted by the struggles of capitalists against already won positions by labour. Indeed such struggle against labour is an essential component of any explanation of nineteenth and twentieth-century economic history, from factories onwards, let alone social and political history. The situation of the late twentieth century British economy, indeed, cannot be explained without reference to the recalcitrance of labour. The British sickness is labour's obstinate health.

The relatively autonomous life of associations of working people needs separate and lengthy descriptions elsewhere. Here I can only urge that the pompous language surrounding the smallest happenings in the associational life, particularly of the second half of the nineteenth century, should be listened to *as* aspiration meaning something of what is said, rather than dismissed as quaint rhetorical decoration. Society, as in the authentic liberalism of the period more generally, was not seen as end-stopped, with existing institutions defining its goals. And Co-operators, for example, had not yet vested the goals of co-operation entirely in the health of their own organization (Carr-Saunders, 1938: 469). To the extent that society was seen as 'system' (which it was from above more than from below), it was seen as an open one. It was tolerant of educated progress, growth and improvement, capable of changing the world and thereby being changed. Given such confidence, there was much organizational fertility and inventiveness. The Webbs, who were great classifiers and collectors of associational forms, recognized, in forms such as the trade-unionism of the miners and cotton workers, creative, highly skilled production of new social forms and relations. For some time indeed, and in many branches, associations of working people held the initiative. They were the most dynamic, progressive and fertile forms of undertaking in their branch. Hence they pioneered and precipitated, in more specifically capitalist forms, the rationalization and modernization of their branch of production, to the extent that such modernization occurred in Britain. Co-operation is only the most obvious example, being a pioneer in retailing forms (e.g. self-service) as well as in specifically co-operative practices right up until the 1950s.

The aspiration was for autonomy and independence and freedom from external control or subordination. An anthology of anti-Statist speeches and writings could be compiled from amongst organized working people, particularly between 1850 and 1890. Such sentiments have so far not been recognized as 'political', still less as 'socialist', in any sense, even when they explain that it is *State* socialism to which they object. They have been seen as 'liberal', 'corporate', 'reformist', or, with a dash of added snobbery, 'petty-bourgeois'. Pre-1850 working-class anti-Statism has had less trouble in making its way as part of our conscious socialist inheritance, partly because there was a large element of programmatic State reform in it, notably the six points of the Charter. After 1890, working-class anti-Statism has become private, and sometimes genuinely reactionary, and needs digging out of a range of familial concerns concealed under blankets like 'privatization' and 'apathy'. But such were the growths of Statism, and discontinuously large capitalist and 'socialist' States, from the 1890s onwards (with much longer roots of course – Corrigan, 1977), and such was the extent to which socialism itself (even Marxism) came to mirror this Statism from the early twentieth century onwards, that working class creativity in its specifically anti-Statist forms during the immediately preceding years has mainly been seen as reactionary. It was indeed a reaction, to things like the defeat of Chartism, Chadwickian Centralization, incipient forms of machine politics around it from the 1870s onwards, sinister 'Liberal' populist imperialists like J. Chamberlain, and to State 'welfare' initiatives which looked as though they might de-skill working-class social production entirely. And in the end, the liberal England of which it was a part did not die – as in Dangerfield's classic *The Strange Death of Liberal England* – it was murdered, albeit more slowly, humanely and with more resistance than elsewhere. But the fact that 'the power is there, latent to be awakened one day,' as Braithwaite noted after a major episode in the subordination of Friendly Societies, is the achievement of the anti-Statism of the second half of the nineteenth century, and is part of our own socialist resources and inheritance. There has been accumulation by labour, for itself; there is some sleeping capital for labour waiting to be roused through accurate history, accurate politics.

In the day-to-day practice of working-class association, co-operative, as opposed to competitive, practices very different from the 'spirit of capitalism' were evident. They were not always articulated as such, but they were there and could be listed at length. In a sense, however, they are not the point. The potential scandal of these associations for capital was not that they constituted another, essentially proletarian, way of life, whole and entire, waiting to break through from underground, and of which there could be no initimations before immortality 'after the revolution'. Rather the opposite: the problem for capital was how seriously they took 'bourgeois values'. They had their own disciplines and rationalities controlled by their own associations. These were not in substance always that different from 'middle-class values'. Indeed, to have allowed rational values, of the kind necessary to build and sustain 'social production controlled by social foresight' in *any* state of affairs, to be called 'middle-class', is a bourgeois trick which marxists, labour historians, or anyone else, should never have allowed to be played. There is a sense in which imitation of 'its' values, growing from relatively autonomous working-class bases, is more dangerous to capital than rejection in the name of 'not working within the system'.

Initiative in labour's hands was not confined to the 'voluntary sector' either. By the end of the nineteenth century, there was a basis for working-class penetration and innovation within elected bodies like School Boards, Guardians, or local Councils. Such bodies had access to public finance and the capacity to control, to some extent independently of a State 'system' which indeed had to be systematized in order to bring them to heel, key areas of social policy production. Believers in a national, professional and central 'system' can be watched as they tried, both in thier histories and in their politics, to cut their way through 'muddle' and 'primitive' untidinesses around them in order to find an efficient 'way out'. The case of the School Boards struggle, culminating in their abolition in 1902, is only the most obvious example. Indeed, the evident possibilities for labour within elected bodies – Labour 'captured' West Ham in 1898 – alongside parallel potentials with which they could conceivably have linked up, for example, in the trade-union and co-operative movements, may explain the timing of an intensified period of counter-attack on labour's forms between c. 1890 and c. 1930, the story of which remains as yet largely untold.[27]

Imagine and Remember

The task, as always, is to make space between what has been and is, and what could be: or to use what has been, as a resource for making a different future.

The task is to imagine what would have been involved during the twentieth century in a successful generalization of the partial, preliminary achievements of working-class associations during the nineteenth century; while remembering that the exciting thing, in the British case, is that we have a material medium for our imagination and memory in the historical thoughts and practices of large numbers of working people. (In any case, British or otherwise, once those historical thoughts and practices are considered irrelevant, something other than socialism-for-labour is being attempted). Before explaining what *did* happen, which would involve the detailed history of each branch of social production, and before being able to think materially about what could happen, for labour, in the future, we have to be able to see, in a more than Utopian manner, what could have happened. To make possible the exercise of the collective memory (i.e. history) and to liberate the exercise of the collective hope (i.e. politics)[28] we need the play of imagination. 'Let us image, for a change . . .'

This means going backwards, in a more detailed way than I have been able to do here, rooting out the not-only-but-also points already made concerning the period *c*. 1850–90, then tracing the period of intensified counter-attack by capital, through the State, *c*. 1890–1930. It is important to emphasize that I am not suggesting that, left to themselves (which, anyway, they had not been), 'English Associations of Working Men' would have constructed the Co-operative Commonwealth. I *am* saying that, in form as well as in substance, such associations represented enough of an actually-existing alternative potential, for 'the State', private capitals, and working people to have been deeply involved in prolonged struggle over their shape and future presence. Such struggle – best seen in class terms – was, and perhaps (see the obvious case of trade unions) still is, open and able to go either way.

To make general the achievements of working-class associations, and to transform them in such a way as to make this possible, would have involved – and did involve for capital doing the transformation predominantly in its direction during the twentieth century – going through public, political relations of production which it is convenient to call 'the State'. For capital this meant, for example, cabinet discussions about the dangers of autochthonous working-class education in the post-1917 crisis, followed by artificial selection of the W.E.A. as a Responsible Body in 1924, the equivalent of Friendly Societies as Approved Societies in 1911. There were, of course, real financial difficulties in the previous twenty-year history of autochthonous efforts which made such intervention appear partly as a genuine rescue and achievement for labour. Again, for the Combine of private Industrial Insurance Companies in 1911, going through the public area of social relations meant getting Lloyd George to define in their precise interests what the status of 'Approved Societies' (including the Friendly Societies) under National Insurance Legislation would be. With W. H. Lever it meant taking twenty-two Co-operative societies to court in 1910 in an attempt, which failed, to make them legally bound to stock his soap, rather than to challenge his empire through exclusive dealing (Yeo, 1977). The fight was on, the battleground was public, and there was and can be no escape from that, no exit to the diminishing territory 'behind society's back'.

Indeed the working class, to fulfil its maximum potential and reach its goal (sometimes called Socialism, perhaps better called a social or associated mode of production) needs the public branch of production of social relations – the State – more, earlier, and in different forms from its predecessor, the carriers of capitalism. There are material differences between the forms as well as the substances of a bourgeois as compared with a proletarian revolution. For labour, the forms are the substance. There can be no promising of the one without the other, as in capitalism (some substance without the forms), or State Socialism (some forms without the substance). This is partly for the elementary reason that there are more labourers than owners and the 'socialist' project cannot be achieved until every worker (every human) is in some associated complex-co-operative (as opposed to competitive) sense, his or her own boss. This is what capitalism promises but cannot, without total transformation or revolution, deliver. 'All previous historical movements,' the Communist Manifesto suggested, 'were movements of minorities, or in the interests of minorities. The proletarian movement is the self-conscious, independent movement of the immense majority, in the interest of the immense majority. The proletariat, the lowest stratum of our present society, cannot stir, cannot raise itself up, without the whole superincumbent strata of official society being sprung into the air.' Capitalism must involve formal, real and then systematic subordination and division into two (historically active) classes: whereas socialism or an associated mode must involve systematic, universal mutuality, fraternity, equality. Society cannot be rescued for the working class behind its back, or its head, or on its base or in any other twisted posture, whereas it can and must for the bourgeoisie. For them, *coup d'états,* followed by night-watchmen states, 'holding the ring', are entirely adequate forms of revolution and post-revolutionary politics. The State can even be left in other hands, in the hands of those predominantly or partially representing an earlier (or even a later, as in the case of social democracy) mode, for long stretches of time, while, back at the 'economic' ranch, material production is developed entirely adequately for capital. Such a separation of the economic from the political is impossible for the working class, if it is to realize its own potential: for the proletariat to rule by dictatorship is a contradiction in terms. If the proletariat is ruling by dictatorship someone else is ruling and pretending to be the proletariat.

But this is where imagination is tempted towards evasion-by-words, or immaterial incantation. I am already slipping into such incantation. Alongside its realism, there is some of this evasion in the Communist Manifesto too. For example: 'In place of the old bourgeois society, with its classes and class antagonisms, we shall have an association, in which the free development of each is the condition for the free development of all.' 'When, in the course of development, class distinctions have disappeared, and all production has been concentrated in the hands of a vast association of the whole nation, the public power will lose its political character.'

Yes, *we shall have*, in the course of development. . . if we can avoid 'the common ruin of the contending classes'. But that development, must be, like the generation of new means of production and exchange in feudal society, 'a movement going on before our own eyes'.[29] In which case what does it, what can it, look like?

Systematic and universal mutuality, fraternity, equality, 'a vast association of the whole nation', will have to consist of myriads of actual activities. links, administrations in the public sphere. To abolish the political in a complex society will mean so many horizontal lines and bonds that the vertical is entirely constituted by those lines and bonds. Some of these must be visible before all of them can be actual. They cannot all be drawn at a stroke. Thus, the question for labour is not *whether* to employ the State, or how to talk in general, about states of affairs replacing states, but *in what* (changing) *forms*? What is (would be and is) involved for labour is finding the forms (economic, social, cultural, political) which can resolve, rather than abolish, a set of contradictions. By this I mean providing forms within which necessary contradictions have space to move. These contradictions need specifying in as material a way as possible. Elsewhere, I have tried to summarize them as the contradiction between low cost to labour and high-class dividend; the contradiction between accessibility and effectiveness (or capacity for universalization), and the contradiction between autonomy and engagement, with allies and against enemies.[30] Labour's project cannot be achieved without uniting such opposites in an active tension, hard enough mentally even harder to sustain in social practice, through long stretches of times, in a given place. For labour, there can be no real distinction between the problem of agency, or constituting an associated mode, and the problems of realizing and living within and maintaining that mode itself. If the associated mode is to be actually and materially for labour, rather than, say, for a new administrative, technical cadre, all of its problems have to be solved to the extent that they are humanly soluble – away from and as a necessary preliminary – indeed constituent of – the *coup de grace*, the capture, which is also the smashing, of 'the State'. For this we shall need all the resources, historical and otherwise, which we can muster.

6

The State and Social Policy
Chris Jones and Tony Novak

Introduction

Social policy – that wide range of government services concerned with health, education, income maintenance, housing and so forth – constitutes a central activity of the State
in contemporary society. Out of a government expenditure
currently exceeding 60% of the gross national product, over
half is accounted for by spending on welfare services; far
more than is spent on other State activities such as the
military or the judiciary.

This growth in State social welfare is not only quantitative
but also qualitative. It has involved the development of new
State agencies and the expansion of existing institutions,
which in turn have encompassed new and larger areas of
control and regulation that touch directly upon the experience of most people during some part of their lives. For
large clusters of people, especially among the working class,
life from the womb to the grave is monitored by, or is
dependent upon, a vast network of State social legislation
and provision. The State's interest in the working class is by

no means novel, and its history is the history of capitalist development itself, but what we have in the specific instance of the growth of social policy is an aspect of the State's intensification of concern over a broader front and in greater depth. As Titmuss has commented on the State's growing interest in child care: 'In every area of a child's life – its physical health and habits, its emotional development, its educational progress, its clothes, its toys and its play – in all its stages of growth and activity the modern child receives far more care and attention than the child of fifty years ago.' (Titmuss, 1951. 412).

In this chapter we want to consider some of the more important factors which have stimulated this development of social policy and of the State itself. Through such a discussion we wish to refute a number of influential myths about the State which have been perpetuated largely through reference to its activities in the field of social policy. Not least, and incomprehensible as it may seem to many current clients of social work, social-security claimants, or council-house tenants, is the view that the State's expanded role in social welfare is the hall-mark of evolutionary human progress: the road to civilization (cf. Bruce, 1961; Marshall, 1966; Forder, 1966; and the critique by Gettleman, 1974), and that it is humanitarianism and benevolence which have been the prime motive forces in its development, melting away class divisons and antagonisms with the growing 'rights' of citizenship.

This huge distortion regarding the nature of the State, social policy, and social life in general, has significant influence because it resonates to some degree with what appears to have happened. It cannot be dismissed simply as a gross mystification; instead we need to address ourselves to what has actually happened, why and to what purpose, and with what results. This is our concern in this chapter, and although we do not seek to provide any sort of definitive answer, we would like to suggest some fruitful avenues of exploration concerning the nature of the State and its activity in social policy.

Social Policy: the Maintenance and Reproduction of Labour

'It is an admitted maxim of social policy,' wrote Sir George Nicholls, one of the three Poor Law Commissioners appointed in 1834, 'that the first charge upon the land must be the maintenance of those reared upon it. Society exists for the preservation of property; but subject to the condition that the wants of the few shall only be realized by first making provision for the necessities of the many' (Nicholls, 1898, vol. I: 2).

Throughout the history of capitalism, the existence of some form of 'social' policy has been determined in part by the fact that capitalism as a system of production depends upon a workforce that has neither property nor security. Those who, for whatever reason, are unable to work have nothing to sustain them, and the relief of their necessity, for both obvious political and economic reasons, has been 'the first principle of the English Poor Law' (ibid.). In relieving poverty, however, the State has not only assumed part of the responsibility of the maintenance of labour for industry (a role which, through Family Income Supplements, etc., now extends far beyond the formally 'unemployed'), but it has also, through the workhouse, the wage stop, and the general continuing principle of less eligibility, served to reproduce the conditions and necessity of labour. As Bernard de Mandeville wrote: 'those who get their living by their daily labour . . . have nothing to stir them up to be serviceable but their wants which it is prudence to relieve, but folly to cure' (cited in Marx 1867a: 614–15), and in reproducing labour *as* labour, ready to resume its position in the market when conditions dictate, the State has come to provide the indispensable basis for capitalist production.

This simple maintenance and reproduction of labour is, however, only one level at which social policies operate. Capitalism is an expanding system: it constantly creates new methods of production, and requires new and higher levels of skill and ability from its workforce. Labour under capitalism is of course a commodity – something which is bought and sold in return for a wage – but it is also an increasingly valuable commodity, on which increasing resources and time have been spent in order to equip it to carry out its task. Rising standards of health, of housing, and of education have, in part as we shall see, been the product of the determination of workers themselves to demand improvement; but they are also requirements which have been set by the competitive growth and international expansion of capital, and it is in this expanded maintenance and reproduction of labour that the State has again played a decisive part.

Social Policy and National Efficiency

The State's concern, through social policy, to maintain and enhance the wealth-producing power of the working class is in part a simple and pragmatic response to the everyday problems created by capitalist society: the problems of poverty, unemployment, disease, overcrowding, and the general physical and mental consequences of urban life. At certain times, however, this concern has become the subject of conscious debate and deliberation, when under the press of events, the practice and purpose of social policy has been reconsidered and reformulated in order to meet the urgency of the situation.

One such major restructuring of social policy occurred over the beginning of the present century. Set in the context of the Great Depression – out of which Britain emerged no longer with the economic advantage of being the world's first industrial nation, but severely challenged by the emerging industrial and military powers of the United States and

Germany – 'the condition of the people' became a question which fundamentally affected the future growth and prosperity of British capitalism. It was a problem which threatened both military and industrial success; as one observer put it, reflecting on the widespread malnutrition and disability amongst the working class revealed by the recruitment campaign for the Boer War: 'If a man is not good enough to be a soldier, he is in fact, as a general principle . . . unfitted for industrial competition' (Duke, 1903: 8).

Yet industrial competition and military efficiency were the terms on which the future depended, and both depended upon labour. With a working class debilitated through years of poverty, chronic unemployment, privation and disease, it was little wonder that a substantial part of ruling-class opinion was to join with Sidney Webb in demanding 'a new industrial character, imperatively required, not merely or even mainly for the comfort of the workers, but absolutely for the success of our industry in competition with the world.' (Webb, 1890: 8).[1]

The need to do something about social conditions, about unemployment, poverty and disease, was thus set by the recognition that under the need for growing productivity and efficiency, labour was not simply a commodity that could be used up and discarded: that capitalism had both an immediate and a long-term interest in its healthy maintenance and reproduction. As William Beveridge argues: 'In the problem thus outlined the community has a vital interest. It should be its object, other things being equal, to reduce to a minimum the involuntary idleness which means first and directly a present waste of productive power, second and indirectly a depravation of human material and destruction of productive power for the future.' (Beveridge, 1906: 326).

Or as Balfour summed it up for us with a directness that would be difficult to surpass: 'It is a most intolerable thing that we should permit the permanent deterioration of those who are fit for really good work. Putting aside all consideration of morals, all those considerations which move us as men of feeling, as flesh and blood, and looking at it with the hardest heart and the most calculating eye, is it not very poor economy to scrap good machinery?' (Cited in Jackson, 1910: 1)

Thus the introduction of national health and unemployment insurance, the feeding of school children and medical inspection were all to be part of the State's intention, as Beveridge put it, of 'forcing up and holding up of the standard of individual efficiency and production [which] must be the corner-stone of social policy' (Beveridge, 1909: 217).

Similar sentiments also were to be expressed in that other 'great debate' on social policy which accompanied its restructuring immediately after the Second World War. Here, predictions of an imminent collapse in the birth rate, and a consequent shortage of labour, were to lead the State into a new commitment to ensure the future viability, health and maintenance of the labour force (cf. P.E.P., 1948). In contrast to the nineteenth-century 'residuum' of chronic poverty and destitution which previous policies had sought to eradicate in the name of efficiency, the post-war concern with such 'problem families' saw them as a resource to be rescued: 'It should not require the cold statistics of the sociologist to awaken the official conscience. Nevertheless, the declining birth rate and the ageing population make it imperative that, quite apart from humanitarian considerations, every child should be given the maximum chance of survival, and more important still, should reach adult life in as perfect state of physical and mental health as is possible.' (Martin, 1944: 106)

Humanitarian considerations apart, of course, the State had an urgent role to perform. The provision of an improved health service, or of child-care facilities, did not stem primarily from pangs of official conscience; it was in part a response to the political expectations and demands of the post-war period, but it was also a reflection of the general consensus amongst the ruling class that the State could and should play a greater role in ensuring the economic viability of present and future generations of labour. As Lord Stamp put it: 'Regarding labour as the continuous flow of one agent, the provision of children to grow up and replace the worn-out units is an economic necessity, to be included in full current 'cost of production' just as surely as a fund for replacement of other producing agents'. (Cited in Rathbone, 1940: 25).

Social Policy, the State, and Capital

Despite the fact that 'money which is spent on maintaining the health, the vigour, the efficiency of mind and body in our workers is the best investment in the market' (George, 1911: 781), it is the State in Britain, and not private enterprise, which has come to assume primary responsibility for the maintenance and reproduction of labour.[2] At one level, of course, there is no 'market' – no immediate opportunity for profit – in rehabilitating juvenile delinquents or providing relief for the unemployed or elderly. In such instances the State provides the institutional support and infrastructure for capitalism in much the same way as it organizes credit and the money supply, regulates shipping, or collects garbage. At another level, however, the assumption by the State of the functions of social policy is a reflection of the inability (and at times the unwillingness) of individual employers themselves to do so.[3]

Historically, the State in Britain has played a leading role in the creation and development of capitalism. It was, according to Marx, 'the governments of Henry VII, VIII, etc.' which through their relentless suppression of vagrancy and their use of the Poor Law as an instrument of labour discipline, 'appear as conditions of the historic dissolution process and as makers of the conditions for the existence of capital' (Marx, 1858: 507), and since that time social reformers, politicians and civil servants have responded to problems and crises in capitalism's development by calling for an enlarged and more active role of the State in solving such problems on behalf of the bourgeoisie.

The Fabian Society, for example, gained considerable influence within government and reform circles at the end of the nineteenth century precisely because it indicated the manner in which unrestrained pursuit of profit by employers spelt anarchic and potentially dangerous social development, permitting a massive concentration of slums, with its attendant problems of labour degeneration and social unrest (Fabian Society, 1886). It was against this background that numerous factions of the middle and upper classes and gentry, particularly amongst the professions, emerged to press for a more active and enlarged State machinery not only to meet the consequences of such developments, but also to control and curb the activities of certain sections of the bourgeoisie themselves. Thus most reformers were united in denouncing the large employers of sweated and of casual labour in the docks and building industries, pointing to the demoralization and physical degeneration of large stocks of labour, especially in London and Liverpool, for which they were held responsible. There has similarly been an even greater tradition of intra-class conflict with regard to working-class housing, with 'progressive' sections of the ruling class accusing landlords and builders of super-exploitation in the single-minded pursuit of profit regardless of its physical and social consequences.

It is in this respect that social reformers through the years have earned the reputation of 'statesmen', as through their attention to the health and functioning of the social system as a whole they have pressed and agitated for a State or quasi-State apparatus which can contain and modify some of the excesses of capitalist employers, not for the purpose of undermining capitalism, but for encouraging its general viability. Consequently the history and development of social policy is in a large part the history of an economically dominant class organizing to become a ruling class, stamping its authority and control over the entire spectrum of social life. In this process, social reformers have played a crucial role in forcing manufacturers and industrialists to recognize 'the true interests of their own order' (Kay-Shuttleworth, 1832: 10) and to create a total social system which allows for stable development.

The State does not, of course, act wholly independently of the ruling class; at times it will condemn one particular section in the interests of the class as a whole; at others its activities reflect the power and organization of particular factions of the class. The State is an arena of contention and conflict within the ruling class just as much as it is the instrument of that class. In Britain in particular, factional divisions between, for example, industry and finance have long played an important part in the shaping of policy as each faction has sought to exert its power and direct State policy towards its own ends (cf. Semmell, 1960).

It is again at this level of intra-class conflict, right down to the more mundane but equally important level of competition that the State's role in organizing on behalf of capital has been decisive. Social reform is costly process; it is not something which individual employers have been willing to undertake alone while their rivals reap the benefits of unrestricted exploitation. The State, however, compels all to move in line. It establishes a national uniformity, setting standards and practices which individual employers would otherwise be unwilling or unable to undertake. There are of course, even amongst the bourgeoisie, losers in the game: growing State regulation, like the growth of capitalism itself, tends to favour the larger monopolistic concerns. As Beatrice Webb argued: 'What we have to do is to detach the great employers, whose profits are too large to feel the immediate pressure of regulation and who stand to gain by the increased efficiency of the factors of production, from the ruck of small employers or stupid ones' (Cited in Saville, 1957: 9)

The State thus acts as an organizing committee on behalf

of the bourgeoisie. Compelled by economic, social and political crises, it has developed into an institution capable of organizing and maintaining a labour market on a national scale. Partly in conjunction with and partly through superseding 'local' State agencies, it has developed a Poor Law, a national system of labour exchanges, social security provisions, housing policies, redundancy payments, and so forth, which have allowed for the transformation of a peasantry and agricultural proletariat into an urban and industrial working class, and which have secured a more flexible and mobile supply of labour to meet the pace of economic development. It is a task which the State alone is capable of performing, and in doing so it has come to provide an essential prerequisite of modern capitalist production.

Through the provision of social policies, the State also relieves capital of a major part of the cost of maintaining and reproducing labour, providing such a service not only where it might otherwise be absent, but also more effectively and efficiently (cf. the Beveridge Report and its criticisms of private insurance schemes). It also, as Marx put it, knows how to throw this burden onto the shoulders of the lower middle and working class (Marx 1867a: 644; cf. 1858: 609–610). Numerous studies have shown how the working class are made to pay for their own welfare services through direct and indirect taxation. But the State also uses other institutions to defray the expense involved; the history of less eligibility is in part a history of forcing the poor onto their own resources, and onto those of friends, neighbours, and relatives. More centrally, a great part of the burden of producing a healthy, well-fed and ready labour force has been placed on the family and the unpaid labour of wives and mothers (cf. Thane, 1977; and Ch. 4 above).

Current concern with the family and the need for a 'family policy' is nothing new to social policy. State policy has always recognized the importance of the role that the family plays in maintaining and reproducing present and future generations of labour, and has consistently sought to strengthen its functions and responsibilities through such devices as the means test, family allowance, tax relief and social-work intervention. As Beveridge argued plainly in his Report:

> In any measure of social policy in which regard is to be had to the facts, the great majority of married women must be regarded as occupied on work which is vital though unpaid, without which their husbands could not do their paid work and without which the nation could not continue.

> Taken as a whole the Plan for Social Security puts a premium on marriage in place of penalizing it. . . . In the next thirty years housewives as mothers have vital work to do in ensuring the adequate continuance of the British race and of British ideals in the world.
> (Social Insurance and Allied Services, 1942: paras. 107 and 117).

The family of course is not only an institution which relieves capital of a major part of the cost of maintaining and reproducing its labour force.[4] It is, as indeed is social policy as a whole, also concerned with the political reproduction and maintenance of labour: with the inculcation of ideals, of the 'right' values and habits, and attitudes of subordination to authority (cf. Wilson 1977).

Social Policy and Process: the Formation of Ideology

So far we have talked of the State's role in maintaining and reproducing labour primarily in material terms. But for capitalism the problem of securing a supply of labour is only in part a problem of ensuring that the right quantity and quality of labour is available in the right place at the right time. Labour for capital is a commodity, and has to be produced and reproduced as such; but unlike other 'factors of production', labour is also a quality possessed by human beings: by people who are capable of reflecting upon their situation, and of attempting to change it.

The maintenance and reproduction of labour, therefore, is not just a question of the physical reproduction of a class without property and with the necessary level of education, physique and skill; it is also a political reproduction which recreates a class that is both able and willing to work – or which at least accepts wage labour, its inequalities and consequences, as in some degree inevitable or unavoidable. Wage labour of course is not a 'natural' relationship: its creation – the creation of a working class – occurred over centuries through which the development of capitalism, aided by State policy and intervention, was to transform a peasantry into a proletariat, a subsistence mentality into an acquisitive one, and a 'moral' economy into a competitive one (cf. Pollard, 1963, 1965; Thompson, 1967, 1971).

Wage labour, however, is also a relationship which is continually being brought into question, not least as a result of its own consequences of inequality, poverty, and unemployment. It is thus a relationship which has continually to be reinforced – partly through the discipline of the market, but also, and especially in times of crisis, through the practice and ideology of social policy. It is in this active construction and reinforcement of the existing social and economic reality that the major developments in social policy have taken place. As J. P. Kay-Shuttleworth argued in 1832: 'The social body cannot be constructed like a machine, on abstract principles which merely include physical motions and their numerical results in the production of wealth. . . Political economy, though its object be to ascertain the means of increasing the wealth of nations cannot accomplish its designs without at the same time regarding the cultivation . . . of religion and morality' (Kay-Shuttleworth, 1832: 64).

Throughout the nineteenth century 'morality' and political economy (a perhaps more appropriate term for what we now call social policy) went together in guiding further State intervention and regulation of economic and social life (cf. Corrigan, 1977). It was the 'demoralization' of agricultural labour in the early nineteenth century – their notions of a 'right' to employment or relief, to a 'just wage', and their sometimes violent protests against poverty and unemployment – which excited the Poor Law Report of 1834. Similarly it was the 'demoralizing contagion' of the residuum at the end of the nineteenth century – their apparent absence of habits of thrift, of labour discipline, and of respect for private property – which was to provoke schemes for their forced emigration, confinement to labour colonies, or simple extermination. Capitalism needs labour; but it also needs a particular kind of labour: a labour force which is docile, relatively unquestioning, disciplined and obedient, and responsive to the cash stimulus. The creation of such a labour force has involved and continues to involve the use of coercion and the repressive force of the State, but it has also come to rely increasingly upon the creation of an ideological framework which presents the existing structure of society as both natural and inevitable.

In the context of social policy, the role of the education system is perhaps the most obvious example of the creation and cultivation of ideology. It is of course a delicate process; as Kay-Shuttleworth again argued:

> The absence of education is like that of cultivation, the mind untutored becomes a waste, in which prejudices and traditional errors grow as rankly as weeds. In this sphere of labour, as in every other, prudent and diligent culture is necessary to obtain genial products from the soil; noxious agencies are abroad, and, while we refuse to sow the germs of truth and virtue, the winds of heaven bring the winged seeds of error and vice. (Kay-Shuttleworth, 1832: 95; cf. Johnson, 1970).[5]

Nor is 'learning to labour' a process of simple achievement, but is rather met with resistance, hostility and indifference (cf. Willis, 1977). Indeed like all areas of social policy, the ideological battle to mould people's views and expectations of the world is a constant and unending one.

Similar ideological effects run through the whole range of social policy practice, at times more or less covert, and direct at others, in their impact on the population as a whole. Many of the more coercive elements of social policy – the refusal of benefits or the power to take children into care, for example – operate only on relatively small and politically insignificant sections of the population; but policy-makers have long been aware of the 'educational influence' in a wider context. As William Beveridge, for example, put it: 'the decision of the workman to work or not depends to some extent on what happens to those who do not work' (Beveridge, 1909: 195); or, as the Report of the Committee on Abuse of Social Security Benefits has explained at greater length more recently:

> To what extent it is to the advantage of the community to spend public money to persuade or compel people to work who do not wish to work, at a time when there are many thousands who wish to work but cannot find work?. . . The unemployment review officer may be cost effective in the narrow sense of saving the cost of unemployment payments to an individual, but has he reduced the cost of unemployment payments to society as a whole? If there are not enough jobs to go round, has he lowered the national level of production by pushing a reluctant, physically or mentally handicapped, socially inadequate, or simply inexperienced man into a job which might otherwise have gone to a man with the prospect of contributing more to production?. . . If this view is accepted there should therefore be no pressure by unemployment review officers or others in areas of serious unemployment. The problem has only to be stated in these terms to indicate how much is left out by the state-

ment of it: the psychological damage to the individual of allowing him to recline on benefit and abandon the search for work; the general effect on public attitudes to work and self-help. . . . We have had the advantage of discussions with officials of the D.E. and D.H.S.S. on this question, and they have told us of the views held by the regional controllers and those working under them, some in regions where unemployment is especially high. They believe that society does benefit from a continuance of the work of unemployment review officers and others in relation to the long-term unemployed even in times and in areas of high unemployment. (Report, 1973: 95–6).

Social policy is more than an attempt to solve the problems of capitalism; it has and continues to play a very important role in securing the parameters within which capitalism has developed and operates and in constructing the social body in accordance with the changing needs and requirements for labour. One of its central concerns has been the maintenance and reproduction of labour: the creation and recreation of the working class as a working class: in other words, the reproduction of the social relations of production on which capitalist society depends. But this process takes place also on a political terrain, and in a context of struggle in which battles for both sides have been won and lost, and it is to this political aspect of State and social policy formation that we must now turn.

Social Policy and Class Struggle

Every 'social problem' is political and in one way or another reflects the class tensions inherent in capitalist society (cf. Clarke, 1975). Unemployment and poverty, for example, are never just about being without work or adequate resources: they also involve fundamental issues of power, the status of wage labour, and of human rights and needs, all of which are contentious in a class society. Similarly, 'solutions' to such problems – insofar as they attempt to solve them within existing social structures – reproduce and reinforce the economic, social and political relationships through which such inequalities are perpetuated.

The direct threat of working-class unrest and militancy has often been one of the key triggering factors in the timing of social policy development. The Unemployed Workman's Act 1906, for example, which entailed central government support to local authorities in establishing relief works for the 'deserving' and 'genuine' unemployed, was quietly dropped by the Tories until a spate of rioting at the end of 1905 spurred it onto the Statute Books (cf. K. Brown, 1971). Similarly, the Beveridge Report and the promise of wide-spread welfare measures were clearly understood at the time as being part of the strategy to sustain the war effort among the working class by giving them hope of a future qualita-tively distinct from their pre-war experiences of massive unemployment and the means test. The 1942 P.E.P. *Report* on social security had no doubt that reforms in this area were essential to preserve bourgeois democracy (1942:1). Or in the words of Quintin Hogg – which echoed those of countless reformers of the past – 'if you don't give the people reform, they are going to give you social revolution' (cited in Harris, 1961:5 cf. Kaufman, 1907:9).

Working-class agitation on any significant scale, whether it be well-orchestrated or spontaneous, can and does pose a major threat to the stability of the capitalist system. The extent of the threat, which determines in great part the nature of the ruling-class response, depends largely upon the numbers involved, the scale of disruption and its political direction. Certainly since the latter part of the nineteenth century, with the increased concentration of workers often in well-defined areas of cities and towns, along with the growth of trade-unionism and a presence in the formal pol-itical arena with the adult franchise, the working class has had the recognized potential of acting and organizing as a

class: in 'concerted masses' as one late Victorian commen-
tator noted (Burleigh, 1887:771). This capacity for class
mobilization, which was well demonstrated for a few days
in May 1926 and by the National Unemployed Workers'
Movement in the thirties (cf. Hannington, 1940, 1936), has
created certain constraints on the State with regard to the
vital issue of sustaining ruling-class control. While overt
violence and force are still used against workers (cf. Grun-
wick), the State has learned that excessive reliance on force
and brutality is unsuitable in the long term as a means for
securing social stability.

In terms of the history of the British State, it was during
the latter part of the last century when the working class
was emerging as a large, politically active and collective
class force that the necessity arose for an expanded and a
more sophisticated range of class control strategies. As Stedman Jones (1971) has indicated, it was during those years
that increasing numbers of social reformers and politicians
were alarming their own class about the threat from the
growing mass of destitute workers, especially in London,
who 'may swell to such proportion as to render continuance
of our existant social system impossible . . . they might
even, stirred up by designing persons and promises of social
salvation, attempt it by revolutionary outbreaks' (Gorst,
cited in Simon, 1965: 79–80). Since that time there has been
a marked tendency for the State to develop and utilize social
welfare measures as a means of defusing working-class discontent, and, equally importantly, do so by developing policies which secure working-class allegiance and their support
for the existing social order. Consequently, alongside the
coercive thrust of much State social policy, there has developed an increasingly important 'educative' dimension which
has the explicit objective of imbuing certain forms of internal self-control and regulation. Contemporary social work
is a fine example of a welfare activity that retains a coercive
edge but attempts in the first instance a 'softer' approach of

persuading 'clients' to take for themselves dominant values and patterns of behaviour.[6]

This expansion in the range and style of State rule is to a large extent a reflection of the influence of working-class action. National insurance reforms in 1911 and 1947, for example, were not solely concerned with creating a fit and viable reserve of labour, but were also intent upon deflating the great agitations of the unemployed against the punitive and degrading Poor Law and associated means tests; and if space permitted we could give further examples with regard to health, housing and education policies. In a fundamental sense, therefore, the concern over the condition of the working class which has underpinned social policy development is a concern about its physical condition *and* its political mentality.

Social policy measures have attempted to secure such objectives in a number of ways. One strand which has a long history is the use of social welfare reforms as a ransom: what Engels once described as the 'infamous charity' of the Christian bourgeoisie (1845b: 279). And throughout the past 150 years it has been possible to trace many examples where working-class agitation, especially over unemployment, has forced governments to make immediate concessions or has stimulated the creation of 'quasi' State welfare agencies.[7] Moreover, it has often been recognized that it is 'good business sense' to alleviate actual or potential grievances of the working class as quickly as possible in order to pre-empt the danger of escalation and a more generalized agitation against the system as a whole.[8] This greater sensitivity on the part of the State is reflected in the expansion of its monitoring and research apparatus both in the universities and the local authorities as well as in the central government departments (cf. Byrne, 1978). This pursuit and development of social reform 'from above' is a fundamental and ongoing part of the State's response to social problems. Despite popular mythology, direct working-class demands and proposals have played a relatively minor role in the creation of the 'welfare state' (cf. Pelling, 1968). Indeed, the historic demand of the labour movement – the demand for the right to work – remains as pertinent now as it was in the 1900s, the 1830s and earlier. It is of course the pressure and threat of class conflict, the direct and indirect challenge of labour to its continued subordination under capital, which remains the motive force of history, and it is through these struggles that social policy and State formation have taken place. Nevertheless, for the ruling class it can be a fragile exercise, in which greater and sometimes dangerous concessions have had to be made in the attempt to outflank an even more dangerous situation; but social policy remains essentially an instrument for preserving the status quo. As Atherley-Jones noted:

> The present movement for social reform springs from above rather than below. The cry for an eight hours bill, for further factory legislation, for the improvement of sanitation, for the increase of allotments and smallholdings, for the readjustment of the incidence of taxation, for old-age pensions, is less the spontaneous demand of the working classes than the tactical inducement of the political strategist. (1893:629; cf. Novak, 1978: 214–20).

The State has had *some* success through its social policy measures in curbing the extent and degree of class conflict, which has partly borne out Balfour's famous assertion about social reforms being the 'most opposite' and 'most effective antidote' to socialism (cited in Halévy, 1934: 231). Such an achievement has involved complex processes and we would be mistaken to look for simple mono-causal explanations which stressed only the ransom nature of social welfare or its incorporative potential. Indeed, the actual history of social policy and State development in Britain is characterized by shifts, flexibility, change and process which reflects that class control is not a once and for all contest.

An obvious ingredient in the 'success' of social policies

has been the State's monopolization of power. Concessions may have been won by the working class in all spheres of social welfare, but the content and form and not least the administration of the policies have remained firmly within the *control* of State agencies (cf. Harvey and Hood, 1958: 253). This control has ensured that particular social policies reflect and actively support dominant social relationships and arrangements. Equally, it has allowed them to become a means for extending the legitimacy and scope of such relationships and values. Through health visitors, doctors, midwives, teachers, youth workers, social workers, housing officers and the like, plus an array of institutions, the State has physically expanded and penetrated deeper than ever before into the personal and private lives of many workers and their families. Under proclaimed banners of welfare and concern, equipped with supposedly neutral bodies of specialist knowledge and bundles of university certificates to verify their expertise, a veritable army of State officials have entered the lives and homes of families especially among the lower working class with the intent to tell people how to manage their lives, raise their children and generally to monitor their 'progress'.

The differential application and administration of social policies is of the greatest political importance in understanding their effects on the working class. In a crucial sense social policies act on the divisions created in the capitalist process as a whole, including not only those generated at the point of production but also sex, age, and race divisions. By acting on these divisions, supporting and reflecting them and often creating further subdivisions, social welfare measures have had their greatest success in maintaining the social order, dissipating militancy and effecting a marked ideological impact. Even within supposedly universal services such as education and health, differential processes are evident whereby people are sifted and allocated resources in a value-laden and segregated manner. As a building worker noted in recalling his schooling:

It was appalling. I hated school. If you passed for the grammar school then you were in the élitist group and then as now it led to a good job. We always argued that most of the people who went to grammar school didn't get there on their abilities but because of their backgrounds. . . Once you go to school you're told what to do; you're taught what they want you to be taught; you're told about differences between races and religions; your whole creative sense is destroyed. And it continued outside of school. (D. Ayre, 'Strong Words', 1979)

Policies relating to unemployment relief provide one of the most obvious examples of why and how the State responds differentially to problems affecting the working class. At the turn of the present century a primary concern was over the plight of previously 'good' and regular workers who had lost their jobs as a result of foreign competition, industrial restructuring, or trade depression. This section of the unemployed working class not only constituted a pool of good reserve labour which on economic grounds could not be allowed to rot away under the Poor Law or passing charity, but was also seen as a political threat of major importance due to their experience of class organization in the trade unions and other working-class institutions (cf. Lane, 1974: Ch. 3). In order to prevent the physical and 'moral' deterioration of these 'deserving' poor, the cry went up, led by such influential organizations as the Charity Organization Society and the Fabian Society, that those 'who deserve relief must be separated from those who require punitive or restrictive action' (Oakeshott, 1894:9). And in the subsequent cluster of reforms which were ennacted between 1885 and 1914, including pensions, relief works, national health, unemployment insurance, and school meals, a strong discriminatory intent was maintained in order to sustain 'good' workers, rewarding them for past efforts in the labour market and future quiescence, and, conversely, to ensure the exclusion of 'undeserving' workers

and their identification with the much harsher régime of the
Poor Law or the labour colonies (Alden, 1905: 145–47).[9]

Processes of differentiation and segregation, whether in
the school, or over entitlement to welfare benefits, or over
the allocation of a council house, all serve to divide people
from one another. Such policies have engendered distances
between and within the classes, which are both physical and
ideological. By playing on class, gender, age and race, social
policies extend and support a social consciousness whereby
social problems and issues are categorized as discrete and
qualitatively specific to certain individuals and groups. Thus
in individualizing many of the consequences of poverty,
alienated labour and unemployment, the very groups and
individuals caught up in the welfare net are portrayed as
being singularly distinctive and different. Over the years this
process of economic, political and moral classification has
been strengthened by the increasing utilization of the social
sciences as the vocabulary of legitimation and explanation.
In social work, for example, which operates in the heartland
of working-class poverty and despair, we read little in their
texts about structural employment or even simple material
poverty. Instead we are bombarded by psychologistic references to inadequate families, usually the mothers (cf.
Timms and Philp, 1957), and poor techniques of socializa-
tion. Moreover, we are told that all the problems are different and that no two clients are the same – a point which
respects their 'humanity', but denies their problems and
their causation. A welfare zoo has been constructed with all
the animals appropriately labelled and caged: an ongoing
process that is as divisive as the differential distribution and
administration of benefits and other resources.

Activities such as these have enhanced and deepened
sectional identities which are already part and parcel of the
labour market and which are reflected in much trade-unionism. A culture which promotes the 'peculiarities' of the
unemployed, problem families, claimants, the mentally ill,
and so on, is unlikely to challenge the traditional sectarian-

ism of organized labour. For example, we find that the 'submerged tenth', now known as problem or criminal families (Women's Group on Public Welfare, 1943), but previously as the undeserving poor, or earlier still as vagabonds, rogues and sturdy beggars (Corrigan and Corrigan, 1978), have been consistently neglected by organized labour who have often been as stigmatizing, if not more so, than the welfare professionals (cf. Coates and Silburn, 1970; Jones, Novak and Phillipson, 1978).[10] Moreover, given that such a large proportion of welfare benefits are currently discretionary and granted on a 'reward' basis this has carried over and created certain influential ideas about justice and rights. These in turn can influence relationships between people and lead to bitter confrontations between council tenants, clients and claimants, who get caught up in policing each other to ensure that no one gets away with something which the others haven't managed to secure. Communal concerns are often lost sight of in such bitter and decisive struggles. Similarly, those active in the welfare matrix struggling for better provisions and treatment have often defined themselves and their constituencies in relation to the categories given by the State policies. Groups such as claimants' unions, radical pensioners, mental patients' unions etc., have all taken their cues from specific social policy measures. This fragmentation, which is easily understandable and often necessary, does allow the State to pick off and deal with discontent largely on its own ground and retards a more general recognition of, and collective mobilization against, the evils of an exploitative social system. In particular, it masks the specific class dimension of renowned problem groups and their place within the working class. The toil and hardship of poverty, unemployment, old age, one-parent families, mental and physical illness, are the property of the working class, contrary to the proclamations of politicians and policy makers.

Despite and because of the differential application of so many social policies, such State activities have an important part to play in the creation of a stable, class-divided society. We must not forget that one part of the British working class experience is that when the State has eventually intervened in social reform it has often brought with it real and substantial improvements in the standard and quality of life. It is not only in the interests of capital to have a labour force free from epidemics, better housed and educated. The present social security system may be hard and stringent, but it has certainly blunted that mighty weapon of starvation which has smashed many workers' struggles in the past. Unfortunately such improvements have fuelled within sections of the organized working class a pervasive belief in reformism and a peculiar view of the State as being capable of acting in their interests and thus a worthy target for their aspirations. While such reformist tendencies contain certain problems for the ruling class in that they can contain aspirations which cannot be met within the existing social framework, they do fulfil one important requirement of fixing the main strength and energy of the working class within bourgeois 'democratic' institutions and systems of thought. A point which was well grasped by Churchill and demonstrated in his comments on the benefits of national insurance:

> The idea is to increase the stability of our institutions by giving the mass of industrial workers a direct interest in maintaining them. With a 'stake' in the country in the form of insurance against evil days these workers will pay no attention to the vague promises of revolutionary socialism . . . it will make him a better citizen, a more efficient worker and a happier man. (*Daily Mail* 16 September, 1909, cited in Harris, 1972: 365–6)

Conclusions

One revolutionary socialist, writing in 1917, described social reform as one of the most subtle weapons used by the State to defend the interests of the ruling class (Paul, 1917: 132). Social reform, and social policy in general, remain as instruments of class domination. They are activities forged through years of struggle and experience which assist in maintaining and reproducing the existing structure of economic and social relationships, and serve to reinforce and often make palatable its inequalities and consequences. Its subtleties are to be found in its varied and differential administrations; its ability to play down direct coercion with a range of ideological pressures to ensure conformity and the supposed democratic nature of its institutions.

Nevertheless, social policy is not an all-embracing and wholly successful monolith. Created through struggle it inevitably carries with it its own contradictions and paradoxes: contradictions which are as apparent for the ruling class as they are for those on the receiving end of the Welfare State. For the working class, social policy remains a deeply ambiguous activity. There have been victories and improvements but there have also been a great many important losses. Notable amongst these has been the decreasing control that workers themselves can exercise over the formulation and implementation of policy. Not only has the formation of State social policy involved the destruction and suppression of alternative working-class institutions (cf. Corrigan and Gillespie, 1974; Simon, 1965) such as friendly societies, schools and libraries, replacing them with its own 'public' versions in which access and control is severely limited,[11] but it has also presented social policy as an 'expert' activity (cf. Laski, 1931) which has both closed off much political and general discussion and legitimized an ever widening encroachment of the State into new areas of social and personal life.

Even the positive gains for the working class – the removal of the threat of starvation (much to Mrs Thatcher's anger), and the increased financial security that the Welfare State has provided – have their own limitations and negative implications. The provision of unemployment benefit, for example, is no real substitute for a society where unemployment is abolished, and, as we have also seen, the benefits are provided in such a way as to reproduce and reinforce inequalities both between and within the classes. In this respect social reform is a lure which has often tempted the more powerful and organized sections of the labour movement and fragmented the potential unity of the class as a whole.

But again neither has the intent of social policy been wholly successful. The attempt to create the image of a benevolent and caring State is constantly belied by the experience of social security offices, school discipline and grossly inadequate health and welfare services. Undoubtedly levels of provision have grown, but for many people the Welfare State does not provide a solution to poverty and the many other problems which are constantly being generated by capitalism.

Probably one of the great achievements of social reform has been in increasing confusion. Part of this confusion stems from the divisions and debates within the ruling class who are commonly divided over what constitutes the most appropriate response to the issues discussed above. Mystification can be compounded when those groups of reformers and politicians pressing for greater State intervention and social welfare provision do so in the name of socialism (Paul, 1917: 180–81).

For the ruling class, also, social policy is a contradictory and paradoxical process over which they have at times been and remain deeply divided. In many areas today there are clear signs of bewilderment over how problems are to be dealt with. Current concern over juvenile delinquency clearly illuminates this: the apparent failure of both penal and rehabilitative policies has brought conflict between State agencies such as magistrates, police, teachers and social workers (Jones, 1978a).

If social policy has been a crucial weapon of the State to ensure the stability and viability of capitalism, it has been done only at a price to the ruling class. Financially the growth of State expenditure on welfare has come to present a major problem which is intensified by the political difficulties of effecting major cuts and more recently the future prospects of increasing unemployment and therefore increased dependency on State funds. And dependency like many things in the social policy field is double-edged. On the one hand it is something which has been tolerated because it focuses working-class aspirations on the State rather than socialism as the solution to their problems. But it is also a dependency which, as many conservatives point out, threatens to weaken the work ethic. Such claims are by no means novel; they have always been used as a pretext for tightening up controls on welfare services especially during periods of high unemployment and stress; each successive advance in social policy has seen the further extension of State control and regulation which in part undermines the incentives and moral qualities of the system it seeks to defend.

Such paradoxes are the inevitable consequence of a society which both generates, and yet at the same time has to provide some palliative to, the problems we have discussed. In responding to these problems the State has been forced to make 'concessions' to the workers, which although formulated and implemented in ruling class terms are nevertheless concessions which the bourgeoisie might otherwise have not wished to make. In the process they have created a vast range of bureaucratic institutions and regulations which have to be operationalized by a massive number of state officials. And as the Gould report (1977) noted in respect of teachers and social workers, there is the growing problem of securing the loyalty of the experts themselves and ensuring their suitability as personal representatives of the State (cf. C. Jones, 1978b).

Consequently, social policy and State formation remains as it has always been, a process of continuing struggle between and within the classes. It is a struggle which combines factions and destroys class alliances and which demands flexibility on the part of the State. The die is not cast and can never be in a social system which denies the humanity of the mass of its population in the pursuit of profit. The working class may have yet to seize their historic mission but there is still abundant evidence to support Holyoake's contention that 'no protest that capital is his friend reassures him. Terror has made him deaf and experience unbelieving' (1878: 494).

NOTES

Abbreviations

BM: British Museum, Department of Printed Books and Department of Manuscripts *and* British Library, Reference Division.
BUL: Birmingham University Library.
Hansard: Hansard's Parliamentary Debates (Series III).
MH: see PRO.
MUL: Manchester University Library.
PP: Parliamentary Papers (a complete set is available in the State Paper Room of the BM and in several university libraries; many libraries – for example, central reference departments of public libraries – have purchased the Irish Universities Press reprints of major nineteenth-century reports).
PRO: Public Record Office, Kew and Chancery Lane.
MH: Ministry of Health Files.
SCMT: Socialist Construction and Marxist Theory.
UCL: University College, London.

1　Pages 1 to 25

1 This chapter originated as our paper to the 1977 British Sociological Association Conference on the State held at Sheffield. It also draws on our collective and individual work: in particular, our two joint books *Socialist Construction and Marxist Theory* (1978) and *For Mao* (1979); Sayer's *Marx's Method* (1979); Corrigan's Ph.D. thesis, (1977); Ramsay, (1976, 1977).

2 For example, the Appendix to *Socialist Construction and Marxist Theory: Marx's Method*; or Corrigan and Sayer, 1979.

3 See the four volumes of Hal Draper's excellent study; other shifts can be traced in the work of Holloway and Picciotto, Jessop and others. A major debate took place between Miliband and Poulantzas – summarized by Laclau (1975); subsequent comments are to be found in Poulantzas, (1976, 1978); Miliband, (1977). Apart from the work of Elias and Foucault we would point to two major bodies of writing with which we share broad agreement: (i) the rediscovered work of Bolsheviks of the 1920s, such as Rubin, Volosinov and Pashukanis; (ii) the surveys and analyses of Stuart Hall (e.g. 1977a, 1977b).

4 For fuller documentation see *Marx's Method*, pp. 83–7; *SCMT*, pp. 3–4; and compare Anderson, 1973:203f.; Balibar, 1968:233f.; Bettelheim, 1970:86f.; 1973:91f. – the last two references are discussed further in the second chapter.

5 This is a basic argument in all our works. For an early discussion see Corrigan and Sayer, 1975; one extended study for nineteenth-century England is provided in Corrigan Ph.D. thesis, especially Ch.3.

6. Corrigan Ph.D. thesis Ch.2 traces ambiguities in Marx and Engels; *SCMT* examines Bolshevism.

7 Some have now established (in Stuart Hall's exact phrase) a theory of *necessary non-correspondence* (Cf. Corrigan and Sayer, 1978). This autonomization corresponds to much of the writing (related to the 'wretchedness of the real conditions in Germany') of 'our *philosophic heroes*' criticized by Marx and Engels in *The German Ideology*. We should stress that Marx continued to attack such 'theoretical bubble blowing' including the famous analyses in his 'Notes on Wagner' in 1880.

8 This dimension is located in M. Barrett (*et al.*), *Ideology and Cultural Production* (1979), and forthcoming articles by Philip Corrigan with Paul Willis, in *Screen Education*, and *Media, Culture and Society*. The recent work (and the light it casts on his earlier writings) of Basil Bernstein (e.g. 1977a) is very important here.

9 This stress is established in *Marx's Method*; as is argued in Sayer (1978a) and Corrigan and Sayer (1978) such a stress is also a component of socialist analysis.

10 Edward Thompson's *Poverty of Theory* (1978a) is a major blast against any denial of the materialist/empirical/historical facet of marxist scholarship. A significant debate is in progress in the pages of the journal *History Workshop*, e.g. Richard Johnson in issue no. 6, Keith McClelland and Gavin Williams in issue no. 7.

11 This is in his criticism of Adolph Wagner. The texts are discussed in Corrigan and Sayer (1975, 1978), and in *Marx's Method*.

12 The term 'idealistic superstructure' is used in many places by Marx – for example later in the same book (1845:373); we think this points to a different explanation of the whole base/superstructure metaphor more 'in tune' with Marx's strategic critique of all phenomenal forms (Corrigan and Sayer 1978, pp. 201f.) Prior discussions of this include Sayer, 1975; Corrigan and Sayer, 1975; *SCMT*, pp. 4f.; *Marx's Method* pp. 80f.

13 Apart from Ch. 4 of this book (and note 13 to Ch. 2) the issue of the patriarchal and familial forms of *capitalist* production relations is raised in the final section of Corrigan and Sayer 1978 (a criticism of the Hindess and Hirst project agreed by R. Coward in *m/f* (2) 1978, p. 95). The two best starting points for an examination of patriarchy and familial forms are two sets of essays: *Feminism and Materialism* (Kuhn and Wolpe, 1978) and *Women Take Issue* (CCCS 1978) plus issues of the journals *Feminist Review*, *m/f* and *Women's Studies*. The essays of Wainright (1978) and Bland, McCabe and Mort (1978) introduce further dimensions. It is as well to stress our disagreement with Althusser's notorious suggestion that reproduction was a superstructural phenomenon and that the family was fully Erastianized. For one empirical dimension see Humphries (1977) together with the

resources (reprinted or collected through oral history) of a *materialist* history of working-class women's historical experience now available.

14 'Separation appears as the normal relation in this society . . . in this society *unity* appears as accidental, *separation* as normal' (Marx, 1863a:409). 'Competition is the mode generally in which capital secures the victory of its mode of production' (1858:730). This is discussed at length in Corrigan and Sayer 1979.

15 This is discussed in Sayer's *Marx's Method*.

16 Discussions of fetishism are found in Geras (1971), Mepham (1972) and in *Marx's Method*, Part One.

17 These points are taken further in Corrigan's Ph.D. thesis Ch.2 for Marx and Engels, and in *SCMT* for Lenin and the Bolsheviks and in *For Mao* for Mao. The contrasting modalities, and their relation to the world market, can be seen best (and most tragically) in the People's Republic of China from the mid-1970s onwards.

18 cf. the works of S. Hall and Draper cited in note 3 above; Miliband's 1965 paper is also useful.

19 On these corrections see Lenin 1917b (and his notebooks, 1917a) plus Balibar 1972 – neither had the greatest possible impact upon the policies of the Communist Parties for whom they were written.

20 *SCMT* n. 2, p. 163; *For Mao*, p. xv; Corrigan and Sayer, 1978:209.

21 This formulation of tactical seriousness and strategic contempt is drawn from Mao's remarks in Moscow in 1957. These remarks were shown to be relevant through a study of the historical experience of working class and other struggles in England and elsewhere and reflected upon in Corrigan and Sayer 1975 and Ramsay (1976a,b, 1977) and is displayed at some length in *SCMT* and *For Mao*. For a shorter version see Corrigan and Sayer 1978:198–199.

2   Pages 27 to 48

1 It was originally intended that there would be two chapters in this area in which Richard Saville and Peter Linebaugh would

draw upon their doctoral research into fiscal policy and labour relations in England from c.1660 to c.1720, and crime, waged labour and the Poor Law in eighteenth-century England, respectively. I wish to acknowledge how much I have learned from their published and unpublished writings and to urge readers to watch for their future publications which will substantiate some of my sketches here; this does not, of course, bind them to agree with or even to support my words. Apart from my own doctoral dissertation (1977) material relating to this chapter can be found in Corrigan and Gillespie 1974; Corrigan and Corrigan, 1978; and in Corrigan, 1979, 1980, especially Part One '1066–1776'.

2 In the mid-1970s when I argued for Smith and Bentham as favourable theorists of the State it was a more marginal (if not an heretical) view; nowadays it is commonplace as recent work by Rosenblum (1978; on Bentham) and Winch (1978; on Smith) has shown. In the case of the latter the pioneering work of Rosenberg (1960) should be acknowledged.

3 Particularly important is Thompson's 1965 response (to Anderson and Nairn) 'The Peculiarities of the English' (reprinted 1978) and his two sketches of eighteenth-century society in 1974 and 1977a; but cf. also his *Past and Present* articles 1967, 1971, the latter being particularly important.

4 Apart from the work of Peter Linebaugh (and that collected in *Albion's Fatal Tree*) I am thinking particularly of Malcolmson's *Popular Recreations in English Society 1700–1850* (1973) and two works of an earlier period: Keith Thomas on religion and magic (1971) and Christopher Hill's exceptional *World Turned Upside Down* (1972).

5 Aside from Peter Linebaugh and Jason Ditton's examination of how common customs became privileges of the few and crimes for the rest, see such work as Rusche and Kirscheimer (1939); the essays edited by J. S. Cockburn (1977), Bayley's essay on the police (1975), Friedmann's review of Renner's work on property law (1950) and Gurr's comparative study (1976). 'Patterns of crime' have been studied by Beattie (1972, 1974) whilst Lazonick outlines Marx's views on enclosures (1974).

6 This is what Thompson, Linebaugh and Ditton accomplish in

their work, drawing on the similarly comprehensive analyses of Marx (1858; 1867a: Part VIII; cf. Weber, 1920: Part IV).

7 For example the lectures by Strayer (1970) or the essay by Koenigsberger (1977); earlier work (notably that of O. Hintze) should not be overlooked by readers.

8 Hintze traces some of these Offices and routines, whilst F. M. G. Evans (1923) examines Secretaries of State in England from Elizabeth I onwards; the fullest surveys (in general dating from 1660) have been undertaken by J. C. Sainty, for the Treasury, Secretaries of State (1660–1782), Board of Trade, Admiralty, and the Home Office. These are all published by Athlone Press (1972 onwards). The finest detailed studies we have are two volumes by Aylmer: *The King's Servants* (1961) and *The State's Servants* (1973).

9 The *general* value of Christopher Hill's work on early modern England deserves more general recognition. We now have his contribution towards a proper understanding of the whole period in his *Reformation to Industrial Revolution, 1530–1780* (1967) in which the chapters on agrarian production and on culture are especially helpful. cf. Clark's survey of Kent 1500–1640 (1977).

10 Elton, 1953, 1972, 1973. cf. Hoskins, 1976, and the work of Hill cited in the text. Anderson (1974:120f.) outlines recent work which argues against Thomas Cromwell's achievements as a 'proto-bourgeois revolutionary'. Nevertheless, it seems clear to me that the *cultural revolution* accomplished by the break with Rome and the vernacularization of religion is of the greatest importance; cf. Corrigan, 1980: Ch. 2.

11 Apart from Loades' valuable book (1974), I acknowledge the inspiration I received from a lecture he gave in Newcastle-upon-Tyne in 1971 on the 'political nation' in Tudor England. Another perspective on the political nation is Bellamy's study of treason.

12 Hill's complementary papers on 'The Agrarian Legislation of the Revolution' (1940a; cf. his 1940b pamphlet) and on the Henrician Reformation (1956b) taken with the relevant chapters in his textbook (1967) are major starting-points. But note the value of Marx's comments both in the *Grundisse* (1858:507) and in the

eighth part of volume one of *Capital*, already mentioned in Ch.
1.

13 Changing the labour market (and it should be increasingly less
necessary to make this emphasis in the 1980s) includes changes in
its sexual structure; apart from such major classics as Alice Clark's
Working Life of Women in the Seventeenth Century, there is a
very useful study in Christopher Middleton's 'The Sexual Division
of Labour in Feudal England', *New Left Review* (113–114) 1979.
Vagrancy and vagabondage are considered in Corrigan and Corrigan, 1978, and in the texts by Chambliss, Samaha, Beier, and
Slack (1974) listed in its (and this book's) bibliography. Thompson, 1975; Linebaugh, 1976; and Ditton 1977 raise wider issues;
whilst Stone, 1966 surveys mobility in general.

14 R. Williams has long drawn attention to this connection
between reproduced and performed representations (e.g. his
1978a paper; other essays in the parent collection; edited by
Boyce, especially that by Harris, are very useful). On the press
see Cranfield, 1978; Fox, 1977, 1978, Hendrix, 1976; James, 1978;
Williams, 1978b; Hall, 1978b; for the theatre: Axton, 1977; Williams, 1974. Major studies on popular culture include Burke,
1977, 1978, and Willis, 1977, and the journals *Literature and
History, Theatre Quarterly* and *London Jnl*.

15 Hill pointed out (1956b:47,n.1) that More recognized the revolutionary thrust of Fish. This is typical of Hill's grasp of the
political context of cultural ideas, e.g. his 1972 book and his recent
study of Milton (1977).

16 In his thorough study of the rulers of Elizabethan London,
Foster (1977:7 fn) says that the larger area of 'London' had
c.90,000 population in 1558 with perhaps 250,000 in 1605. Note
his identification of the 'leaders, notables and élite' and the links
between City, Parliament and Crown.

17 I draw here on conversations with Richard Saville but am, of
course, responsible for the words used.

18 Professor Aylmer kindly sent me a photocopy of his text
(1974); his contribution to the supplementary 'Companion' volume of the *Cambridge Modern History* should also be examined.

19 To show the extent of recent work, see the review of 1977

periodical literature in the period 1500–1700 which concerns the fiscal state, *Economic History Review* 32(1) February 1979: 142.

20 In a long and useful communication in January 1979, to P. Corrigan. E. P. Thompson has also pointed to the *Imperial* dimension of English State formation (1977a:139 n.8). Of course, a study of the first and richest of English colonies is very instructive: for Wales, see Gareth Jones, 1977; for India, see Gough, 1978, and Misra, 1960 – the latter's study of the East India Company's State formation needs supplementing by such insights as those of Prothero: 'The big Thames yards were thus essential to the navy, but were also very dependent on it and the East India Company, and so strikingly illustrate the connections between early capitalism and the state.' (1979:47).

21 cf. E. Thompson, 1971; 1977a:146 and recent discussions on Party organization, e.g. Colley, 1977.

22 Corrigan Ph.D. thesis (Ch.1) reviews all this literature, see also Paul Richards' chapter in this volume: major sources are Gretton, 1913; Cohen, 1941; Finer, 1951; Parris, 1968, 1969; a detailed statistical return is available in PP 1828(522)XVI. The *extent* of Excise involvement (and resistance and evasion) is documented for soapmaking 1711–1853 by Gittins, 1977.

23 Apart from material already cited, on Bentham see J. S. Mill, 1838; Coates, 1950; and James 1973. Elie Halévy's study of Philosophic Radicalism is excellent.

24 Peter Linebaugh, *Tyburn: a Study of Crime and the Labouring Poor in London during the First Half of the Eighteenth Century* (Ph.D. Thesis, Warwick University, 1968). cf. Rusche and Kirscheimer,1939.

25 This is, of course, Edward Thompson's story (e.g. his 1963 epic). For recent accounts see Goodwin's *The Friends of Liberty* (1979) and Prothero's *Artisans and politics* (1979).

26 Thompson is clearest on this: 'that State, weak as it was in its bureaucratic and rationalizing functions, was immensely strong and effective as an auxiliary instrument of production in its own right . . . It is this specific combination of weakness and strength which provides the "general illumination" in which all colours of that century are plunged . . .' (1977a:162)

27 cf. D. C. Moore 1965, 1967, 1976, and Brundage 1972, 1974, 1975, 1978. Wrightson (1977) examines earlier changes in social structure and politics.

28 J. R. B. Johnson, *The Education Department 1839–64* (Ph.D. Cambridge 1968, p.509, n). I am most grateful to Richard Johnson for the chance to examine his thesis, and employ this sentence.

3 Pages 49 to 78

1 These labels are meant to indicate *tendencies* within British historiography rather than schools. Hart identified MacDonagh, Lambert, Burn, and Roberts as 'Tories' (Hart, 1965:39–61) but the latter have made no attempt to group the 'Fabians'. Lewis (1952) seems a solid 'Fabian' text whereas Finer (1952) is a more sceptical work. Parris (1969) provides a good survey of the two *tendencies* although he appears to endorse Lewis (292). There can be no doubt that Fabianism owes an intellectual debt to Benthamism as B. Webb herself admitted. (Perkin, 1969:262). But this important subject demands an essay of its own to clarify the labels used here. The very purpose of the 1960s growth of government controversy seems confused. Is the project the *origins* of the Welfare State or how government responded to social evils? What is a Welfare State and a social evil?

2 This present essay has its origins in a Ph.D. thesis (Richards, 1975) although I must thank Dr Richard Johnson of Birmingham University for sound advice in its preparation. The final text is, of course, my own.

3 PRO, *Russell Papers* (2F), Russell to Melbourne, 9 September 1837: 'It is certainly of no use to conceal the difficulty of our situation – I do not at all think, as some do, that the members of the new House of Commons will be more (steady?) to us than the last. On any new question the new House may take a view of its own, and adopt a character of its own, which like the late House it will probably maintain.' This admission of political 'weakness' on the part of the Home Secretary illustrates a crucial shortcoming of academic orthodoxy. Historians of the nineteenth-century State have researched 'government', or the expert/departmental region of the State, and almost ignored its representative/parliamentary region. This is not to play down the significance of nineteenth-

century State Servants whose activities have been explored in a Ph.D. thesis (Corrigan, 1977) which is a strong challenge to 'Tory' and 'Fabian' histories.

4 BM. Add. MSS., 27835, *Place Papers*, f. 67.

5 PRO, *Russell Papers*, (2F), Russell to Melbourne, 13 August 1837.

6 UCL, *Brougham Papers*, 33372, Hume to Brougham, 16 January 1837. This shows a strong reaction to a Whig attempt to assert greater control over their supporters from 'popular' constituencies. Such M.P.s were more or less independent of the formal party system. Local circumstances and the principles of candidates were more vital in elections than allegiance to Peel or Russell while popular constituencies kept a close watch on the parliamentary activities of their representatives. PRO, *Russell Papers*, (4A), Parkes to Russell, 7 May 1841.

7 We are engaged with the politics of class struggle which consists of economic, political and ideological class struggle (Poulantzas, 1968: 75–76) as embodied respectively in the following policy fields: factory/minimum wage legislation; poor law/police and education/public health. The reasons for the latter pairing will become clear. It is recognized that the number of fields could be extended but those taken were central to political class struggle in our period. Information on M.P.s has been taken from C. R. P. Dod's invaluable reference book wherein further biographical details can be obtained. Also useful for the attitudes of M.P.s is Lubenow (1971) although this text does not break through the limitations of the 1960s academic debate.

8 Thomson has no modern biographer but Prouty (1957) and Brown (1958) are useful for filling out the links between the Board of Trade and the Mancunian big bourgeoisie.

9 PP. (1841) X, 'Report of the Handloom Weavers Commission', esp. 402–3.

10 PRO, MH, 32/58, Muggeridge to Nicholls, 25 July 1837.

11 For Roebuck there is a mine of information in Leader (1897), and Hamburger (1965) investigates all the philosophic radicals.

12 *Hansard*, XX, col. 145.

13 Slaney has had no biographer although see Richards (1979). The *Journal* of the M.P. at Shrewsbury Public Library comprises nine volumes and, despite its unevenness, is a valuable record of the life and thought of a member of the landed ruling class.

14 *Hansard*, LI, cols. 1222–34.

15 PP. (1840) XI, 'Report from the Select Committee on the Health of Towns', especially pp. 281–98.

16 When he was elected for Shrewsbury in 1826 Slaney told his father-in-law that he would try to make 'a useful and respectable member and do my duty to the town and neighbourhood'. BUL, *Eyton-Slaney MSS.*, 9/V/I.

17 Significant is Slaney's *Essay on the Beneficial Direction of Rural Expenditure* (1824) which was really a propaganda tract defending industrialism and telling the landowner (and industrial capitalist?) how 'charitable' schemes could make his workers at once more productive and contented. Slaney also burdened the landed ruling class, on account of their wealth and power, with responsibility for the state of society as a whole. And this was, it should be said, often accepted within urban society (F. M. L. Thompson, 1963:276).

18 Slaney was a central figure in the education politics of the late 1830s (Johnson, 1977:98).

19 The *economic* interests of the landed ruling class were, of course, interwoven with those of the industrial bourgeoisie (Aydelotte, 1965:290–305).

20 Fielden deserves more serious study than he has received. Charnley (1960) provides an outline of his political career and Cole (1941) remains useful.

21 PRO, MH. 12/6272, Fielden to the Board of Guardians, Todmorden Union, 2 July 1838.

22 BM. Add. MSS., 40490, *Peel Papers*, fs. 337–8.

23 Just *how* popular and realistic is a peripheral question for this essay but one which needs more research and elaboration. A

fuller discussion is in Richards (1975:97–108). The popular radicals as a whole need more study. Support for the Ten Hours Bill and opposition to the New Poor Law (see *Hansard*, XIX, cols. 913–14 and XXIV, col. 1061) as well as extension of the franchise cemented the party.

24 PRO, *Russell Papers*, (2D) 29 November 1836. The implication that the Whigs and Peelites were simply alternative managers of the central political 'scene' should be treated with caution. But to compare and contrast the two requires an evaluation for which there is no space here.

25 Barker's (1978) criticism of Holloway and Picciotto contains some helpful comments on the making of the modern nation State.

26 PRO, MH. 32/48, Kay to Lewis, 27 October 1835. For Kay the New Poor Law was the basis of 'all plans of social improvement'. Cf. Corrigan, 1977:Chs. 3 and 4.

27 The general unionism of 1834 and the propaganda of the 'Regeneration Society' caused some panic among liberals. Fielden and Owen were involved in plans for a campaign (Foster, 1974:110) whereby all workers were to refuse to work more than eight hours and to force a more equal distribution of wealth. The Bolton M.P., R. Torrens, solicited Brougham's aid to publish lectures on profits and wages to 'rapidly communicate to the people the correct views of the essential principles on which their well-being depends' in order to counter the 'spirit of combination which if unchecked would overthrow the government' (UCL, *Brougham Papers*, 32563, 19 April 1834). But the 'whole duty of government', said Melbourne, 'is to prevent crime and to preserve contracts' (Cecil, 1955:214). At the Home Office (1830–34) Melbourne expressed this 'duty' in the suppression of the Swing labourers and persecution of the Tolpuddle martyrs.

28 This figure was the estimate of the 1834–35 select committee. (E. P. Thompson, 1963:344). The numerous cotton handloom weavers were not only the worst hit by slumps but 'had to serve the bourgeoisie as a handle in meeting attacks upon the factory system' (Engels, 1845a:169).

29 Paisley Public Library, *Paisley Advertiser*, 23 January 1836.

30 *Westminster Review*, XXXVI (1841): 132.

31 This will be argued through in a forthcoming article although it should be noted that trade boards in some Scottish towns did achieve some success. See *Hansard*, XXIII, cols. 370–74. If the Bill had given only slight relief it might have made the difference between 'death and survival' (E. P. Thompson, 1963:333–4).

32 Oldham Public Library, *Fielden Letters*, Fielden to Knott, 16 June 1834.

33 PP. (1835) XIII, 'Report of the Select Committee on the Petitions presented by the Hand-Loom Weavers', esp. pp. 3–15.

34 For the parliamentary attack on the Bill see *Hansard*, XXIX, cols. 1160–83. Thomson described the Bill as 'an act of tyranny' and called on M.P.s finally to reject all such measures.

35 The Tillys (1975:275:76) make some interesting comments on the early 1830s in Britain: 'they marked the transition from predominantly reactive to predominantly proactive popular movements; after that point, the food riot, the tax rebellion, machine-breaking, and kindred actions faded fast away. From the 1830s on, petitions, demonstrations, strikes, mass meetings, special-purpose associations predominated in British collective action. Essentially the same transition occurred in France and Germany two or three decades later.'

36 UCL., *Chadwick Papers*, Russell to Chadwick, 9 September 1836. The Poor Law Commission secretary was told that 'in the improvement of our institutions . . . we must beware not to lose the co-operation of the country. . . some faults must be indulged for the sake of carrying improvement in the mass.'

37 PRO, *Russell Papers* (4A), Normanby to Russell, 14 June 1841. This and other Whig communications demonstrate the unpopularity of Chadwick, the man most associated with aggressive liberalism, who clashed with Normanby as well as his superiors at the Poor Law Commission (Finer, 1952:210–12).

38 Shrewsbury Public Library, *Slaney Journals*, vols. 6 and 7 substantiate all this. The Shrewsbury M.P. attended meetings of the statistical societies and the British Association in most of the major industrial towns where the 'statistics' had been gathered.

39 *On the Employment of Children, in Factories and Other Works in the U.K., and some Foreign Countries* (1840), p. 16.

40 UCL, *Brougham Papers*, 25058, 8 August 1840.

41 This is confirmed by the membership of what is usually known as the public health movement (Finer, 1952:238) and the overlapping group involved in the extension and promotion of factory legislation. Horner thought it 'a happy thing to bring men of different politics together, to unite in such a work of humanity and justice, and sound policy' (Lyell, 1890:18). Corrigan (1977:ch.3) shows at length that Horner's views were shared by apparently different State Servants and the liberal philanthropist M.P.s did much to persuade the Manchester liberals that their 'individualism' of the 1830s now had to be abandoned in favour of collective ruling class action.

42 Gramsci's concept of hegemony has sparked much controversy within marxist circles which cannot be joined here. Two useful articles are Hall, Lumley, McLennan (1977:45–73) and Anderson (1977:5–78). We should note, however, that the hegemonic class or fraction is not always the class or fraction in charge of the state: 'This was so in Britain after 1832, where the landed aristocracy occupied the political scene and provided the top bureaucratic – military personnel, whereas the bourgeoisie held hegemony' (Poulantzas, 1968:250).

43 G. P. Scrope, *Principles of Political Economy* (1833), p. 7. The title of this tract emphasizes its propaganda character. Scrope was the brother of C. P. Thomson of the Board of Trade.

44 Although the Conservatives had attacked the 1839 education plan proposed by the Whigs, the Peelites, once in office, were convinced that the new Education Department ought to expand its funds and powers. Lansdowne had assured Dr Kay, the Department's Secretary, of Peel's intentions: 'I know that it is P's desire to conciliate on this and some other points, on which he can do so without breaking with any of the interests on which he relies for support, and I have little doubt that he will now take the system under his protection.' MUL, *Kay-Shuttleworth Papers*, 10 September 1841.

45 The Anti-Corn Law League had not been a broad-based middle-class movement even in Manchester itself (Fraser, 1976:203).

46 In the general interpretation of the period I acknowledge the influence of a review of Foster (1974) which needs a wider audience (Jones, 1975:35–69).

4 Pages 79 to 109
1 Bob Jessop, in his analysis of political class struggle and its relation to the state, does refer to the importance of 'other political forces besides wage-labour and capital' (1977:12). Poulantzas, in a similar context, insists that 'relations of power do not exhaust class relations . . . and this is so most notably in the case of relations between men and women' (1978:43). However, in neither case is the importance of these other power relations and struggles specified or investigated.

2 We are aware that, theoretically, the term 'patriarchy' or 'patriarchal relations' remains problematic. As Mark Cousins points out, 'the concept can imply a teleological unfolding over time of the effects of a 'first cause' of women's oppression – whether that cause is located in women's reproductive functions, violence, or the incest taboo' (Cousins, 1978:64). Our use of the term 'patriarchal relations' attempts descriptively to locate the way in which the category 'women' is constructed in a subordinate power relation within particular practices and apparatuses of the State; it does not imply a more general theory of 'patriarchy'.

3 A distinction should be made between classic 'logic of capital' accounts of the State, which are exclusively *class* analyses (e.g. Holloway and Piccioto, 1978), and the way in which a logic of capital approach has informed feminist debates on the state (e.g. Political Economy of Women Group, 1975; Wilson, 1977; Bland, McCabe, and Mort, 1978).

4 The *Contagious Diseases Acts* of 1864, 1866 and 1869 gave to the police in certain garrison towns special powers to arrest a woman suspected of being a common prostitute, and detain her for medical treatment. For an account of Josephine Butler's campaign in the 1860s and 1870s for the repeal of the acts see Nield (1973) and Sigsworth and Wyke (1973).

5 Karl Renner refers to the 'bourgeois fiction' of the separation of public and private (Renner, 1949:115).

6 The system of primogeniture was attacked by the Chamberlainite radicals in the 1880s and by the Liberals in 1909 and 1914 (Harding 1966:374).

7 Under the common law system of coverture, property rested in the hands of the father or husband. Both testate succession (the will of the father) and intestate succession (where no will was made) favoured sons, the eldest in particular, leaving daughters in a position of relative dependence. After coverture was abolished in 1882 intestate succession was less likely to discriminate in favour of sons, though testate succession was characterized by discrimination as before. The increasing freedom of testation also gave the husband the right to disinherit the wife: his control over her chastity was absolute. Our thanks are due to Albie Sachs for these details (personal communication 25 May 1978).

8 As Renner points out: 'Ownership taken by itself is incapable of serving the organization of modern industry. It can only do so with a number of satellite or complementary institutions: company law, the contract of sale and the contract of employment. A single economic process, sometimes corresponds to a whole group of legal categories' (Renner, 1949:5).

9 Settlements were replete with such clauses as the 'restraint on anticipation' clause, which prevented a wife from disposing of her own property.

10 For a more detailed account see Holcombe (1977:19).

11 They gave as an example of the reform of common law 'working well' the case of New York, where women had enjoyed absolute control over their property since 1848, and over their earnings since 1860, with no ill effects on marital relations (*Report of the Select Committee on Married Women's Property 1867–68*:83).

12 Obviously, that is not to imply that all nineteenth century feminist politics were middle-class in character. The struggles of women at work and in the Trade Union Movement in the late 1880s and the 1890s are significant examples of working-class feminism during the period.

13 The classic expression of that ideology of complementarity and equality through difference is to be found in the *Beveridge Report on Social Insurance and Allied Services* (1942; cf. Bland *et al.*, 1978).

14 Veronica Beechey (1977) discusses this in detail.

15 For an account of divorce procedure prior to 1857 see Finer and McGregor, (1971:91–96). Between 1551 and 1856 a total of 317 Parliamentary Divorce Acts were passed.

16 The 1909 *Royal Commission on Divorce and Matrimonial Causes* was explicitly appointed: 'to inquire into the present state of the law . . . in divorce and matrimonial causes and applications for separation orders, especially with regard to the position of the poorer classes'. The Majority Report of 1912 recommended amendments to the existing divorce law, to secure 'the equal treatment of men and women in regard to the grounds on which divorce could be attained'. and also recommended 'a simplification and decentralization of procedure . . . so that none should be excluded from relief by poverty' (McGregor, 1957:27). The Commission's recommendations were enacted through the two *Matrimonial Causes Acts* of 1923 and 1937, which are consolidated in the Act of 1950.

17 Lord Hardwicke's Marriage Act of 1753 specified that henceforward marriages were to be celebrated and registered only in Anglican Churches or chapels, after the proper publication of banns and the production of a licence. The two acts of 1836 (*An Act for Marriage in England,* and *An Act for Registering Births, Deaths and Marriages*) established a central Register Office, with local registrars throughout the country who had the power to celebrate marriage by a civil ceremony. The position of the Established Church remained as before, but the act now gave nonconformist places of worship the licence to conduct marriages.

18 However, individualist ideologies of romance do not normally inflect accounts of *marital* relations in the fiction of the period. Romance is usually seen to occur outside the structures of marriage, often as the preparation and prelude to it (e.g. Charlotte Brontë's *Jane Eyre* and Mrs Gaskell's *North and South*).

19 It is not until the 'permissive' legislation of the 1950s and 60s,

addressing such practices as divorce, abortion, homosexuality, family planning, that ideologies of individual, private 'consent' between contracting parties (as opposed to public moral sanction) come to structure the regulation of sexual and moral practices (see Hall, 1978a).

20 Debates around the repeal of the *Contagious Diseases Act* in the 1860s and 1870s frequently focused on the relative merits and dangers of state intervention in the sphere of sexuality. The argument surfaced extensively in the various government reports and commissions on venereal disease and prostitution in the period. For example: 'Prostitution may be said to be tolerated by the law, because it is not an offence; but toleration is a negative quality, and the bound of toleration is overstepped when the law interferes to place prostitutes under regulation with the avowed object of protecting those with them from the dangerous consequences to which illicit commerce is liable. Thus, it is said, prostitution is indirectly if not directly recognized as a necessity . . . It is difficult . . . to escape from the inference that the State, in making provision for alleviating its evils has assumed that prostitution is a necessity.' (*Report of the Committee Appointed into the Pathology and Treatment of Venereal Disease*, 1868, reprinted in *British Parliamentary Papers*, Irish University Press, 1963).

21 The 1826 amendment removed the need to prove 'emission of seed' and penetration for prosecutions, and re-enacted the death penalty for sodomy (Weeks, 1977:13).

22 See Montgomery-Hyde (1970) and Weeks (1977) for discussion of the Labouchère Amendment.

23 Slightly later, Freudian psychoanalysis can be seen to categorize sexual perversion in a similar way; though perhaps with less of an explicit moralism. See, for example, Freud's *Three Essays on the Theory of Sexuality*, 1905.

24 See, for example, the Reports of the Committees of 1864, 1868 and 1869.

25 The *Wolfenden Report* (1957) on homosexuality and prostitution forms the most significant example of the strategy of categorization and individualization. The Report contains detailed discussion of the aetiology of both homosexuality and prostitution,

and recommends that various 'extra-legal disciplines' should be used to regulate the homosexual subject (e.g. sociology, orthodox medicine, psychology).

26 At particular points in *La Volonté du savoir* Foucault does indicate that discourses around the family, sexuality and procreation are crossed by determinations from other practices (e.g. the reference to the inter-relation of racist and familial discourses, p. 37). However, those relations are never explored in depth in the analysis.

27 See Hindess (1977) and, for an explicitly feminist use of the same problematic, Coward (1978).

5   pages 111–141

1 As Natalie Davis put in an important theoretical Introduction to her *Society and Culture in Early Modern France*: 'It (research) was also a matter of recognizing that forms of associational life and collective behaviour are cultural artefacts, not just items in the history of the Reformation or of political centralization. A journeyman's initiation rite, a village festive organization, an informal gathering of women for a lying-in or of men and women for storytelling, or a street disturbance could be 'read' as fruitfully as a diary, a political tract, a sermon, or a body of laws.'

2 Against 'the selfish misconception that induces you (the bourgeoisie) to transform into eternal laws of nature and of reason the social forms springing from your present mode of production and form of property – historical relations that rise and disappear in the progress of production – this misconception you share with every ruling class that has preceded you.' (Marx and Engels, 1848: 83).

3 'Let us uproot this habit of thinking of individuals according to certain artificial so-called 'classes'. Nothing is more unjust and nothing could be more dangerous,' Lord Leverhulme (W. H. Lever), *The Six Hour Day and Other Industrial Questions* (1918: 294).

4 Such as the atomized, mechanized world of E. M. Forster's frightening story 'The Machine Stops' (1909), or the better-known, drugged world of Aldous Huxley's *Brave New World* (1932).

5 The quotations in this paragraph are all from *Capital*, I, Ch. 15, section 9, 'The Health and Education Clauses of the Factory Acts', (1867b).

6 See, for example, the excellent article by Gareth Stedman Jones, 'Engels and the Genesis of Marxism', in *New Left Review*, 106, (Nov.–Dec. 1977), particularly pp. 85 and 102–3. 'Theoretical ability, even when possessed in as exceptional a degree as in Marx, is a necessary but not sufficient condition of a theoretical revolution: especially in the social domain. For such revolutions to occur, disturbing phenomena are also necessary, which not only point to the inadequacy of the existing theoretical problematic, but are suggestive of the raw components of a new theoretical structure. It was Engels in his writings of 1844 and 1845 who provided these decisive new components.' 'The importance of Engels' contribution derived less from his moments of theoretical originality than from his ability to transmit elements of thinking and practice developed within the working-class movement itself in a form in which it could become an intrinsic part of the architecture of the new theory.' 'It was the process itself rather than the intervention of the philosopher which had awakened workers to a consciousness of the class position, and which he hoped would lead to the emergence of a "proletarian socialism".'

7 See also the section in the *Grundrisse* (Marx, 1858: 704–706) on the 'contradiction between the foundation of bourgeois production . . . and its development.' These pages consider 'to what degree the powers of social production have been produced, not only in the form of knowledge, but also as immediate organs of social practice, of the real life process.' 'Forces of production and social relations – two different sides of the development of the social individual – appear to capital [and to many modern Marxists, S.Y.] as mere means, and are merely means for it to produce on its limited foundation. In fact, however, they are the material conditions to blow this foundation sky-high.' I was led to these pages by Corrigan and Sayer 1975: 18.

8 For the honourable history of such forms, see T. M. Parssinen, 'Association, Convention and Anti-Parliament in British Radical Politics, 1771–1848', in *English Historical Review*, 88, (July 1973) pp. 504–33; and for O'Connor's defence of one of them (the 1839

Chartist Convention) see *Northern Star* 22 June 1839, p. 8: 'To the existence of that Convention, you are to attribute the difference between our present revolution and any revolution which has hitherto taken place among nations. (Cheers). Look to the several French revolutions. They failed of producing the promised result because men attacked abuses, and fought for a shadow, without being prepared with a substitute. (Cheers). Your case is now different for, upon an emergency, you have a Parliament which would act, and one whose orders you would obey or to appoint *instanter* another, whose orders you could more cheerfully obey. (Loud cheers). Herein then lies all the difference: you cannot move without the consent of all. You cannot move partially, because you are one link in the great chain. (Cheers). There is an end to sectional agitation; you are each answerable to the other for the manner in which you shall handle this cause. (Cheers).' Quoted in J. A. Epstein, 'Feargus O'Connor and the English Working-class Radical Movement, 1832–1841: a Study in National Chartist Leadership', unpublished Ph.D. (Birmingham, 1977).

9 So that the third of the Provisional Rules of the International, drafted by Marx, read: 'That the economical emancipation of the working-classes is therefore the great end to which every political movement ought to be subordinate as a means.'

10 See Marx, 'The Association for Administrative Reform (People's Charter)' (1855) for a comparison of the implications of universal suffrage in Britain and in France, made necessary because 'the continentals are prone to under-rate the importance and meaning of the English Charter.' Marx's point underlines that of Feargus O'Connor in note 8 above. Whereas in France, owing to historical development and social structure, suffrage reform was a mere political question, in Britain it had become a social one: since 1842 'there has no longer been any doubt as to the meaning of universal' suffrage. Nor as to its name. It is the *Charter* of the classes of the people and implies the assumption of political power as a means of meeting their social requirements. That is why universal suffrage, a watchword of universal fraternization in the France of 1848, is taken as a war slogan in England. There the immediate content of the revolution is universal suffrage, here

the immediate content of universal suffrage is the revolution.' In Marx–Engels, *Articles on Britain*, (Moscow, 1975: 234).

11 'Educated' in the sense of what Marx calls Hegel's 'very heretical views on the division of labour.' In his *Philosophy of Right* he says: 'By educated men we may *prima facie* understand those who . . . can do what others do' (Marx, 1867b: 485 n. 51). As large-scale industry develops, the proportion of such people, for capital (but potentially also for labour), presumably increases greatly.

12 'The mind which believes only in its own magic strength will disappear. For the revolutionary struggle is not fought between capitalism and mind. It is fought between capitalism and the proletariat.' Walter Benjamin, *Understanding Brecht* (1973; 103).

13 Philip Corrigan's clarity in his thesis (1977: 378) helps here: 'Just as Marx was able to refer to a "political economy of Labour" which was different from that of Capital, so we can point to different moral relations. The dominant moral order works – i.e. is in being – because it is based upon a material order (that is a world) *held one way up* by historically specific relations of production and State apparatuses formed for their maintenance. In experiencing that moral order, the working classes also experience the power and force which holds the world one way up. *Their experience of the State is therefore quite analytically separable from their role performance which sustains that order without internalizing it* [my emphasis, S.Y.]. For this reason apart from the tensions and structural crises of the world-wide mode of capitalist production – the State apparatuses of modern Britain are constantly engaged (flexibly and subtly) in reproducing and enforcing *a* moral order. These investigation have shown how that order was both a selection from available alternatives (moral economy, social economy) and acted to suppress or marginalize other images of social life.'

14 Two essays in E. J. Hobsbawm's *Revolutionaries* (1973) pose this question of interpreting the second half of the nineteenth century in Britain very sharply: 'Lenin and the "Aristocracy of Labour" ', 121–29; and particularly, 'Karl Marx and the British Labour Movement', 95–108. In the latter, Hobsbawm suggests a revolutionary (Chartist etc.) phase for British labour, followed by

the 'phase of modest reformism which succeeded it in the 1850s, 1860s and 1870s' during which 'it became clear (to Marx-Engels) that they could no longer expect very much from the British labour movement.' Hobsbawm can see that 'looking at the mid-Victorian decade with the wisdom of hindsight, we can observe that the retreat concealed elements of a new advance', but for him that advance consisted of anticipation of the continuous *organization* of the socialist/trade union revival of the 1880s onwards as opposed to the earlier 'succession of waves of militancy'.

Hobsbawm's judgement of the second phase is clear: and it can stand as representative of a whole school of labour history – not just marxist – and not yet spent: 'It (the British labour movement) still led the world in a special form of organization, namely trade unionism and probably also in the narrower form of class consciousness which simply consists in recognizing the working class as a separate class, whose members have different (but not necessarily opposed) interests to other classes. However, it had abandoned the effort and perhaps even the hope of overthrowing capitalism, and accepted not only the existence of this system, seeking merely to improve the condition of its members within it, but also, and increasingly, it accepted with certain specific exceptions – the bourgeois-liberal theories about how much improvement could be achieved. It was no longer revolutionary, and socialism virtually disappeared from it.' Marx, he argues, 'recognized the adaptation of the labour movement to the bourgeois system; but he regarded it as a historical phase, and indeed, as we know, it was a temporary phase. A socialist labour movement in Britain had disappeared; but it was to reappear'.

It is towards qualifying and enriching such partly-true judgments that the second half of my chapter here is directed. Hobsbawm goes on to argue that this reformist phase for British labour, while increasingly disappointing for Marx-Engels, did not lead Marx into Fabianism/revisionism. 'They may have led him to become pessimistic about the short-term prospects of the working class movement in western Europe, especially after 1871. But *they neither led him to abandon the belief that the emancipation of the human race was possible nor that it would be based on the movement of the proletariat* (my italics). He was and continued to be a revolutionary socialist.' The question which now needs putting is: if the italicized sentence above constitutes qualification for being revolutionary, don't many 'reformist' working people, co-operators and others, during this second phase, also qualify, along with Marx?

15 J. T. W. Mitchell (1828–95): 'the most remarkable personality that the British Co-operative Movement has thrown up', (according to Beatrice Webb, *My Apprenticeship* (Pelican, 1938: 406, n.I). Bastard son of a beerhouse and lodgings keeper, he worked as a piecer in a cotton-mill from ten years old, stayed in the textile industry, until he was forty-five, then worked for the Co-op. movement. Re-elected chairman of C.W.S. from 1874–95, quarter by quarter. 'Throughout these twenty-one years of complete absorption in building up the most varied if not the largest business enterprise in the world at that time, Mitchell lived on the minute fees, never exceeding £150 a year, that this vast enterprise then allowed its Chairman, in a small lodging at Rochdale, his total estate on death amounting to the magnificent sum of £350 17s 8d.' See also Percy Redfern, *John T. W. Mitchell* (1923); and *Dictionary of Labour Biography* I, (1972: 241–42).

16 The best work on Friendly Societies is that of P.H.J.H. Gosden *The Friendly Societies in England 1815–1875* (Manchester, 1961) and *Self-Help, Voluntary Associations in Nineteenth-Century Britain* (1973); see also Barry Supple, 'Legislation and Virtue: An Essay on Working Class Self-Help and the State in the Early Nineteenth Century' in *Historical Perspectives: Studies in English Thought and Society in Honour of J. H. Plumb* (1974), and Geoffrey Crossick, *'An Artisan Elite in Victorian Society Kentish London 1840–1880'* (1978: Ch. 9, 174–198).

17 For concern, as late as 1928, about changes in the format of Congresses of the T.U.C. such as introducing the rostrum instead of speaking from the floor, see W. Citrine, *Men and Work* (1964: 248–49). For a typically 'smart', modern dismissive, cynical tone about Congresses see Peter Jenkins' 'Annual Ritual of Democracy', *Guardian* 5 September 1967.

18 For tensions within the Reading Co-op., for example, between the editor of the *Reading Co-operative Record* (Esrom) and the Trade sub-Committee, over the ideological/political education of

the adverts in the *Record*, see Stephen Yeo, *Religion and Voluntary Organization in Crisis* (1976: 283–9).

19 See E. J. Cleary, *The Building Society Movement* (1965), particularly Ch. 6 'Starr-Bowkett Buildings Societies', pp. 101–115; and Stephen Yeo, 'Class Struggle and Associational Form: a Way of Seeing Co-operation and Other Working-Class Forms, Particularly during the Late-Nineteenth and Early-Twentieth Centuries', Xeroxed paper, September 1977, available from author.

20 This situation and the specific choices faced and made by associations of many kinds within it – religious, leisure, welfare, educational and political – between 1890 and 1914 is a major theme of my *Religion and Voluntary Organization in Crisis* (1976).

21 Faced by deficit in 1911, the Reading W. E. A. appealed to branches in other towns to raise a 1d. tax on members to save 'the pioneer branch': they were unusually self-conscious about vice-presidential domination and its subordinating tendencies. Gradually, however, they lost autonomy – see Yeo, 1976: 235-241. For the Statist background to the W.E.A. becoming a Responsible Body in 1924 (as opposed to the W.E.A. reasons) see R. Challinor, *The Origins of British Bolshevism* (1977: 261).

22 Rich material for making up one's mind on these questions is in Geoffrey Crossick's 'Social Structure and Working-Class Behaviour', D. Phil. (London, 1976); and his *An Artisan Élite in Victorian Society: Kentish London 1840–1880* (1978). He produces fascinating evidence, such as that 12% of Royal Arsenal Co-operative Society members were unskilled or semi-skilled in the period 1872–80, and that (1978: 196): 'It was a central tenet of friendly society exclusiveness that this independence and this capacity for self-government must theoretically be attainable by all'; and that (1976: 182) 'It is clear from both the national and the local evidence that the élitist position of the aristocracy of labour rested upon earnings differentials and relative job security.' But, with a lot of careful argument and qualification, he would probably disagree with my sentences here.

23 Yeo, 1976: 286, and Board of Trade Labour Department, *Report of Workmen's Co-operative Societies in the U.K.*, Cd. 698

(1901: xviii-xix), for examples of Co-operators discussing the problem of moving beyond their better-paid base.

24 The analogy is with manufacture and machine production or 'large-scale industry' in *Capital*, I, 504: 'Manufacture produced the machinery with which large-scale industry abolished the handicraft and manufacturing systems in the spheres of production it first seized hold of. The system of machine production therefore grew spontaneously on a material basis which was inadequate to it. When the system had attained a certain degree of development, it had to overthrow this ready-made foundation, which had meanwhile undergone further development in its old form, and create for itself a new basis appropriate to its own mode of production'. (1867b) See also Gramsci's view that what makes intellectuals/ philosophy 'organic' and what makes ideas into material forces, and what unites theory and practice, are adequate-for-labour parties or movements or, in the language of my chapter here, associational forms. Parties or 'the party' are/will be more or less adequate-for-labour forms of 'political', and other, production: *Prison Notebooks* (1934: 330–31) and elsewhere.

25 Just as it is 'quite possible that socialism will remain a sect till the very eve of the last stroke that completes the Revolution, after which it will melt into the new society,' William Morris, *Commonweal*, 3 July 1886. I owe this reference to Ian Bullock.

26 See Bentley Gilbert, 'The British National Insurance Act of 1911 and the Commercial Insurance Lobby', in *Journal of British Studies*, IV (1965: 127–48); W. J. Braithwaite, *Lloyd George's Ambulance Wagon* (1957); Stephen Yeo (1978), 'Working-Class Association, Private Capital, Welfare and the State in the Late-Nineteenth and Early-Twentieth Centuries'. in Noel Parry, Michael Rustin and Carole Satyamurti, *Social Work and the State* (1979).

27 Neil Killingback of the Graduate School (Politics), University of Sussex, is doing doctoral work which includes the details and politics of this story.

28 See Karl Liebknecht's reaction to 'politics as the art of the possible'. 'The extreme limit of the possible can only be attained by grasping for the impossible. The realized possibility is the

resultant of the impossibilities which have been striven for. Willing what is objectively impossible does not, therefore, signify sense-less fantasy-spinning and self-delusion, but practical politics in the deepest sense. To demonstrate the impossibility of realizing a political goal is not to show its senselessness. All it shows, at most, is the critic's lack of insight into society's laws of motion, particularly the laws that govern the formation of the social will. What is the true and strongest policy? It is the art of the imposs-ible,' quoted in Rudolph Bahro, 'The Alternative in Eastern Europe', in *New Left Review*, 106 (Nov.–Dec. 1977: 31).

29 'Socialism does not claim to speak the truths of an abstract society: it portrays the relational understanding of social forma-tions from a particular, materialist and thoroughly experiential basis. The material base of socialism is simultaneously its moral base: how direct producers are, and the thousands of struggles involved in understanding what it is to be a direct producer under the dictatorship of the bourgeosie,' (Corrigan and Sayer, 1975: 21–22). Or, for an older, late Owenite view: 'Instead of wasting time, energy and money on palliatives, which under existing con-ditions will be palliatives to some only, whilst they are bound to be aggravatives to others – all reformers, and especially all social-ists, ought to unite their efforts to establish the new society side by side with present institutions, so that the superiority of the new may show the inferiority of the old, and that will be the best way to get rid of it. . . The new society must be established . . . by its evident superiority over the old. I can see no way to replace individualism and competition, except by showing in actual ever-yday life, the great superiority of organized co-operation in labour for the common good, and a community of interest in the results,' R. J. Derfel, *An Unauthorized Programme* . . . (Manchester, 1895).

30 Stephen Yeo, 'Some Problems in Realizing a General Work-ing-Class Strategy in Twentieth-Century Britain', duplicated paper presented to the British Sociological Association annual confer-ence, 1977. The distinction between 'abolition' of contradictions and finding forms 'within which they have room to move' is based on *Capital*, I, 198. 'We saw in a former chapter that the exchange of commodities implies contradictory and mutually exclusive con-ditions. The further development of the commodity does not abol-

ish these contradictions, but rather provides the form within which they have room to move. This is, in general, the way in which real contradictions are resolved. For instance, it is a contradiction to depict one body as constantly falling towards another and at the same time constantly flying from it. The ellipse is a form of motion within which this contradiction is both realized and resolved.' (1867b).

6 Pages 143–170

1 As Winston Churchill noted in contrast: 'The American labourer is a stronger, larger, healthier, better fed and consequently more efficient animal than a large proportion of our population' (Cited in Bruce, 1973: 128).

2 This, for example, contrasted again with the case of America where, despite the development of local and national State legislation (on which see Weinstein, 1969), 'company welfare' schemes were and remain of vital importance (cf. Brandes, 1970).

3 This is not to argue that certain employers in Britain failed to recognize the need for and develop their own welfare schemes (cf. Cadbury). Similarly, the development of State legislation has owed much to the 'private' initiatives of reform groups who in recognizing, investigating, and proposing solutions for potential social problems, have often undertaken the groundwork on which the State builds (cf. Kirkman Gray, 1908).

4 Helen Bosanquet's book, *The Family* although published in 1906 and much neglected today, remains one of the most concise and succint statements regarding the centrality of the family in capitalist society. Bosanquet, a leading member of the Charity Organization Society, and with her husband, the Idealist philosopher Bernard Bosanquet, a leading theorist of the C.O.S. – her importance in the social policy field at the time being reflected in her membership of the Royal Commission on the Poor Laws (1905–9) – was clearly aware of the importance of the family as the most suitable means for the moral and material reproduction of labour and its general power as regulatory force on the working class: 'The home is the centre, both in the material and the moral sense, from which he starts each day afresh, and to which each day takes him back at night' (H. Bosanquet, 1906: 204). And: 'It

seems clear than, that this grouping together of individuals into economic units comprising both the weak and the strong elements [the family] would be in itself, if it were nothing more, a most successful device for maximizing the economic efficiency of the people. There are other conceivable methods of providing for the weaker members of the community, but none which call out the best qualities of the average man and woman to the same extent' (ibid: 224).

The recent emphasis on 'community care' and 'neighbourliness' is in the main an attempt to shift and keep the burden of ill health and old age on the family rather than on expensive State institutions such as hospitals and old people's homes. We have a clear statement of this in the Younghusband Report on health und welfare services: 'There is also clearer understanding of maintaining the elderly and the mentally and physically handicapped in the community wherever practicable . . . The services are now more consciously planned and administered so as to help the family care for its own member. It has been put to us that the new emphasis on preventive and domiciliary care is sound economy as well as sound social policy, and that it is certain to prove less costly than the alternatives of admission to residential care' (1959: para 551).

5 Nor, like much else in social policy, is the recent call for the extension of 'political education' in schools of any novel significance. As Kay-Shuttleworth put it: 'A little knowledge is inevitable, and it is proverbially a dangerous thing. Alarming disturbances of social order generally commence with *a people only partially instructed*. The preservation of *internal peace* not less than the improvement of our national institutions, depends on the education of the working classes . . . Unacquainted with the real sources of their own distress . . . the people have too frequently neglected the constitutional expedients by which redress ought only to have been sought, and have brought obloquy on their just cause by the blind ferocity of those insurrectionary movements in which they have assaulted the institutions of society. That good government may be stable, the people must be so instructed that they may love that *which they know to be right* . . . The ascertained truths of political science should be early taught to the labouring classes, and *correct* political information should be constantly and industriously disseminated amongst

them.' (1832: 95–7, his emphases; cf. Corrigan, 1977: Ch. 3 where this is shown to be a *general* perspective of several 'States-men').

6 As early as 1895 the Charity Organization Society through its monthly magazine was informing its members and workers that 'discourtesy, harshness and dryness are never more deprecated than dealing with the poor. Brusque words frighten the timid . . . they discompose the nervous and put out the dull and slow' (*C.O.R.* 1895: 144). In other words, if the strategy is intended to persuade people to change their attitudes, their way of life and attendant values, then one's approach is of crucial importance. As the United Nations Report on social work training indicated, if clients have some 'motivation to change this is enhanced if they are respected, understood and believed in. They do not change through being exhorted to behave differently or told what they ought to do, unless they have a strong emotional bond with those who make these demands' (1958: 198); '. . . the great bulk of social work practice has internal change as its goal. Here we find that imposing, telling, or giving orders do not work well. Only as the client is thoroughly involved and comes to accept on deepening levels the process of change can our methods be effective in relation to our goals' (Bernstein, 1960:8).
Strangely enough social work seems to be ignorant of the work of the other Bernstein who discovered in the school context that working-class kids find it difficult to comprehend middle-class teachers. The little research done on social work clients would suggest that most find their social workers incomprehensible.

7 In Hannington's valuable and stirring accounts of the activities of the National Unemployed Workers' Movement we have innumerable examples where mass demonstrations won immediate concessions. It is worth noting, however, that in the past the bourgeoisie has as a class often responded more rapidly than the State to working-class agitation and disturbance. This was especially the case in the East End of London at the end of the nineteenth century where literally hundreds of small charitable groups flourished and emerged as trade depressions swept through the vast pools of casual labour. One notable example was in 1886 when after a riot by the unemployed and destitute had swept through St. James' damaging the much-hallowed property of the

clubs, 'carriages' of money arrived at the Mansion House for the Lord Mayor's relief fund (see Stedman Jones, 1971).

8 It has long been recognized that one of the great potential dangers of sectionalized or partial working-class agitation is that it could expand to include other groups and become a more generalized agitation against the social system. This is especially the case when the disturbances are focused around poverty and unemployment, and can easily spill over into criticisms of profits, wages, overtime, investment and so forth. The emergence of a tangible socialist dimension to many of the workers' criticisms about the character of the Poor Law and unemployment at the turn of the last century was certainly a crucial factor in stimulating State action for here was a clear case of a potentially major threat to ongoing stability. As one contemporary recognized: 'Not that it can be said that there is anything novel or unusual in the fact that many working men and women are laid idle through want of work. This has at all times been a regular occurrence, and it is only now when the socialist unrest by which we are surrounded becomes accentuated that attempts are made to find 'cures' whereby the cloud of unemployment which lowers darkly over many a workman's home can be dispelled' (Hutchinson, 1908: 331).

In that particular context the British ruling class were not slow in grasping the lessons to be learnt from Bismarck's Germany where a package of social reform measures had been ennacted, both as a strategy to improve the quality of labour and to deal a decisive blow against German socialism. As Spender noted in 1909: 'It is not enough for the social thinker in this country to meet the socialist with a negative. The English progressive will be wise if, in this at any rate, he takes a leaf from the book of Bismarck who dealt the heaviest blow against German socialism not by his laws of oppression . . . but by that great system of State insurance which now safeguards the German workman at almost every point of his industrial career' (cited in Gilbert, 1966: 257).

9 Llewellyn Smith who as Permanent Secretary of the Board of Trade was a key figure in the framing of the National Insurance Act 1911, clearly outlined the differential intent of the Act with respect to the various categories of labour: 'The crucial question from a practical point of view is, therefore, whether it is possible

to devise a scheme of insurance which, while nominally covering unemployment due to all causes other than those which can be definitely excluded, shall automatically discriminate between the classes of unemployment . . . Armed with this double weapon of a maximum limit to benefit and of a minimum contribution, the operation of the scheme itself will automatically exclude the loafer . . . The scheme must aim at encouraging the regular employer and workman, and discriminating against casual employments . . . the rules relating to benefit being so devised as to discriminate effectively against unemployment which is due to personal defects while giving a substantial allowance to those whose unemployment results from industrial causes beyond the control of the individual' (cited in Beveridge, 1939: 265–66).

10 As early as 1908, Ramsay MacDonald had asserted while electioneering for the Labour Party that they would 'never willingly touch a slum population, or one that has shown no signs of intelligent initiative like trade-unionism and co-operation' (1908: 343).

11 We gain some indication of this loss of working-class control from the records of the Crook Co-operative Society which was by no means a revolutionary organization but nevertheless recognized the implications of the 1902 Education Act which abolished School Boards: 'The May Quarterly Meeting was notable for the following motion being carried unanimously: "That we, as a Society, protest against the taxes imposed by the Government upon the working class; and, also, we protest against the Education measure, as a retrograde step in the abolition of School Boards, and in which the working classes are denied of popular control and their rights ignored" ' (Lloyd, 1916: 194).
It should be noted that the denial of popular control has generally proceeded along two related fronts: one being the actual structural closure of working-class participation or working-class institutions, and the other being through the proclamations of expertise. In the latter instance, an area or sphere of social life is proclaimed to require the control of experts and that those without appropriate training, education, certificates or diplomas, are not qualified to judge on the issues concerned. In this way vast areas have been removed from public and political discourse and challenge to the sphere of full-time State officials and satellite professionals. Such closure procedures are further assisted by the development of

specialist vocabularies usually draped with scientific gloss which enhances their supposedly expert and neutral status.

BIBLIOGRAPHY

Note: Unless otherwise indicated place of publication is London. Abbreviations: U = University; P = Press; NLR = New Left Review:

P Abrams:
1968: *The Origins of British Sociology, 1834–1914*, Chicago UP.
1972a: 'The Sense of the Past and the Origins of Sociology', *Past and Present*, (55).
1972b: *Being and Becoming in Sociology*, Inaugural lecture, Durham City, The University.
1978: (ed.) *Work, Urbanism and Inequality*, Weidenfeld.
P. Alden: (1905) *The Unemployed: a National Question*, P. S. King.
P. Anderson:
1963: 'Origins of the Present Crisis', *NLR*, (23); reprinted in *Towards Socialism*, Fontana, 1965.
1968: 'Components of a National Culture', *NLR*, (50).
1973: *Passages from Antiquity to Feudalism*, NL Books, 1974.
1974: *Lineages of the Absolutist State*, NL Books.
1977: 'The Antimonies of Antonio Gramsci', *NLR*, (100).

205

P. Ariès: (1973) *Centuries of Childhood*, Penguin.
L. A. Atherley-Jones: (1893) 'Liberalism and Social Reform: a Warning', *The New Review*, 9.
M. Axton and R. Williams: (1977) *English Drama: Forms and Development*, Cambridge UP.
W. O. Aydelotte: (1965) 'The Business Interests of the Gentry in the Parliament of 1841–1847' in G. Kitson-Clark, *The Making of Victorian England*, Methuen.
G. Aylmer:
1961: *The King's Servants: the Civil Service of Charles I*, Cambridge UP.
1973: *The State's Servants: the Civil Service in the English Republic 1649–1660*, Routledge.
1974: 'Office Holding, Wealth and Social Structure in England, c.1580–c.1720', *Datini Inglo*, 1978.
D. Ayre: (1979) *Durham Pit Villages*, forthcoming 'Strong Words' pamphlet, Erdesdun Publications, Whitley Bay.

J. M. Baernreither: (1893) *English Associations of Working Men*, Swan Sonnenschein.
R. Bahro: (1977) 'The Alternative in Eastern Europe', *NLR*, (106).
E. Balibar:
1968: 'The Basic Concepts of Historical Materialism' in L. Althusser and E. Balibar, *Reading Capital*, NL Books, 1970.
1972: 'La Rectification du Manifeste Communiste', *La Pensée*, (164).
C. Barker: (1978) 'A note on the Theory of the Capitalist State', *Capital and Class*, (4).
M. Barrett, P. Corrigan, A. Kuhn, J. Wolff (eds.): (1979), *Ideology and Cultural Production*, Croom Helm.
D. H. Bayley: (1975) 'The Police and Political Development', Ch. 5 in Tilly, 1975.
J. M. Beattie:
1972: 'Towards a Study of Crime in Eighteenth Century England', in *The Triumph of Culture*, Hakkert, Toronto.
1974: 'The Pattern of Crime in England 1660–1800', *Past and Present*, (62).
V. Beechey: (1977) 'Female Wage Labour in Capitalist Production', *Capital and Class*, (3).

A. L. Beier: (1974) 'Vagrants and the Social Order in Elizabethan England', *Past and Present*, (64).
J. Bellamy: (1979) *The Tudor Law of Treason*, Routledge.
W. Benjamin: (1973) *Understanding Brecht*, NL Books.
B. Bernstein:
1977a: 'Aspects of the Relations between Education and Production'.
1977b: *Class, Codes and Control*, III, rev. ed. Routledge (Ch. 8).
S. Bernstein: (1960) 'Self-Determination: King or Citizen in the Realm of Values', *Social Work*, January.
C. Bettelheim:
1970: *Economic Calculation and Forms of Property*, Routledge, 1972.
1973: *Cultural Revolution and Industrial Organization in China*, Monthly Review Press, 1974.
W. H. Beveridge:
1906: 'The Problem of the Unemployed', *Sociological Papers*, 3.
1909: *Unemployment: a Problem of Industry*, Longmans, Green & Co. rev. ed., 1930.
1942: *Social Insurance and Allied Services*, (The Beveridge Report), H.M.S.O.
Birmingham University, Centre for Contemporary Cultural Studies, Women's Studies Group: *Women Take Issue*, Hutchinson, 1978.
L. Bland, T. McCabe, F. Mort: (1978) 'Sexuality and Reproduction: Three Official Instances', in M. Barrett *et al.*, (1979).
H. Bosanquet: (1906) *The Family*, Macmillan.
P. Bourdieu: (1976) 'Marriage Strategies as Strategies of Social Reproduction', in R. Forster and P. Ranum (eds.) *Family and Society: Selections for the 'Annales'*, Johns Hopkins UP.
J. Bowring:
1838–1843 (ed.): *The Works of Jeremy Bentham*, 2 vols., Edinburgh, Tait.
1877 (ed.): *Autobiographical Reflections*, H. S. King.
G. Boyce, J. Curran, P. Wingate: (1978) *Newspaper History from the Seventeenth Century to the Present Day*, Constable.
W. J. Braithwaite: (1957) *Lloyd George's Ambulance Wagon*, Methuen.

S. D. Brandes: (1970) *American Welfare Capitalism, 1880–1940*, Chicago UP.
A. Briggs:
1956: 'Middle-Class Consciousness in British Politics 1780–1846', *Past and Present*, (9).
1959: *Age of Improvement*, Longman.
1960: *Mass Entertainment: the Origins of a Modern Industry*, Adelaide, University.
1961: 'The Welfare State in Historical Perspective', *Archives Européenes de sociologie*, 2.
C. Brooks: (1974) 'Public Finance and Political Stability', *Historical Journal*, 17(2).
K. Brown: (1971) *Labour and Unemployment*, Rowan and Littlefield.
L. Brown: (1958) *The Board of Trade and the Free Trade Movement, 1830–1842*, Clarendon Press, Oxford.
M. Bruce:
1961: *The Coming of the Welfare State*, Batsford.
1973: *Rise of the Welfare State: English Social Policy, 1601–1971*, Weidenfeld.
A. Brundage:
1972: The Landed Interest and the New Poor Law, *English Historical Review*, 87.
1974: The English Poor Law and the Cohesion of Agricultural Society, *Agricultural History Review*.
1978: *The Making of the New Poor Law, 1832–1839*, Rutgers UP and Hutchinson.
A. Buck: (1976) 'Dress as a Social Record', *Folk Life*, 14.
J. Buckley: (1926) *Joseph Parkes of Birmingham*, Methuen.
P. Burke:
1977: 'Popular Culture in Seventeenth Century London', *London Journal*, 3(2).
1978: *Popular Culture in Early Modern Europe*, Temple Smith.
B. Burleigh: (1887) 'The Unemployed', *Contemporary Review*, 52.
W. L. Burn: (1968) *The Age of Equipoise; a Study of the Mid-Victorian Generation*, Allen and Unwin.
D. Byrne: (1978) 'Social Research and the State', *Bulletin on Social Policy*, (1).
D. Bythell: (1969) *The Handloom Weavers: a Study in the*

English Cotton Industry during the Industrial Revolution, Cambridge UP.

A. M. Carr-Saunders *et al.*: (1938) *Consumers Co-operation in Great Britain: an Examination of the British Co-operative Movement,* Allen and Unwin.
C.C.C.S. *see* Birmingham University.
D. Cecil: (1955) *Melbourne,* Constable.
R. Challinor: (1977) *The Origins of British Bolshevism,* Croom Helm.
W. J. Chambliss:
1964: 'Sociological Analysis of the Law of Vagrancy', *Social Problems,* 11.
1975a: 'Towards a Political Economy of Crime', *Theory and Society,* 2.
1975b: 'The State, the Law and the Definition of Behaviour as Criminal and Delinquent', Ch. 1 in *Handbook of Criminology,* Rand McNally.
Charity Organization Review: (1895) 'How to Take Down a Case'.
C. A. Charnley: (1960) *John Fielden (1784–1849): a Study in Radicalism,* University of Birmingham B. A. Dissertation.
W. Citrine: (1964): *Men and Work,* Hutchinson.
P. Clark: (1977) *English Provincial Society from the Reformation to the Revolution: Religion, Politics and Society in Kent 1500–1640,* Harvester Press.
P. Clark and P. Slack: (1976) *English Towns in Transition 1500–1700,* Oxford UP.
M. Clarke: (1975) 'Social Problem Ideologies', *British Journal of Sociology,* 26(4).
E. J. Cleary: (1965) *The Building Society Movement,* Elek.
A. W. Coates (ed.): (1971) *The Classical Economists and Economic Policy,* Methuen.
K. Coates and R. Silburn: (1970) *Poverty: the Forgotten Englishmen,* Penguin.
W. H. Coates: (1950) 'Bentham, Laissez-faire and Collectivism', *Journal for the History of Ideas,* 11.
J. S. Cockburn (ed.): (1977) *Crime in England 1550–1800,* Methuen.
E. W. Cohen: (1941) *The Growth of the British Civil Service*

1780–1939, Allen and Unwin; reprinted F. Cass, 1965.

G. D. H. Cole: (1928) Introduction to Defoe, *A Tour through the Whole Island of Great Britain*, 1726 (Everyman Edition). (1941): *Chartist Portraits*, Macmillan.

D. C. Coleman and A. H. John (eds.): (1976) *Trade, Government and Economy in Pre-Industrial England*, Weidenfeld.

L. J. Colley: (1977) ' "The Loyal Brotherhood of the Cocoa Tree": the London Organization of the Tory Party, 1727–1760', *Historical Journal*, 20(1).

P. Cominos: (1973) 'Late-Victorian Sexual Respectability and the Social System', *International Review of Social History*, 8.

Committee on Abuse of Social Security Benefits (1973): *Report*, H.M.S.O. (Cmnd. 5228).

P. Corfield: (1976) 'Urban Development in England and Wales in the 16th and 17 Centuries', Ch. 11 in D. C. Coleman and A. H. John, op. cit.

P. Corrigan:

1977: *State Formation and Moral Regulation in Nineteenth-Century Britain: Sociological Investigations*, Durham University PhD. thesis.

1979: 'Capitalism's Cultural Revolution' in Corrigan and S. Yeo: *Class-Culture and History: two essays*, forthcoming.

1980: *State Formation and Moral Regulation: the Elementary Forms of English Political Life*, Macmillan.

1981: *Culture and Control*, Macmillan.

    and P. Corrigan: (1977) *Labour and the State*, Paper to the 1977 B.S.A. Conference, University of Sheffield.

    and V. Corrigan: (1978) 'State Formation and Social Policy until 1871', in *Social Work, Welfare, and the State*, Edward Arnold, Leeds.

P. Corrigan and V. Gillespie: (1974) *Class Struggle, Social Literacy and Idle Time*, Labour History Monographs, Brighton 1978.

P. Corrigan, H. Ramsay, D. Sayer:

1977: *The State as a Relation of Production*, Paper to the 1977 BSA Conference, University of Sheffield (Revised form as Ch.1 of this book).

1978: *Socialist Construction and Marxist Theory: Bolshevism and its Critique*, Macmillan and Monthly Review Press, New York.

1979: *For Mao*, Macmillan.
P. Corrigan, D. Sayer:
1975: 'Class Struggle, Moral Relations and Political Economy',
Radical Philosophy, 12.
1978: 'Hindess and Hirst: a Critical Review', *Socialist Register*.
1979: *How the law rules*, Paper to the 1979 BSA Conference,
University of Warwick; revised version: in *Law, State and
Society*, Croom Helm, 1980.
M. Cousins: (1978) 'Material Arguments and Feminism', *m/f*(2).
R. Coward: (1978) 'Rethinking Marxism', *m/f* (2).
F. R. Crane: (1977) 'Family Settlement and Succession' in R.
H. Grayson and F. R. Crane, *A Century of Family Law
1857–1957*, Sweet and Maxwell.
G. A. Cranfield: (1978) *The Press and Society: from Caxton to
Northcliffe*, Longman.
G. Crossick:
1976: *Social Structure and Working-Class Behaviour*, London
University Ph.D. thesis.
1978: *An Artisan Élite in Victorian Society: Kentish London
1840–1880*, Croom Helm.
M. J. Cullen: (1975) *The Statistical Movement in Early Victorian
Britain*, Harvester Press.
J. Curran (ed.): (1978) *The British Press: a Manifesto*,
Macmillan.

L. Davidoff, J. Esperance, H. Newby: (1976) 'Landscape with
Figures: Home and Community in English Society', in *Rights
and Wrongs of Women*, Penguin.
A. Davin: (1978) 'Imperialism and Motherhood', *History
Workshop*, (5).
N. Z. Davis: (1975) *Society and Culture in Early Modern
France*, Duckworth.
D. Defoe: (1726) *A Tour through the Whole Island of Great
Britain*, Everyman Edition. Dent, 2 vols., 1962.
J. Ditton:
1976: 'Moral Horror vs Folk Terror', *Sociological Review*, 24.
1977: 'Perks, Pilferage and the Fiddle: the Historical Structure
of Invisible Wages', *Theory and Society*, 4.
C. R. P. Dod: (1832–1885) *Parliamentary Pocket Companion* in
M. Stenton (ed.) *Who's Who of British Members of Parliament*,

Harvester Press 1976.
H. Draper:
1977: *Karl Marx's Theory of Revolution*, Part I, 2 vols.
1978: *Idem*, Part II. 2 vols. Both sets, Monthly Review Press.
O. Duke: (1903) 'Physical Education', unpublished paper read
to the Council, Charity Organization Society, 13 July 1903.

N. Elias:
1978: *The Civilizing Process*, Blackwell, Oxford.
1979: *The Dynamics of the State*, Blackwell, Oxford.
G. Elton:
1953: *Tudor Revolution in Government*, Cambridge UP.
1972: *Policy and Police*, Cambridge UP.
1973: *Reform and Renewal*, Cambridge UP.
F. Engels: (*see also* Karl Marx)
1845a: *The Condition of the Working Class in England*,
Granada, 1969.
1845b: *Idem*, Allen and Unwin, 1952.
1885: Note to the rev. ed. of Marx and Engels 1850, *MECW*,
10.
1889: 'The Abdication of the Bourgeoisie', in Marx/Engels:
Articles on Britain, Progress, Moscow, 1975.
J. A. Epstein: (1977) *Feargus O'Connor and the English
Working-Class Radical Movement 1832–1841*, Birmingham
University, Ph.D. thesis.
F. M. G. Evans: (1923) *The Principal Secretary of State,
1558–1660,* Manchester UP; reprinted F. Cass.

Fabian Society: (1886) *The Government Organization of
Unemployed Labour*, Strandring.
M. Falkus: (1976) 'Lighting in the Dark Ages of English
Economic History', Ch. 12 in D. C. Coleman and A. H. John,
op. cit.
J. Fielden: (1836) *The Curse of the Factory System*, Privately
published.
M. Finer and O. McGregor: (1971) 'The History of the
Obligation to Maintain', in *The Finer Report*, H.M.S.O.
S. E. Finer:
1951: 'Patronage and the Public Service', *Public Administration*,
30, 1952.

1952: *The Life and Times of Sir Edwin Chadwick*, Methuen.
S. Fish: (1528) *The Supplication of Beggars*, reprinted, Primary
Publications, 1970.
N. Forder: (1966) *Social Casework and Administration*, Faber.
E. M. Forster: (1909) 'The Machine Stops', in *The Eternal
Moment*, Sidgwick, 1928.
J. Foster: (1974) *Class Struggle and the Industrial Revolution*,
Weidenfeld.
M. Foucault:
1975: *Discipline and Punish*, Allen Lane, 1977.
1976: *La Volonté du savoir*, Gallimard, Paris (English
translation, Allen Lane, 1979).
C. Fox:
1977 'The Development of Social Reportage in English
Periodical Literature during the 1840s and Early 1850s', *Past
and Present* (74).
1978: 'Political Caricature', in Boyce *et al.*, 1978.
D. Fraser: (1976) *Urban Politics in Victorian England*, Leicester
UP.
W. Friedman: (1950) 'The Function of Property in Modern
English Law', Review of K. Renner (1928/1949) in *British
Journal of Sociology*, 1.

N. Gash: (1972) *Sir Robert Peel*, Longman.
N. Geras: (1971) 'Essence and Appearance', *NLR* (65);
reprinted in R. Blackburn (ed.), *Ideology in Social Science*,
Fontana, 1972.
M. Gettleman: (1974) 'The Whig Interpretation of Social
Welfare History', *Smith College Studies in Social Work*, 44(3).
B. Gilbert:
1965: 'The British National Insurance Act of 1911 and the
Commercial Insurance Lobby', *Journal of British Studies*, 4.
1966: 'Winston Churchill versus the Webbs: the Origins of
British Unemployment Insurance', *American Historical Review*,
71(3).
L. Gittins: (1977) 'Soapmaking and the Excise Laws 1711–1853',
Industrial Archeology Review, 1(3).
A. Goodwin: (1979) *The Friends of Liberty*, Hutchinson.
J. Goody:
1976a: 'Inheritance, Property and Women', in Goody *et al.*,

1976b.

1976b (*et. al.*, eds.) *Family and Inheritance*, Cambridge UP.

P. J. J. H. Gosden:

1961: *The Friendly Societies in England 1815–1875*, Manchester UP.

1973: *Self-Help Voluntary Associations in Nineteenth-Century Britain*, Batsford.

K. Gough: (1978) 'Agrarian Relations in South India 1750–1976', *The Review*, 2(1).

A. Gramsci: (1934) *The Prison Notebooks*, (Selections), Lawrence and Wishart, 1971.

R. H. Gretton: (1913) *The King's Government*, Bell.

T. R. Gurr: (1976) *Rogues, Rebels and Reformers*, Sage.

E. Halévy:

1912: *England in 1815*, Benn, 1949.

1923: *A History of the English People in the Nineteenth Century*, vol. III, Benn, 1964.

1934: *The Growth of Philosophic Radicalism*, rev. ed., Faber, 1972.

B. T. Hall: (1912) *Our Fifty Years: the Story of the Working Men's Club and Institute Union*, C.I.U.

S. Hall:

1977a: 'Rethinking the "Base and Superstructure" Metaphor', in J. Bloomfield (ed.), *Class, Hegemony and Politics*, Lawrence and Wishart.

1977b: 'The "Political" and the "Economic" in Marx's Theory of Classes', in A. Hunt (ed.), *Class and Class Structure*, Lawrence and Wishart.

1978a: 'Reformism and the Legislation of Consent', unpublished paper (to appear in *Permissiveness and Control*, Macmillan).

1978b: 'Newspapers, Parties and Class', in Curran, 1978.

and B. Lumley and G. McLennan: (1977) 'Politics and Ideology: Gramsci' in *Working Papers in Cultural Studies*, (10), now also available as *On Ideology*, Hutchinson, 1979.

J. Hamburger: (1965) *Intellectuals in Politics: John Stuart Mill and the Philosophic Radicals*, Yale UP.

G. Hammersley: (1976) 'The State and the English Iron Industry in the Sixteenth and Seventeenth Centuries', Ch. 9 in D. C. Coleman and A. H. John, op. cit.

J. L. Hammond and B. Hammond: (1923) *Lord Shaftesbury*, Constable.

W. Hannington:

1936: *Unemployed Struggles, 1919–1936*, reprinted, Lawrence and Wishart, 1977.

1940: *Ten Lean Years*, republished, E. P. Publishing Wakefield, 1978.

A. Harding: (1966) *The Social History of English Law*, Penguin.

J. Harris: (1972) *Unemployment and Politics: Study in English Social Policy 1886–1914*, Oxford UP.

N. Harris: (1961) 'The Decline of Welfare', *International Socialism*, (7).

R. Harrison: (1964) 'The British Labour Movement and the International in 1864', *Socialist Register*.

J. Hart: (1965) 'Nineteenth-Century Social Reform: a Tory Interpretation of History', *Past and Present*, (31).

N. B. Harte: (1976) 'State Control of Dress and Social Change in Pre-Industrial England', Ch. 8 in D. C. Coleman and A. H. John, op. cit.

J. Harvey and K. Hood: (1958) *The British State*, Lawrence and Wishart.

D. Hay *et al.* (eds.): (1975) *Albion's Fatal Tree*, Allen Lane.

R. Hendrix: (1976) 'Popular Humour in "The Black Dwarf" ', *Journal of British Studies*, 16(1).

C. Hill:

1940a: 'The Agrarian Legislation of the Revolution', *English Historical Review*, (218), reprinted as Ch. 5 of Hill, 1958.

1940b: *The English Revolution, 1640*, Lawrence and Wishart, 1955.

1952: 'William Perkins and the Poor', *Past and Present*, (2), 1952.

1954: 'The Norman Yoke' in R. Saville (ed.) 1954, *Democracy and the Labour Movement*; reprinted in Hill, 1958: Ch. 3.

1956a: 'Recent Interpretations of the Civil War', *History* (141/3), reprinted as Ch. 1 in Hill, 1958.

1956b: 'Social and Economic Consequences of the Henrician Reformation', Ch. 2 in Hill, 1958.

1958: *Puritanism and Revolution*, Panther, 1968.

1967: *Reformation to Industrial Revolution, 1530–1780*, Penguin, 1969.

1972: *World Turned Upside Down*, Temple Smith.
1977: *Milton and the English Revolution*, Faber.
1978: 'Sex, Marriage and the Family in England', *Economic History Review*, 31(3).
B. Hindess: (1977) 'The Concept of Class in Marxist Theory and Marxist Politics', in J. Bloomfield (ed.), *Class, Hegemony and Party*, Lawrence and Wishart.
O. Hintze: (1975) *Historical Essays*, Oxford UP, New York.
E. J. Hobsbawm: (1973) *Revolutionaries*, Weidenfeld.
E. Hodder: (1886) *The Life and Work of the Seventh Earl of Shaftesbury*, Volume 1, Cassell.
L. Holcombe: (1977) 'Victorian Wives and Property Reform', in M. Vicinus (ed.), *A Widening Sphere*, Indiana UP.
J. Holloway and S Picciotto: (1978) 'Towards a Materialist Theory of the State', in J. Holloway and S. Picciotto (eds.), *State and Capital*, Edward Arnold, Leeds.
G. Holyoake: (1878) 'The New Principle of Industry', *Nineteenth Century*, 4.
L. Horner: (1840) *On the Employment of Children, in Factories and Other Works in the U.K. and Some Foreign Countries*, Longman.
W. G. Hoskins:
1976: *The Age of Plunder: the England of Henry VIII*, Longman.
1977: *The Making of the English Landscape*, rev. ed., Hodder.
J. Humphries: (1977) 'Class Struggle and the Resistance of the Working-Class Family', *Cambridge Journal of Economics*, 1.
J. G. Hutchinson: (1908) 'A Workman's View of the Remedy for Unemployment', *Nineteenth Century*, 64.

C. Jackson: (1910) *Unemployment and Trade Unions*, Longmans, Green and Co.
L. James: (1978) 'Cruikshank and Early Victorian Caricature', *History Workshop*, (6).
M. James (ed.) (1973) *Bentham and Legal Theory*, Northern Ireland Legal Quarterly Supplement, Belfast.
B. Jessop:
1977: 'Capitalism and Democracy: the Best Possible Political Shell', in G. Littlejohn *et al.* (eds.), *Power and the State*, Croom Helm 1978.

1978: 'Marx and Engels on the State', in S. Hibbin (ed.), *Politics, Ideology and the State*, Lawrence and Wishart.
R. Johnson:
1970: 'Educational Policy and Social Control . . .' *Past and Present*, (49).
1975: *Peculiarities of the English Route*, Birmingham C.C.C.S. Occasional Papers, 26.
1976: 'Barrington Moore, Perry Anderson and English Social Development', in *Working Papers in Cultural Studies*, 9.
1977: 'Educating the Educators: "Experts" and the State 1833–1839', in A. P. Donajgrodzki (ed.), *Social Control in Nineteenth-Century Britain*, Croom Helm.
T. Johnston: (1974) *The History of the Working Classes in Scotland*, reprinted, EP. Publishing, Wakefield.
C. Jones:
1978: *An Analysis of the Development of Social Work and Social Work Education 1869–1977*, Durham University Ph.D. thesis.
1978a: 'The State of Contemporary British Social Work', *Catalyst*, 1(2).
1978b: 'Notes on Social Work Education', in N. Parry *et al.* (eds.), *Social Work, Welfare and the State*, Edward Arnold, Leeds.
and T. Novak, C. Phillipson: (1978) 'The Politics of Welfare', *Bulletin on Social Policy*, (1).
G. Jones: (1977) *The Gentry and the Elizabethan State* C. Davies, Swansea.
Gareth Stedman Jones:
1971: *Outcast London*, Clarendon Press, Oxford.
1975: ' "England's First Proletariat" ', *NLR*, (90).
K. Joseph:
1975: 'Is Beckerman amongst the Sociologists?' *New Statesman*, 18 April.
1976: *Reversing the Trend*, Rose Books.

M. Kaufman: (1907) *The Housing of the Working Classes and the Poor*, republished, E.P. Publishing, Wakefield, 1975.
J. P. Kay-Shuttleworth: (1832) *The Moral and Physical Condition of the Working Classes Employed in the Cotton Manufacture in Manchester*, reprinted, F. Cass, 1978; originally published under authorship of Dr J. P. Kay.

V. Kiernan: (1965) 'State and Nation in Western Europe', *Past and Present*, (31).

M. Kishlansky: (1978) 'The Case of the Army Truly Stated', *Past and Present*, (81).

H. S. Koenigsberger: (1977) 'Dominum Regale or Dominum Politicum et Regale? Monarchies and Politics in Early Modern Europe', in *Der Moderne Parliamentarismus*, Duncker und Humboldt, Berlin.

A. Kuhn and A. M. Wolpe (eds.) (1978) *Feminism and Materialism: Women and Modes of Production*, Routledge.

E. Laclau: (1975) 'The Specificity of the Political: the Poulantzas-Miliband Debate', *Economy and Society*, 4.

R. Lambert: (1963) *Sir John Simon (1816–1904) and English Social Administration*, MacGibbon and Kee.

T. Lane: (1974) *The Union Makes Us Strong*, Arrow.

H. J. Laski: (1931) *The Limitation of the Expert*, Fabian Society (Tract, no. 235).

W. Lazonick: (1974) 'Karl Marx and Enclosures in England', *Review of Radical Political Economy*, 6(2).

R. E. Leader (ed.): (1897) *Life and Letters of John Arthur Roebuck,* Edward Arnold, Leeds.

V. I. Lenin:

1917a: *Marxism and the State*, Progress, Moscow, 1972.

1917b: *State and Revolution*, Lawrence and Wishart, 1933.

W. H. Lever, Lord Leverhulme: (1918) *The Six-Hour Day and Other Industrial Questions*, Allen and Unwin.

R. A. Lewis: (1952) *Edwin Chadwick and the Public Health Movement*, Longman.

P. Linebaugh: (1976) 'Karl Marx, the Thefts of Wood and Working-Class Composition', *Crime and Social Justice*, 1976.

C. M. L. Lloyd: (1916) *The Reorganisation of Local Government*. Labour Research Department.

D. M. Loades: (1974) *Politics and the Nation, 1450–1660: Obedience, Resistance and Public Order*, Fontana.

W. C. Lubenow: (1971) *The Politics of Government Growth*, David & Charles, Newton Abbot.

K. M. Lyell: (1890) *Memoir of Leonard Horner*, vol. 2., Women's Printing Society Ltd.

O. MacDonagh: (1958) 'The Nineteenth-Century Revolution in Government: a Re-appraisal', *Historical Journal*, 1.

O. McGregor: (1957) *Divorce in England*, Heinemann.

M. McIntosh: (1978) 'The State and the Oppression of Women', in Kuhn and Wolpe, 1978.

R. W. Malcolmson: (1978) *Popular Recreations in English Society, 1700–1850*, Cambridge UP.

E. Mandel: (1975) *Late Capitalism*, NL Books.

P. Mantoux: (1928) *The Industrial Revolution in the Eighteenth Century*, Methuen, 1964.

S. Marcus: (1966) *The Other Victorians*, Weidenfeld.

T. H. Marshall: (1966) 'Welfare in the Context of Social Development', in J. S. Morgan (ed.), *Welfare and Wisdom*, University of Toronto Press.

A. G. Martin: (1944) 'Child Neglect: a Problem of Social Administration', *Public Administration*, 22(2).

K. Marx and F. Engels: (*see also* Engels)

(*Note*: For the fullest listing of works by Marx and Engels in English see the Bibliography to Sayer's *Marx's Method*).

COLLECTED WORKS, 1975 onwards, Lawrence and Wishart, cited as MECW below.

1843: *On the Jewish Question*, MECW, 3.

1845: *The German Ideology*, MECW, 5.

1847a: *Moralizing Criticism and Critical Morality*, MECW, 6.

1847b: *The Poverty of Philosophy*, MECW, 6.

1848: *Manifesto of the Communist Party*, MECW, 7; *Political Writings*, I (Penguin); in 1968 *Selected Works*.

1849: *Wage, Labour and Capital*, in 1968 *Selected Works*.

1850: 'Address of the Central Authority to the League (March 1850)', MECW, 10.

1852: *Eighteenth Brumaire*, in 1968 *Selected Works* and *Political Writings*, II (Penguin).

1854: *Letter to the Labour Parliament*, in *Political Writings*. II (Penguin).

1855: 'The Association for Administrative Reform' – People's Charter (1855)' in Marx and Engels: *Articles on Britain*, Progress, Moscow.

1858: *Grundrisse*, M. Nicolaus (ed.), Penguin, 1973.

1863a,b,c: *Capital*, IV: Theories of Surplus Value, I, II, III. Progress Moscow.

1864: *Inaugural Address of the International Working Man's Association, Political Writings, III*, Penguin.
1865: *Capital*, III, Progress, Moscow (Ch. 1) revised edition 1894, Kerr, Chicago, 1909 (Ch. 5).
1867a: *Capital*, I, Lawrence and Wishart, 1967.
1867b: *Capital*, I, Penguin, 1976.
1871a: First draft of 1871c.
1871b: Second draft of 1871c.
1871c: *The Civil War in France*, FLP, Peking, 1970.
1872: 'Preface' to the German edition of the *Manifesto*: in 1968 *Selected Works*.
1878: *Capital*, II, rev. ed., Progress, Moscow, 1967.
1879: 'Circular Letter to Bebel, Liebknecht, Bakke, *et al.*', in *Political writings, III*, Penguin.
1880: 'Notes on Adolph Wagner' in Marx: *Texts on Method*; Carver (ed.), Blackwell, Oxford, 1975.
1962: *On Britain*. F.L.P.H. Moscow.
1968: *Selected Works in One Volume*, Progress, Moscow.
F. C. Mather: (1974) 'The General Strike of 1842', in J. Stevenson and R. Quihault (eds.), *Popular Protest and Public Order*, Allen Lane.
J. Mepham: (1972) 'The Theory of Ideology in "Capital" ', *Radical Philosophy*, (2); reprinted in *WPCS*, (6) 1975.
R. Miliband:
1965: 'Marx and the State', *Socialist Register*.
1977: *Marxism and Politics*, Oxford UP.
J. S. Mill:
1838: 'Bentham', *Westminster Review*; reprinted in *Mill on Bentham and Coleridge*, (ed. F. R. Leavis), Chatto, 1950.
1964: *Autobiography*, New American Library, New York.
B. B. Misra: (1960) *Central Administration of the East India Company 1773–1834*, Manchester UP.
H. Montgomery-Hyde: (1970) *The Other Love*, Heinemann.
D. C. Moore:
1965: 'The Corn Laws and High Farming', *Economic History Review*, 18.
1967: 'Social Structure, Political Structure and Public Opinion in Mid-Victorian England', Ch. 2 in R. Robson (ed.) *Ideas and Institutions in Mid-Victorian England*, Bell.
1976: *Politics of Deference*, Harvester Press.

W. Müller and C. Neussüs: (1978) 'The "Welfare-State Illusion" and the Contradiction between Wage-Labour and Capital', in J. Holloway and S. Picciotto (eds.), *State and Capital*, Edward Arnold, Leeds.

R. S. Neale: (1972) *Class and Ideology in the Nineteenth Century*, Routledge.
G. Newman: (1975) 'Anti-French Propaganda and British Liberal Nationalism', *Victorian Studies* 18 (4).
K. Nield: (1973) *Prostitution in the Victorian Age*, Gregg International.
G. Nicholls: (1898) *A History of the English Poor Law*, P. S. King.
T. Novak: (1978) *Poverty and the State: a Study of Unemployment and Social Security in Britain*, Durham University, Ph.D. thesis.

J. F. Oakeshott: (1894) *The Humanizing of the Poor Law*, Fabian Society (Tract, no. 54).

H. Parris
1968: 'Origins of the Permanent Civil Service, 1780–1830', *Public Administration*, 46.
1969: *Constitutional Bureaucracy*, Allen and Unwin.
N. Parry, M. Rustin and C. Satyamurti: (1979) *Social Work and the State*, Edward Arnold.
T. M. Parssinen: (1973) 'Association, Convention and Anti-Parliament in British Radical Politics, 1771–1848', *English Historical Review*, 88.
B. Pashukanis: (1929): *Law and Marxism: a General Theory*, third edition, Ink Links, 1978.
W. Paul: (1917) *The State: its Origin and Function*, reprinted, Proletarian Publishing, Edinburgh, 1974.
R. Pearsall: (1969) *The Worm in the Bud: the World of Victorian Sexuality*, Penguin.
J. D. Y. Peel: (1971) *Herbert Spencer*, Heinemann.
H. Pelling: (1968) 'The Working Class and the Origins of the Welfare State', in his *Popular Politics and Society in Late Victorian Britain*, Macmillan.
H. Perkin: (1969) *The Origins of Modern English Society*.

1760–1880, Routledge.
POLITICAL and Economic Planning:
1942: 'Planning for Social Security', *Planning*, 9(190).
1948: *Population Policy in Great Britain*, P.E.P.
POLITICAL Economy of Women Group: (1975) *On the Political Economy of Women*, Stage One (CSE Pamphlets, 2).
S. Pollard:
1963: 'Factory Discipline in the Industrial Revolution', *Economic History Review*, 16.
1965: *The Genesis of Modern Management*, Penguin, 1968.
N. Poulantzas:
1968: *Political Power and Social Classes*, NL Books, 1975.
1976: 'The Capitalist State', *NLR*, (95).
1978: *State, Power, Socialism*, NL Books;
J. Prest: (1972) *Lord John Russell*, Macmillan.
I. Prothero: (1979) *Artisans and Politics in the Early Nineteenth Century*, Dawson.
R. Prouty: (1957) *The Transformation of the Board of Trade, 1830–1855*, Heinemann.

H. Ramsay:
1967a: 'Participation: the Shop Floor View', *British Journal of Industrial Relations*, 13.
1976b: 'Who Wants Participation?' *New Society*, 30 September.
1977: 'Cycles of Control: Worker Participation in Sociological and Historical Perspective', *Sociology*, 11.
E. Rathbone: (1940) *The Case for Family Allowances*, Penguin.
D. Read: (1964) *The English Provinces, c. 1760–1960*, Edward Arnold, Leeds.
P. Redfern: (1923) *John T. W. Mitchell*, Co-operative Union, Manchester.
K. Renner (1949) *The Institutions of Private Law and their Social Functions* English translation of 1928 edition, Routledge.
P. Richards:
1975: *The State and the Working Class, 1833–1841: M.P.s and the Making of Social Policy*, Birmingham University Ph.D. thesis.
1979: 'R. A. Slaney, the Industrial Town and Early Victorian Social Policy, *Social History*, 4.
C. Roberts: (1977) 'The Constitutional Significance of the

Financial Settlement of 1690' *Historical Journal,* 20(1).
D. Roberts: (1960) *The Victorian Origins of the British Welfare State,* Yale UP.
N. Rosenberg: (1960) 'Some Institutional Aspects of the "Wealth of Nations" ' *Journal of Political Economy,* 68.
N. L. Rosenblum: (1978) *Bentham's Theory of the Modern State,* Harvard UP.
H. Roseveare: (1973) *The Treasury, 1660–1870,* Allen and Unwin.
ROYAL COMMISSION on Law of Divorce: (1853) *Report,* Parliamentary Papers.
I. Rubin: (1928) *Essays on Marx's Theory of Value,* Black and Red, Detroit 1972.
G. Rusche and O. Kirscheimer: (1939) *Punishment and Social Structure,* reprinted, Russell and Russell, New York, 1970.

A. Sachs: (1978) 'The Myth of Male Protectiveness and the Legal Subordination of Women: an Historical Analysis', in B. Smart and C. Smart (eds.), *Women, Sexuality and Social Control,* Routledge.
J. Samaha: (1974) *Law and Order in Historical Perspective: the Case of Elizabethan Essex,* Academic Press.
J. Saville:
1957: 'The Welfare State: an Historical Approach', *New Reasoner.*
1960: 'Trade Unions and Free Labour', *Essays in Labour History, I,* Macmillan.
1969: 'Primitive Accumulation and Early Industrialization in Britain', *Socialist Register.*
D. Sayer:
1975: 'Method and Dogma in Historical Materialism', *Sociological Review,* 23.
1978a: 'Science as Critique' in J. Mepham *et al.*: *Issues in Marxist Philosophy,* Harvester Press, 1979.
1978b: *Marx's Method,* Harvester Press, 1979.
G. P. Scrope: (1833) *Principles of Political Economy,* privately published.
SELECT Committee on Marriage and Divorce: (1867–1868), *Report,* Parliamentary Papers.
B. Semmell: (1960) *'Imperialism and Social Reform: English*

Social Imperial Thought, 1895–1914, Allen and Unwin.
E. Sigsworth and J. Wyke: (1973) 'A Study of Victorian
Prostitution and Venereal Disease', in M. Vicinus (ed.), *Suffer
and be still*, Indiana UP.
B. Simon: (1965) *Education and the Labour Movement*,
Lawrence and Wishart.
Q. Skinner: (1978) *The Foundation of Modern Political
Thought*, two volumes, Cambridge UP.
P. A. Slack: (1974) 'Vagrants and Vagrancy in England,
1598–1664', *Economic History Review*, 27.
R. A. Slaney: (1824) *Essay on the Beneficial Direction of Rural
Expenditure*, privately published.
SOCIAL INSURANCE and Allied Services, 1942, H.M.S.O.
(Cmd. 6404) *The Beveridge Report*.
W. Stern: (1950) 'U.K. Public Expenditure by Votes of Supply,
1793–1812', *Economica*, 17.
L. Stone:
1966: 'Social Mobility in England, 1500–1700', *Past and Present*
(33).
1977: *The Family. Sex and Marriage in England, 1500–1800*,
Yale UP.
R. D. Storch: (1979) 'The Study of Urban Crime', (review
essay), *Social History*, 4(1).
J. P. Strayer: (1970) *On the Medieval Origins of the Modern
State*, Princeton UP.
B. Supple:
1971: 'The State and the Industrial Revolution', in C. M.
Cipolla (ed.) *The Industrial Revolution*, Fontana, 1973.
1974: 'Legislation and Virtue', in *Historical Perspectives* Europa.

H. Taylor: (1832) *On the Best Mode of Constituting Public
Offices* reprinted *Political Studies*, 9, 1961.
P. Thane: (1977) 'Women and the Poor Law in Victorian and
Edwardian England', *History Workshop* (6) 1978.
J. Thirsk: (1977) *Economic Policy and Projects: the
Development of a Consumer Society in Early Modern England*,
Clarendon Press, Oxford.
K. Thomas:
1971: *Religion and the Decline of Magic*, Penguin.
1976: 'Age and Authority in Early Modern England',

Proceedings of the British Academy, 62, 1977.
E. P. Thompson
1963: *The Making of the English Working Class*, Penguin, 1968.
1964: 'Working-Class Culture and the Transition to
Industrialism', *Bulletin of the Society for the Study of Labour
History*, (9).
1965: 'Peculiarities of the English', *Socialist Register:* reprinted
in his 1978b.
1967: 'Time Work-Discipline and Industrial Capitalism', *Past
and Present*, (38); reprinted in *Essays in Social History* (ed.
Smout), Oxford UP. 1974.
1968: Postscript to the Penguin edition of his 1963 book.
1971: 'The Moral Economy of the English Crowd in the
Eighteenth Century', *Past and Present* (50).
1973: 'Open Letter to Leszek Kolakowski', *Socialist Register*,
1974; reprinted in his 1978b.
1974: 'Patrician Society, Plebian Culture', *Journal of Social
History*, 7.
1975: *Whigs and Hunters*, Allen Lane.
1976a: 'Interview with E. P. Thompson', *Radical History
Review*, 3(4).
1976b: 'The Grid of Inheritance: a Comment', in J. Goody *et
al.*, 1976b.
1977a: 'Eighteenth-Century English Society', *Social History*,
3(2), 1978.
1977b: Review essay on the family, *New Society*, 8 September.
1978a: 'The Poverty of Theory or an Orrery of Errors' in 1978b.
1978b: *The Poverty of Theory*, Merlin Press.
1978c: 'The State versus its Enemies', *New Society* 19 October.
1978d: 'The Secret State within the State', *New Statesman*, 10
November.
1978e: Introduction to *Review of Security and the State, I.*,
Julian Friedmann.
1979: 'Interview with E. P. Thompson', *Leveller*, January.
F. M. L. Thompson: (1963) *English Landed Society in the
Nineteenth Century*, Routledge.
C. Tilly:
1975 (ed.): *The Formation of National States in Europe*,
Princeton UP.
and L. Tilly, R. Tilly: (1975) *The Rebellious Century*,

1839–1930, Dent.

N. Timms and A. Philp. (1957) *The Problem of the Problem Family,* Family Service Units.

R. Titmuss: (1951): 'Family Relations in the Welfare State', *Listener*, 15 March.

J. R. Torrance: (1978): 'Social class and bureaucratic innovation', *Past and Present*, (78).

(1968): 'Sir George Harrison', *English Historical Review*, 83.

A. S. Turberville: (1958) *The House of Lords in the Age of Reform, 1784–1837,* Clarendon Press, Oxford.

United Nations: (1958) *Training for Social Work*, third survey, U.N. New York.

J. Vincent: (1966) *The Formation of the British Liberal Party 1857–1868*, Penguin, 1972.

V. Volosinov: (1930) *Marxism and the Philosophy of Language*, Seminar Press, New York, 1973.

H. Wainwright:
1977: *The Labour Party's Monopoly of Working-Class Representation: its Conditions and its Limits,* paper to the 1977 Conference of Socialist Economists.
1978: 'Women and the Division of Labour', Ch. 3 in Abrams, 1978.

J. T. Ward: (1962) *The Factory Movement, 1830–1855,* Macmillan.

B. Webb: (1926) *My Apprenticeship*, Penguin, 1938.

S. Webb: (1890) 'The Reform of the Poor Law', *Contemporary Review*, 58.

M. Weber:
1918: 'Politics as a Vocation' in his 1948 essays.
1920: *General Economic History*, Collier-Macmillan, New York, 1961.
1948: *Essays*; ed. Gerth and Mills, Routledge.

J. Weeks: (1977) *Coming Out*, Quartet.

J. Weinstein: (1969) *The Corporate Ideal in the Liberal State, 1900–1918,* Beacon Press, Boston.

R. Williams:
1958: *Culture and Society*, rev. ed., Penguin, 1963.

1961: *The Long Revolution*, Penguin, 1965.
1972: 'Social Darwinism', *Listener*, 23 November.
1973: *The Country and the City*, Paladin, 1975.
1973a: 'Base and Superstructure in Marxist Cultural Theory', *NLR* (82).
1974: *Drama in a Dramatized Society* [Inaugural lecture], Cambridge UP, 1975.
1975: *Developments in the Sociology of Culture*, paper to the 1975 B.S.A. Conference; revised version: *Sociology* 10(3).
1976: 'Notes on Marxism in Britain since 1945', *NLR*, (100).
1977a: 'Two Interviews with Raymond Williams', *Red Shift* (3) and (4).
1977b: *Marxism and Literature*, Oxford UP.
1978a 'The Press and Popular Culture' in Boyce *et al.*, 1978.
1978b: 'The Press We Don't Deserve', in Curran, 1978.
P. Willis: (1977) *Learning to Labour*, Saxon House.
E. Wilson: (1977) *Women and the Welfare State*, Tavistock.
D. Winch: (1978) *Adam Smith's Politics*, Cambridge UP.
WOMEN'S GROUP on public welfare: (1943) *Our Towns*, Oxford UP.
K. Wrightson: (1977) 'Aspects of Social Differentiation in Rural England c.1580–1660', *Journal of Peasant Studies*, 5(1).

S. Yeo:
1976: *Religion and Voluntary Organization in Crisis*, Croom Helm.
1977: 'Class Struggle and Associational Form, xeroxed paper.
1978: 'Working-Class Association, Private Capital, Welfare and the State', in N. Parry, et. al., *Social Work, Welfare and the State*, Arnold, 1979.
YOUNGHUSBAND REPORT, 1959: Being the *Report of the Working Party on Social Workers in the Local Authority Health and Welfare Services*, H.M.S.O.

INDEX

Carr, R., xviii
Chadwick, E., 58–9, 71, 73, 76, 98, 135, 183*n*
Chamberlain, J., 135
Charity Organization Society, 163, 198*n*, 200*n*
Chartism, 52, 72f., 119, 134–5, 191*n*
Christianity, 12, 118, 160; *sa* Church of England; Methodism
Church of England, 30, 33, 93, 97–8, 99; *sa* Anglicans
Churchill, W., 198*n*
Cinematograph Act, 1910, 132
civil society, 8–10
Civil War, English, *s* English Revolution
class, classes, Chs. 1, 3, 5 (especially 116–17)
clubs, 127–8
Cobbett, W., 62, 68
commodity(ies), 7, 23, 114, 117, 146, 153–4
Common Law, 84
Commonwealth, *s* English Revolution
Committee on Abuse of Social Security Benefits, 1973, 156–7
Commune, Paris (1871), 21–2, 119
Communism, 5 *def*
consensus, consent, *s* legitimacy
Conservatives, Party, 54, 75; *sa* Tories
Contagious Diseases Acts, 100, 105, 185*n*, 188*n*
contradiction(s), 14–15, 16f., 19, 122, 140
co-operation, co-operatives, Ch. 5, 202*n*
Co-operative Wholesale Society, 112, 194*n*
Corrigan, P. R. D., 119, 134, 180*n*, 184*n*, 190*n*, 192*n*, 197*n*, 200*n*, 210–11 *bib*
cultural revolution, Chs. 2, 5 and *passim*
Cowper, W., 60
Cromwell, T., 30–31, 45

Dangerfield, G., 135
Defoe, D., 37
Denning, Lord, xix
difference(s), 10–11, 14, 18, 22, 23–4, Ch. 4, 156, 162, 164
division of Labour, *s* Labour, division of
divorce, 91, 187*n*
Duncannon, Lord, 60
Duncombe, T., 63

economics, Chs. 1, 5; *sa* political economy, social economy
Edelman, M., xix
Education, State System, 58, 75, 83, 98, 155–6, 162–3, 168; *sa* School Boards
Egerton, Lord, 60
Enclosures, 37–8, 45
Engels, F., Ch. 1, 49, 52, 119, 122, 124, 190*n*
English Revolution, 31
expertise, experts, xxiv, 66, 69, 77, 164, 167, 169, 202–3*n*

'Fabian interpretations', 50, 77, 179*n*
Fabian Society, 150, 163
Factory Inspection/Legislation, 11, 56, 59, 67, 71–2, 77, 83, 121–2
family, xxiv, Ch. 4, 115, 152, 173*n*
Family Income Supplements, 145
fetishism, 14, Ch. 5
Fielden, J., 62–4, 68, 69–71
forms, associations, Ch. 5
Foster, J., 51–2, 72–3
Foucault, M., 39, 104, 106–8
Franchise Reform, Ch. 3, 121–2
Friendly Societies, 112, 127, 131, 138, 194*n*

gender, Ch. 4; *sa* difference(s)
General Strikes, 1842, 72f.
1926, 159
Gillan, W. D., 63
Gorell Commission on Divorces and Matrimonial Causes, 1909, 96

230 *Index*

Morris, W., 122
'mutuality', Ch. 5

Nairn, T., xvii, xviii
National Insurance, 112, 126, 138, 160, 196*n*
National Unemployed Workers' Movement, 159
nations, nationalism, 8, 41–3, 65–6
needs, 111–12, 114
Nicholls, Sir G., 145
'Normal regime', 29
Normanby, Lord, 60

Oastler, R., 63
'Old Corruption', 35–6, 44–5, 99
Oldham Political Association, 63

Patten, J. W., 55
Parliament: Commons, 40, Ch. 3, 179*n*, 180*n*
   Lords, 94; *sa* Legislation
patriarchy, xxiv, Ch. 4, 173*n*
Peel, Sir Robert, 54, 63, 75, 76
phenomenal forms, 4–6, 12–15, 78, Ch. 5 *passim*
Philips, M., 55, 60
political economy, xx, 119, 154f.
Poor Law, 30, 45, 59, 63, 67, 69, 71, 72, 73, 82–3, 98, 145, 149, 152, 155, 160, 163, 182*n*; *sa* Guardians; 'Welfare State'
'Popular Radicals', 62–4, 66, 71
Porter, G. R., 56
poverty, Ch. 6
production, Chs. 1, 5, 111f.
proletariat, *s* working class
property, Ch. 1, 39f., Ch. 4
prostitution, Ch. 4
Prudential Assurance, 114
Public Employment Act, 1817, 45
public opinion, 46

Raeburn Committee, 1932, 131
Reading Co-operative Society, 130, 194–5*n*
registration (regulation), 30, 97–9, 133f.

Relief Act, 1757, 45
'Relief function', 163f.
Roebuck, J. A., 57, 59, 71
Royal Arsenal Co-operative Society, Woolwich, London, 129
Royal Commission on Income Tax, 1920, 131
Russell, Lord John, 54, 179–80*n*, 183*n*
Ryan, A., xxii

Sandon, Lord, 60
Saville, R., 174–5*n*
Sayer, D., 190*n*, 197*n*, 223 *bib*
School Boards, 136
Senior, N., 56, 69
'separation', *s* phenomenal forms
sexuality, Ch. 4; *sa* difference(s)
Skinner, Q., xxii–xxiii
Slaney, R. A., 60, 73, 181*n*
Smith, A., 27, 39, 57
Smith, Dr Southwood, 60
social economy, xx
socialism, socialist construction, 20–25, Ch. 5, 166f.
sons, *s* men, males, heirs
Stamp, Lord, 149
Stanley, Lord Edward G. (later 14th Earl of Derby), 55
State, images of:
   'instrumental', 13
   'superstructural', 13
   'relational', Ch. 1 (esp. 24)
   'organizational', 20, 150–51
'State Servants', 17–18, 29, 43, 52, 66, 73, 77–8, 149, 184*n*, 202*n*
'Stuart Regime', 31

Thompson, E. P., xx, 12, 17, 27–8, 34–6, 43–4, 47–8, 52–3, 225 *bib*
Thomson, C. P., 55, 57, 68, 71
Three Great Differences, 23 *def*
Ten Hours Bill, Act, Campaign, 52, 72f., 121f., 182*n*
Times, The, xvi, xviii, xix
Titmuss, R., 144
Tories, xviii, 52, Ch. 3, 99; *sa* Conservatives, Party